The Philosophic Thought of Ayn Rand

The
Philosophic
Thought
of
Ayn Rand

Edited by
Douglas J. Den Uyl
and
Douglas B. Rasmussen

1984

University of Illinois Press
Urbana and Chicago

Illini Books edition, 1986
© 1984 by the Board of Trustees of the University of Illinois
Manufactured in the United States of America
2   3   4   5   C   P   5   4   3   2

This book is printed on acid-free paper.

Library of Congress Cataloging in Publication Data

Main entry under title:

The Philosophic thought of Ayn Rand.

Includes index.
I. Rand, Ayn.   I. Den Uyl, Douglas J., 1950–
II. Rasmussen, Douglas B., 1948–
B945.R234P48   1984   191   83-5844
ISBN 0-252-01033-7 (cloth)
ISBN 0-252-0140-7 (paper)

And now I see the face of god, and I raise
this god over the earth, this god whom men have
sought since men came into being, this god who
will grant them joy and peace and pride.

This god, this one word: I.

Ayn Rand, *Anthem*
(New York: Signet Books, 1946)

Contents

Contents

Preface

Ayn Rand is among the most controversial figures of our age. The sense of vehemence emanating from the pens and mouths of her critics is matched only by the devotion she commands from her admirers. She has been heralded as bringing forth a new vision for mankind and also for advocating the destruction of the very roots of western civilization. Many of these charges and countercharges stem from Ayn Rand's public image—that is, out of claims made for and against her in the press, on television, and on the covers of her books. Media "hype," however, should not be confused with substantive analysis. The best that can be said for Rand's public image is that it urges us to look more carefully into the ideas of such a disquieting thinker. It is to that end that this volume has been cast.

Two theses come immediately to mind when one thinks of Ayn Rand. On the one hand, there is her contention that selfishness is a virtue and altruism a vice. On the other, there is her uncompromising defense of laissez-faire capitalism. As if these two theses were not provocative enough when separately considered, Rand continues to fuel controversy by claiming that capitalism cannot be defended unless one first accepts the truth of ethical egoism! All this would seem to play right into the hands of those leftists who have claimed all along that capitalism and egoism go hand in hand. Nevertheless, and to the consternation of these same leftists who believe Rand can be impaled on some well-known ideological spike, Rand unquestionably repudiates those thinkers who normally constitute the traditional background of capitalist intellectual history. Neither Hobbes, nor Spencer, nor Nietzsche characterizes Rand's philosophical teaching; and she has no use for the utilitarian approach of Bentham and the early J. S. Mill. Furthermore, no sympathy is shown for Adam Smith's moral philosophy, and an approach like Edmund Burke's would not even be given serious consideration.

For all the foregoing reasons, and for other reasons discussed in this book, Rand cannot be labeled as either a conservative or a liberal. Present day conservatives are all too happy to accept her desire not to be associated with that movement. And although few have mistaken her for what we now call a liberal, many of Rand's admirers once considered themselves to be liberals. Evidently Rand does not fit into any of the ideological boxes we are accustomed to using when categorizing any given thinker's political leanings.

In order to defend what might appear to some to be paradoxical theses at best, Rand felt that she had to develop her own systematic philosophy. The political positions Rand is most noted for depend on her defense of natural rights. To defend natural rights Rand believes she must formulate an ethical theory, and an ethical theory in turn requires a position on metaphysical and epistemological questions. Because she believes that a number of the major fields of philosophy are interdependent and because she herself claims to have developed a philosophic system, this book is devoted to an assessment of Ayn Rand the philosopher. All the contributors to this volume agree that she is a philosopher and not a mere popularizer. Moreover, all agree that many of her insights on philosophy and her own philosophic theories deserve critical attention by professional philosophers, whatever the final merits of those insights and theories. It is appropriate, therefore, that our contributors are themselves professional philosophers.

In any collection of essays devoted to a single thinker's ideas, there are variations of interpretation and disagreements over the soundness of that thinker's doctrines. Despite these differences we have sought to maintain a consistent level of professional standards throughout this book. To satisfy this aim, the contributors are not only academicians, but also independent theorists in their own right. No one (including the editors) should be considered a spokesman for Rand's views in the sense that any interpretation given below has been sanctioned by Rand herself. By the same token, it would be false to conclude that anyone writing here is motivated simply by a desire to see her theories discredited. There are, to be sure, more and less favorable treatments of Rand to be found in these pages. But in each case the contributor has sought to evaluate Rand according to the same scholarly standards that would apply to any philosopher.

This volume is organized into three sections that correspond to the three central divisions of Rand's philosophy—metaphysics and epistemology, ethics, and political and social theory. Her aesthetic philosophy is not discussed. Although the editors do not profess to be spokesmen for Rand's views, we begin each of the three sections of the book with an expository essay designed to introduce the reader to the basic Randian argument on the topic for that section. These introductory essays are thus more interpretative than critical. The critical work is to be found in the essays of the other contributors.

It should be noted here that when, in various places in certain of the essays in this book, the terms *objectivism* and *objectivist* are used, they are generally meant to refer to Rand's philosophy. When this is not the case, the context should make this clear.

Since the focus of this volume is on the nonfiction writings of Ayn Rand, this seems an appropriate place to mention her major nonfiction works. These include: *The Virtue of Selfishness* (New York: New American Library, 1964), *For the New Intellectual* (New York: New American Library, 1961), *Capitalism: The Unknown Ideal* (New York: New American Library, 1967), and *Introduction to Objectivist Epistemology* (New York: The Objectivist, 1966–67; reprint ed., New York: New American Library, 1979). Other nonfiction writings could be mentioned, but either these works are not as significant philosophically as the above or they are not readily available to the public.

Ayn Rand claims to have stood for the supremacy of reason in human existence. It is our sincere hope that this volume will contribute something to moving the discussion away from the emotional aura surrounding Ayn Rand to a more rational discussion. We thus hope the book will help move the focus to what is essential, rather than accidental, about Ayn Rand. Since Ayn Rand is no longer alive, it is only what is significantly essential about her that now matters.

We wish to give special thanks to Frank Williams of the University of Illinois Press for his encouragement and assistance on this project. We would also like to thank Rita Zelewsky and Judith McCulloh, also of the University of Illinois Press, for their helpful assistance. Thanks must also be given to the Liberty Fund (Indianapolis) and the Reason Foundation (Santa Barbara) for making it possible (both financially and otherwise) for both of us to be together in the summer of 1979 to work on this book. Finally, we wish to thank our wives, whose patience and indirect support of this project contributed to its completion.

I

Metaphysics and Epistemology

1

Ayn Rand's
Realism

⌒

Douglas J. Den Uyl
and
Douglas B. Rasmussen

John Frederick Peifer has written:

An error lurking in the roots of a system of thought does not become a truth simply by being evolved. It remains an error; and if thought is consistent, that consistency can mean only a more intricate enmeshing in error. Usually it requires a mistake in logic to produce correct conclusions from false premises, but false conclusions can be drawn from false premises with strict logical accuracy. In this way, integral and elaborate systems of thought can be unravelled in which the rules of logical procedure are rigidly adhered to, and yet the entire system can be invalidated by an error at its base.[1]

As a philosopher Ayn Rand has abided by this insight. She has always been acutely aware that it is the answers offered to fundamental metaphysical and epistemological questions that are crucial to any system of thought. Careful thinking on fundamental problems is a most pressing demand. It is in terms of fundamentals that Rand approaches philosophy, both her own and that of others; and it will be in terms of the fundamentals of Rand's metaphysics and epistemology that this essay will proceed.

I

The first thing that should be said about Rand's philosophy is that it is a form of Aristotelianism. Rand holds that there are beings which exist and are what they are quite independently of anyone's knowledge of them. Moreover, these beings are capable of being known as they are. Rand's acceptance of metaphysical realism and rejection of idealism is illustrated by the following argument: "If nothing exists, there can be no consciousness: a consciousness with nothing to be conscious of is a contradiction in terms. *A consciousness conscious of nothing but itself is a contradiction in terms: before it could identify itself as consciousness, it had to be conscious of something.*"[2] The very nature of awareness, no matter what its mode may be, is to be *of* or *about* something other than itself. In traditional Aristotelian thought, this character of consciousness is described as "intentionality";[3] and one implication of this theory of consciousness is that the existence of reality is not something one demonstrates, but rather something that is self-evident.

Yet Rand's Aristotelianism goes beyond the mere insistence on an independently existing world of beings. Rand also insists that "to exist is to be something, as distinguished from the nothing of non-existence, it is to be an entity of a specific nature made of specific attributes. . . . A is A. A thing is itself."[4] To exist, for Rand, is not bare existence that somehow *has* a character, as a pincushion has pins. Rather, the very being or existence of a thing *is* to be something. Or, in Aristotelian terms, the identity or what-it-is-to-be (in Greek τὸ τί ἦν εἶναι) is the cause of each thing's existence; and identity is the cause not just in the sense of *what* a thing is, but in an ontological sense of that in virtue of which a thing *exists*. Rand formulates this position succinctly; existence *is* identity.[5] Independently of Rand, Emerson Buchanan has also formulated this idea. He states that "τὸ τί ἦν εἶναι should be taken literally as meaning what it is for a thing to be; that it is an ontological principle and, as the Being (*ousia*) of each thing, is that in the thing which is the cause of its being or existing."[6] To understand what something is, to grasp the identity of a thing, is to reach rock-bottom—the point where inquiry ends and explanation begins. This is the crucial Aristotelian metaphysical insight, one Rand fully endorses— perhaps more than any contemporary thinker.

Though Rand accepts the validity of the metaphysical enterprise, she does not countenance many of its so-called questions: Why is there something rather than nothing? or Why could not something just be without being something? She regards such questions as mistaken, because their *viability as questions* presupposes that which they want explained. As Aristotle has stated: "'why a thing is itself' is a meaningless inquiry, for the fact or existence of the thing must already be evident . . . but the fact that a thing is itself is the single reason and the single cause to be given to all such questions as 'why is man man' or 'the musician musical'."[7] In other words, if we ask Why is there something rather than nothing? or Why could not something just be without being something? Rand would reply, as Aristotle suggests, that these questions would not be significant if the facts for which they demand explanation were not already presupposed. These questions assume that something already exists and is something or other. If these questions did not assume these most basic facts, there would not be anything that could be explained and nothing would be referred to that could be differentiated from anything else. The "nothing" of the first question and the "something" of the second would be mere marks or noises devoid of significance.

Rand would consider this line of argument applicable to the Thomistic approach to metaphysics, where the distinction between *what* a thing is and *that* a thing is requires a separate ontological principle, an *esse*, in virtue of which a thing is said to be *simpliciter*. She recognizes what Aristotle said in *Posterior Analytics*, namely, that "*to know what something is is the same as knowing why it is*; and this is *either* why it *exists simply* and not why it is one of the things predicated of it *or* why it is one of the predicates."[8] Rand, therefore, rejects attempts to explain existence as such. "Existence exists" is a primary fact and needs no explanation[9] beyond the particular explanations offered for the various types of beings that constitute existence. Rand's Aristotelianism is much like that ascribed to William of Ockham by E. A. Moody: "Ockham's Aristotelianism is indicated by his complete adoption of the thesis that the reason of the fact is the being of the things of which the fact is true. It is in defense of this principle that Ockham opposes the traditional 'real distinction' between essence and existence within finite things."[10] Rand fully accepts the view that explanations come to an end somewhere, and the somewhere is the nature, the what-it-is-to-be, of a thing.

Rand, furthermore, accepts two central Aristotelian metaphysical tenets: (1) there are many senses in which something may be said to be, and (2) what exists primarily are individuals and nothing exists apart from them. The first tenet commits Rand to metaphysical pluralism and the rejection of reductionism. The second commits her to individualism and the rejection of Platonism in logic.

(1) The general character of existence, according to Rand, is that it is noncontradictory. To be is to be something, and a thing cannot be other than it is. Yet within this limit there can be a wide diversity of beings: existence must be in some form, but it can be in any form.[11] Indeed, sometimes metaphysicians (and scientists qua metaphysicians) attempt to legislate what can be, in order to insulate their theories and methodologies from criticism. Yet, this is nothing more than a kind of a priorism that Rand thoroughly rejects.

Rand is very reluctant to engage in armchair pronouncements on what the world's ontological furniture *must* be. She is, for example, not a materialist, despite her naturalism. She holds that consciousness is an attribute of certain living organisms; it is neither a spiritual substance within a body nor a mere linguistic fiction referring to nothing more than a set of electrochemical processes and/or observable forms of behavior. Consciousness exists. It is a faculty of awareness by which living things relate themselves to what exists. Consciousness is ultimately *of* or *about* something other than itself—it is inherently relational. Moreover, consciousness always involves action—it is an activity exercised by some types of living entities but not by others. And consciousness allows for different *levels* of awareness as well—e.g., conceptual as differentiated from perceptual—which some living entities can attain and some cannot. Consciousness, wherever it is found, is distinguished by these two fundamental attributes—content and action.[12] Since material things are not intentional in character, viz., inherently relational, consciousness cannot be reduced to a material state; and since awareness is an activity that certain living things do, consciousness cannot be explained[13] as some sort of spiritual entity. Rand's pluralistic approach to existence demands neither a mind/body dualism nor a reductive materialism.

Another example of Rand's pluralism is her recognition that

entities, attributes, motions, and relations all exist, but in different ways. Entities are the only primary existents. Attributes, motions, and relations exist only *in*, *of*, and *among* entities;[14] they do not exist by themselves. Though Rand never explicitly mentions the Aristotelian distinction between substance and accident—between beings that exist primarily (in virtue of themselves) and beings that exist secondarily (in virtue of being related in some way to those primarily existing beings)—she does seem to recognize this distinction as having a real foundation. It is not merely language or man's mode of cognition that makes "brownish bears" the correct expression and "bearish browns" incorrect. Rand's acceptance of the substance/accident distinction illustrates not only her metaphysical pluralism but also her commitment to individuals as the primary existents.

(2) Rand considers entities to be ontologically whole in the sense that the existence of individuals is metaphysically given and basic. Accordingly, she rejects the attempt to ontologically bifurcate entities into metaphysical constituents, such as form and matter. Such bifurcation is at root Platonic, for it makes the individual ontologically derivative and causes doubt as to whether conceptual knowledge can pertain to individuals. Although Rand does not see herself as offering a new interpretation of Aristotle on this issue, but rather as advancing her own modification and correction, she is clearly, nevertheless, advocating a view consistent with certain contemporary interpretations of Aristotle.

The works of Walter Leszl, E. A. Moody, and Edward Regis, Jr., all present a view of Aristotle in which the individual is considered ontologically ultimate. Leszl, in *Logic and Metaphysics in Aristotle*, argues that it is a mistake to interpret matter for Aristotle as some "independent factor or force which causes the individuality of things."[15] Further, he contends that the existence of a universal for Aristotle is nothing more than an identity between certain individuals—the individuals are so and so and require no explanation beyond the fact that they are indeed so.[16] Leszl argues that interpreters of Aristotle tend to Platonize form and matter and that this Platonic rendition, more than anything else, is the cause of difficulties for Aristotelianism.[17]

E. A. Moody, in his ground-breaking work *The Logic of Wil-*

liam of Ockham, presents Ockham as advancing a pure Aristotelianism, free of any admixture of Platonic/Augustinian thought. Ockham thus objects to the tendency among certain medieval Scholastics to regard "genera and species or 'universal things' corresponding to them, [as] exist[ing] outside the mind as *parts* of individual substances, in such manner that substances are 'individuated' by something distinct from the essential nature signified by the substantial term."[18] The entire development of Aristotelianism is affected, Moody contends, by a failure on the part of some Scholastics[19] to distinguish between a concept understood as a sign—that is, as an immediate significative relation that requires no third thing beyond the mind—and a concept understood as the thing known—that is, as an object of reflective consideration whose relation to other concepts logic studies. Traditionally this distinction is understood as the distinction between first and second intentions. The former are the concern of epistemology and metaphysics and signify *beings in rerum natura*; the latter are the concern of logic and are only concepts of concepts, not real beings. Moody argues that it is the confusion between concepts considered as first intentions and second intentions that is the source of the temptation to treat concepts, "universal things" such as man, animal, form, and matter as constituting ontological elements within the existing individual. It is also, he holds, responsible for the seemingly endless and largely unnecessary debate as to whether universals exist *in re*.

Edward Regis, Jr., in a recent article entitled "Aristotle's Principle of Individuation," points out that form and matter are both only aspects or features of the individual. The "problem of individuation" has been considered a problem because it has been assumed that "(a) the existence of numerically different but specifically identical individuals is something which itself stands in need of causal explanation, and (b) that matter or form can provide it."[20] Regis argues, on the contrary, that the existence of individuals is not for Aristotle an *explanandum* but an *explanans* and, thus, that nothing has more fundamental ontological status than the individual. Aristotle, Regis claims, is one of the few naturalistic realists in philosophy.

Rand can be clearly understood as the naturalistic realist

Regis describes Aristotle to be, the Aristotelian Ockhamite of Moody's work who refuses to grant extramental reality to logic's objects, and a thoroughly de-Platonized Aristotle for which Leszl argues. Rand's commitment to the ontological primacy of individuals is endemic to her whole manner of philosophizing. She never forgets that concepts are derived from concretes, that thought is a tool, and that the natural world of existing individuals is ultimate.

There is only one other point that must be made regarding Rand's approach to metaphysics, and this concerns metaphysical argumentation. She accepts what is sometimes called the transcendental question—namely, asking "What makes x possible?" This method of inquiry, however, is not necessarily Kantian; for this type of question goes back to Aristotle's defense of the principle of noncontradiction.[21] Rand explicitly states that the failure to keep the presuppositions of certain activities in mind is a major philosophical error. She describes how one argues for something that is fundamental:

An axiom is a statement that identifies the base of knowledge and of any further statement pertaining to that knowledge, a statement necessarily contained in all others, whether any particular speaker chooses to identify it or not. An axiom is a proposition that defeats its opponents by the fact that they have to accept it and use it in the process of any attempt to deny it.[22]

The foregoing approach to metaphysical argumentation has been fruitfully employed in recent works by T. H. Irwin[23] and Joseph M. Boyle.[24] We cannot go into this most interesting approach to metaphysics, but it was necessary to indicate the type of argumentation in metaphysics Rand finds acceptable.

II

Rand's theory of knowledge is clearly in the Aristotelian tradition also. The following theses should bear this out.

1. All our knowledge begins and arises out of sense experience. The senses are valid.[25]

2. The existence of the external world and our knowledge of it is self-evident; and the attempt to prove the existence of

such a world, or our knowledge of it, is the central error of modern philosophy.

3. The mode of our knowledge should not be confused with the content of our knowledge.

4. It is meaningful to speak of conceptual knowledge, not just propositional knowledge; and a theory of abstraction is crucial to the validation of man's knowledge—that is, crucial to making the process of forming real definitions intelligible.

5. The meaning of words is their semantic reference, *not* their use; and concepts are necessary for there to be meaning.[26]

6. The necessity exhibited in logic is not a function of purely formal or linguistic considerations, but ultimately of reality itself. The analytic/synthetic distinction should be rejected and replaced with a theory of propositions that allows one to identify the nature of things.[27]

7. Skepticism is self-refuting, and the question for epistemology is not *whether* man has knowledge, but how.[28]

8. It is illegitimate to render any proposition dubitable simply because the proposition *Human beings are limited and fallible* is true.[29]

With the possible exception of thesis 4, none of these eight theses is fully developed by Rand. The essentials of some are developed, but others are only adumbrated.

It should be mentioned that it is probably because Rand views philosophy from a classical perspective that she has been largely ignored by philosophers in epistemology. Their paradigm is much different from Rand's own. Rand's relationship to the history of philosophy is given a detailed discussion in Robert Hollinger's essay. But at this stage we can say that most contemporary epistemologists are still operating from a largely Kantian perspective in which the human knower is viewed as conditioning what is known. Thus, knowledge of the world *as it is* is not considered possible or, if not that, then not important. Yet, the history of philosophy offers what could be called the *Aristotelian alternative*, and Rand can be understood as trying to call the attention of contemporary philosophy to such an alternative.

In this section it will be impossible to discuss all eight of these theses. In fact we can do no more than just indicate the type of argument Rand would offer for three of the eight listed above. We shall discuss theses two, three, and four because we believe these are the most central of the eight. The other five theses are made possible by these three.

Thesis 2. We stated above that Rand regards consciousness—awareness—as being fundamentally *of* or *about* something other than itself. We called this feature of consciousness "intentionality" and described this feature as being inherently relational. Though Rand does not use the term *intentionality*, it certainly describes her view of consciousness. "Directly or indirectly, every phenomenon of consciousness is derived from one's awareness of the external world. . . . *It is only in relation to the external world* that various actions of a consciousness can be experienced, grasped, defined, or communicated."[30] It is impossible, then, for one to consider the contents of one's awareness and doubt (à la Descartes) whether there really is a world independent of such awareness or whether one is knowing anything. Such doubt would privatize thought and make consciousness the starting point for philosophy.[31] Rand correctly concludes that Descartes's starting point leads down a blind alley and cannot be the true origin of an account of the cognitive relation. The alternative is to be found in the Aristotelian tradition. As Aquinas writes: "The intelligible species [i.e., the concept] is to the intellect what the sensible species [i.e., the percept] is to the sense. But the sensible species is not *what* is perceived, but rather that *by which* the sense perceives. Therefore the intelligible species is not what is actually understood, but that by which the intellect understands."[32] Thought does not need to be related to things; it *is* the relation—the way we cognitively contact the world—and not something we know directly and somehow relate to things.

As a result of the foregoing, it can be seen that Rand's use of the term *concept* is not to be construed as Locke construes the term *idea*.[33] Rand's view of awareness—that consciousness is inherently relational—prevents her view of concepts from being regarded in a Cartesian/Lockean fashion and lends credence to her claim that *existence exists* is an axiomatic and informative truth. Or, as Peifer has put the issue, "that thought, while being immanent, does not know things, does not attain the real, is *not evident*. What *is evident* is that it does!"[34]

Thesis 3. Rand accepts Gilson's claim that any attempt on the part of a philosopher to avoid the logical conclusion of his position is destined to failure. "What he himself declines to say will be said by his disciples."[35] Rand applies this insight to Kant when she quotes Henry Mansel, a nineteenth-century follower of Kant, as declaring explicitly what was only implied by Kant's "Copernican Revolution."

With him (Kant) all is phenomenal (mere appearance) which is relative, and all is relative which is an object to a conscious subject. The conceptions of the understanding as much depend on the constitution of our thinking faculties, as the perceptions of the senses do on the constitution of our intuitive feelings. Both *might* be different, were our mental constitution changed; both probably *are* different to beings differently constituted. The *real* thus becomes identical with the absolute, with the object as it is in itself, out of all relation to a subject; and, as all consciousness is a relation between subject and object, it follows that to attain a knowledge of the real we must go out of consciousness.[36]

According to Rand, Kant's "Copernican Revolution" is the climax of an attack on man's consciousness (both perceptual and conceptual) that took place throughout modern philosophy. Rand states that the attack rests on the unchallenged premise that "any knowledge acquired by a *process* of consciousness is necessarily subjective and cannot correspond to the facts of reality, since it is *processed* knowledge."[37] Indeed, the uncritical move from that which is relational to that which is appearance is evident in Mansel's remark.

But, even more important, Rand is arguing for a distinction long forgotten in modern philosophy: "For although it be necessary for the truth of 'cognition' that the cognition answer to the thing known, still it is not necessary that the mode of the thing known be the same as the mode of its cognition."[38] Consciousness must of necessity operate in a certain fashion or manner—there must be a mode of cognition—otherwise it makes knowing something miraculous. Rand states that "the last stand of the believers in the miraculous consists of their frantic attempts to regard *identity* as the *disqualifying* element of consciousness." [39] The identity of consciousness, the mode of cognition, must be acknowledged, but the claim that knowledge of reality is not possible does not follow from such an admission. There is a difference between the mode of knowing and the content of knowing. Kant conflates these.

Thesis 4. It is impossible to give a full account of Rand's theory of concept formation in this essay, let alone in this subsection. We must, therefore, confine ourselves to two areas: (a) her view of concept formation as a form of measurement, and (b) her view that concepts are cognitively rich. However, the reader is directed to Wallace Matson's essay for a contemporary critique of Rand's overall theory.

(a) Rand refers to concepts as tools of cognition. Yet, the use of these tools is not automatic. It requires an act of focus on the part of the knower. Conceptual knowing is for Rand a process of grasping relationships among entities by grasping the similarities and differences of their identities. In particular it is "the ability to regard entities as units that is man's distinctive mode of cognition" [40] and the key to conceptual awareness.

A unit is an existent *regarded as* a separate member of a group of two or more similar members. . . . The concept "unit" involves an act of consciousness (a selective focus, a certain way of regarding things), but . . . it is not an arbitrary creation of consciousness: it is a method of identification or classification according to the attributes which a consciousness observes in reality. [41]

The concept "unit" is the bridge between existence and consciousness.

Entities exist and are what they are, but they can, in virtue of their identities, be regarded in certain existing relationships. When this is done, a unit is formed; a unit is a way of looking at an existent—it is a relating of one existent to another on the basis of some foundation. Essentially, a unit is a relation. This is so because what is crucial to an existent's becoming a unit is its *being regarded as* a such-and-such, and this being-regarded-as is just what the very character of relation is. "A relation does not *have* a respect to something else but it *is*, by its very nature, a respect." [42] This is why Rand can say that units qua units do not exist *in rerum natura* as things or parts of things and still maintain that to consider something a unit is not necessarily an arbitrary process. All that a relation requires to exist is distinct terms and a foundation, not inherence as such in the terms.

As already stated, the basis for something being related to something else—something being a unit—is the identities of the entities involved. Rand states that the same characteristic possessed in different degree or measure is the foundation for this relating. "If a child considers a match, a pencil, and a stick, he observes that length is the attribute they have in common but their specific lengths differ. The *difference is one of measurement.* In order to form the concept 'length,' the child retains the attribute and omits its particular measurements."[43] The principle at work here is that the attribute in question exists in some quantity but may exist in any quantity. This is the principle by which something is regarded as being a member of a group of similar things and is Rand's characterization of the process by which abstraction is accomplished and concepts are formed. The process involves a selective mental focus that separates an aspect of reality from others on the basis of some characteristic(s) and unites it with other aspects possessing the same characteristic(s) in different degree. The process involves differentiation *and* integration.

Though Rand does not mention it, her account of concept formation—particularly her view of the foundation for concept formation—is very much akin to Aquinas's view of relations. Aquinas holds that the character of a relation is the ordination of one thing to another and that two distinct terms are necessary for the foundation of that ordering. The foundation for a relation is something that is itself not a relation, for it is the basis for the relation. For Aquinas quantity provides the principal foundation for numerical relation and even the relations of likeness or similarity. As Robert W. Schmidt, S.J., states:

Quantity serves to refer one thing to another because . . . it is capable of being applied to an external thing as measure. . . . [U]nity, the principle of all number, is a form of quantity. *Upon unity are founded various relations. . . . Other relations which are not evidently quantitative are also founded upon numerical unity.* The relation of likeness . . . , as Aquinas frequently says, *is based upon unity in quality.*[44]

And Rand states: "With the grasp of the (implicit) concept 'unit,' man reaches the conceptual level of cognition which consists of two interrelated fields; the *conceptual* and *mathematical*. The process of concept-formation is, in large part, a mathematical process."[45]

Rand, indeed, uses the category of quantity as the foundation for concept formation, for she considers abstraction to be essentially a process of measurement, of treating an aspect of reality as a *unit* of a group sharing the same characteristic(s) but possessed in different degree. Rand states that "the relationship of concepts to their constituent particulars is the same as the relation of algebraic symbols to numbers."[46] This does not mean that all knowing is mathematical. Rather, it means that concept formation and mathematical reasoning are both forms of measuring, of relating. We must, however, leave this comparison, for it takes us into areas we cannot properly handle here.

(b) Rand rejects any conceptualist or nominalist theory of concepts. She regards the former as considering meaning to be nothing more than a product of consciousness that bears little or no relation to the world and the latter as treating concepts as arbitrary groupings of existents based on nothing more than inexplicable relations of resemblance. Instead, she seems to agree with Maritain that a concept must signify more than just what we explicitly consider and more than a collection of individuals.[47] A concept signifies individuals that are something or other. Sheer extension does not suffice. There must be an intelligible feature in virtue of which classifications are made.

Rand is clearly following the "moderate realist" tradition in regard to the "problem of universals." She is, however, emphasizing the more Aristotelian/naturalist side of that tradition.[48] Rand holds that concepts are tools and that individuals, not universalized natures existing "in" concretes, are the primary objects of thought. As a result, she does not confine a concept's significance to the defining characteristics of a certain class. She states, "It is important to remember that a definition *implies all the characteristics of the units*, since it identifies the *essential*, not their *exhaustive*, characteristics, since it designates existents, not their isolated aspects; and since it is a condensation of, not a substitute for, a wider knowledge of the existents involved."[49] Rand never forgets that concepts are *formed* and that *the process of discovering* what distinguishes one group of existents from another implies a vast amount of knowledge from which the fundamentally distinguishing characteristic is determined. Thus, it should not be assumed that what a concept signifies is confined to the definition or what can be deduced from it.

It is important to realize that Rand does not consider a concept to signify all the characteristics of its referents in a Leibnizian way—that is, as being deduced from the definition. The Leibnizian approach to a concept's significance implies that one somehow knows the definition without any process of differentiation and integration, viz., that the definition is somehow epistemologically prior to the other characteristics. Yet, this is the very point Rand seeks to deny. There is a difference between the epistemological order and the logical order. Rand does not view a concept as "analytically containing" or "completely mirroring" the rest of the universe. Since concepts are tools by which we come to know the world, viz., intentions, they cannot but consist of all the characteristics of their referents. But the foregoing does not mean that everything we need to know can be deduced from our concepts. The *specific measurements*, to use Rand's terms, must exist in *some* form but can exist in *any* form; and there is no way that the latter can be known from just a consideration of the definition. Such is the error of rationalism.

The central reason Rand offers for contending that a concept signifies more than its defining characteristics is that "essences are epistemological."[50] Rand does not look upon the essential characteristic of something as a metaphysical constituent and criticizes Aristotle for allegedly doing this. She rather regards essence to be a result of a classificatory process that represents the best we know about the entity in question. She is against the so-called intuitionist view of Aristotle, which allegedly states that the essential characteristic is just "intellectually seen." Rand considers the intuitionist theory part of the miraculous view of cognition that plays into Kantian hands; for if anything seems obvious in epistemology, it is that the essential characteristic of something is discovered by much cognitive blood, sweat, and tears. Rand admits that human interest and concerns (our cognitive needs) have a place in the classificatory process. She holds, however, that the role our interests and concerns play in the process in no way makes essences arbitrary. She states her "epistemological" view of essence as follows:

The essence of a concept is that fundamental characteristic(s) of its units on which the greatest number of other characteristics depend, and which distinguishes these units from all other existents within the field of man's knowledge. Thus the essence of a concept is determined *contextually* and may be altered with the growth of man's knowledge. The metaphysical referent of man's concepts is not a special, separate metaphysical essence, but the total of the facts of reality he has observed, and this total determines which characteristics of a given group of existents he designates as essential.[51]

Rand takes both nominalism and conceptualism as belonging to the school of thought that regards "essence" as simply an arbitrary grouping of existents resulting from linguistic or pragmatic concerns. However, she sees both extreme realism and moderate realism as trying to reduce the conceptual process to the perceptual—that is, as trying to reduce conception to an automatic function that requires no effort on our part.

Leaving aside the question of whether Rand has accurately assessed the nature of nominalism and conceptualism (surely she has accurately described at least some nominalists and conceptualists), a crucial difference between Rand's use of the term *essence* and the use made of it by certain Aristotelians should be noted. Maritain means by *essence* both differentia (distinguishing characteristic) and genus. Henry Veatch means by *essence* simply "what something is"—much like Rand's use of the term *identity*. Rand, however, seems to mean by *essence* the fundamental distinguishing characteristic—the differentia. It is quite doubtful that Aristotelians have ever meant, for example, by the phrase *essence of man* just rationality. It seems then that Rand, in criticizing the Aristotelian commitment to metaphysical essences, is, at worst, attacking a straw-man or, at best, attacking ill-formed statements of the position. It might be said, in fact, that the belief that there are essences is nothing more than the belief that to be is to be something—that existence *is* identity.

Surely, Rand does not wish to deny this. Rather, she is trying to show that concept formation is not an automatic process, and it depends on human effort in order to occur.

Yet, it must be admitted that there are times when Aristotelians do seem to talk as if the essence of a being were a constitutive *part* of the thing. It seems, therefore, that Rand may have an important insight after all. Her insight is even more credible when we recall the tendency of some "Scholastics" to confuse the second intentional status of genus and species with that of things, the objects of our first intentions. This error is a form of Platonism, and Rand is not the first Aristotelian to find such Platonism among proponents of Aristotelianism. She will, no doubt, not be the last. The tendency to confuse thought with things thus seems to be a perennial philosophical problem and the source of recurrent difficulties.

Rand's theory of concepts is still, despite her criticism of Aristotle, a type of moderate realism, because it approaches the metaphysical question of whether there are universals as primarily a pseudoissue. Although our conceptual tools can be considered as second intentions and thus viewed as universals, universality is only the mode of our cognition. There is no reason to posit the existence of universals or essences as such—either as separate from individuals or existing "in" them. Rand's version of moderate realism shows promise in coming to grips with just what it is that concepts signify; and in expressing her view, she asks us to reconsider our view of meaning. Rand's theory of concepts is, like its author, quite radical.

NOTES

1. John Frederick Peifer, *The Concept in Thomism* (New York: Bookman Associates, 1952), p. 9.

2. Ayn Rand, "This Is John Galt Speaking," in *For the New Intellectual* (New York: New American Library, 1961), p. 124. Emphasis added.

3. Cf. Peifer, *Concept in Thomism*; Henry B. Veatch, *Intentional Logic: A Logic Based on Philosophical Realism* (New Haven: Yale University Press, 1952); and id., *Two Logics: The Conflict between Classical and Neo-Analytical Philosophy* (Evanston: Northwestern University Press, 1969).

4. Rand, "John Galt Speaking," p. 125.

5. Ayn Rand, *Introduction to Objectivist Epistemology* (New York: The Objectivist, 1966–67), p. 55. Hereafter cited as *IOE*.

6. Emerson Buchanan, *Aristotle's Theory of Being* (Cambridge, Mass.: Greek, Roman, and Byzantine Monographs, 1962), p. 50.

7. Aristotle *Metaphysics* 7.16.1041a15–18.

8. Aristotle *Posterior Analytics* 2.2.90a31–34. Emphasis added.

9. Rand, *IOE*, pp. 52–53.

10. E. A. Moody, *The Logic of William of Ockham* (New York: Russell & Russell, 1965), p. 311.

11. This statement results from an application of Rand's principle of concept formation to metaphysics. See thesis 4 starting on page 13.

12. Rand, *IOE*, p. 31.

13. Ibid., p. 52. Rand holds that the existence of consciousness is a fundamental axiom. Also, cf. John Deely, "How to Use Words to Mention," *New Scholasticism* 51, no. 4 (1977).

14. Rand, *IOE*, p. 19.

15. Walter Leszel, *Logic and Metaphysics in Aristotle* (Padua, Italy: Editrice Anenore, 1970), p. 497.

16. Ibid., p. 500.

17. Ibid., pp. 500–502.

18. Moody, *Logic of William of Ockham*, p. 79.

19. Porphyry and Scotus are the most prominent figures for Moody. Aquinas, however, is explicitly excluded. Ibid., ch. 3.

20. Edward Regis, Jr., "Aristotle's Principle of Individuation," *Phronesis* 21 (1976): 165.

21. Cf. Douglas Rasmussen, "Aristotle and the Defense of the Law of Contradiction," *The Personalist*, Spring, 1973.

22. Rand, "John Galt Speaking," p. 155.

23. T. H. Irwin, "Aristotle's Discovery of Metaphysics," *Review of Metaphysics*, December, 1977.

24. Joseph M. Boyle, "Self-Referential Inconsistency, Inevitable Falsity and Metaphysical Argumentation," *Metaphilosophy*, January, 1972.

25. Rand, *IOE*, p. 9. Cf. Nathaniel Branden, "The Stolen Concept," *Objectivist Newsletter*, January, 1963. Also, cf. Veatch, *Intentional Logic*, p. 90, and David Kelley, "The Evidence of the Senses" (Ph.D. diss., Princeton University, 1974).

26. Rand, *IOE*, chs. 2 and 3, also pp. 62–63. For a related approach, cf. John A. Oesterle, "Another Approach to the Problem of Meaning," *The Thomist*, April, 1944; also, Mortimer Adler, *Some Questions about Language* (La Salle, Ill.: Open Court, 1976).

27. Rand, *IOE*, p. 68. Cf. Leonard Peikoff, "The Analytic-Synthetic Dichotomy," *The Objectivist*, May–Sept., 1967. For related approaches, cf. Veatch, *Intentional Logic*, Brand Blanshard, *Reason and Analysis* (La Salle, Ill.: Open Court, 1962); Milton Fisk, *Nature and Necessity* (Bloomington: Indiana University Press, 1973); and Edward Madden and Rom Harré, *Causal Powers* (Totowa, N.J.: Rowman & Littlefield, 1975).

28. Rand, "John Galt Speaking," pp. 154–55; also, id., *IOE*, esp. chs. 1, 5, and 7.

29. Rand, *IOE*, chs. 5 and 7. For a related approach, cf. Douglas Rasmussen, "Austin and Wittgenstein on 'Doubt' and 'Knowledge'," *Reason Papers* (Fredonia, N.Y.) 1 (Fall 1974).

30. Rand, *IOE*, p. 31. Emphasis added.

31. Rand, in *For the New Intellectual*, p. 28, states: "Descartes began with the basic epistemological premise . . . 'the prior certainty of consciousness,' the belief that the existence of an external world is not self-evident, but must be proved by deduction from the contents of one's consciousness."

32. St. Thomas Aquinas, *Summa Theologiae*, 1.85.2.

33. John Locke seems to hold that ideas are that which the mind knows in thinking; see *Essay Concerning Human Understanding*, vol. 1, ed. A. C. Fraser (New York: Dover, 1959), pp. 32–33.

34. Peifer, *Concept in Thomism*, p. 13.

35. Etienne Gilson, *The Unity of Philosophical Experience* (New York: Charles Scribner's Sons, 1948), p. 302.

36. Henry Mansel, "On the Philosophy of Kant," in *Letters, Lectures and Reviews*, ed. H. W. Chandler (London: John Murray, 1873), p. 171; quoted in Rand, *IOE*, pp. 71–72. The interpolations are Rand's.

37. Rand, *IOE*, p. 72.

38. St. Thomas Aquinas, *Summa Contra Gentiles*, 2.75.

39. Rand, *IOE*, p. 71.

40. Ibid., p. 12.

41. Ibid. Emphasis added.

42. Robert W. Schmidt, S.J., *The Domain of Logic According to Saint Thomas Aquinas* (The Hague: Martinus Nijhoff, 1966), p. 134.

43. Rand, *IOE*, p. 16.

44. Schmidt, *Domain of Logic*, pp. 141–42. Emphasis added.

45. Rand, *IOE*, 12.

46. Ibid., p. 21.

47. Jacques Maritain, *An Introduction to Logic* (New York: Sheed & Ward, 1937), p. 23.

48. Cf. Moody, *Logic of William of Ockham*; however, Aquinas does state, "It is false that the essence of man as such exists in this individual." St. Thomas Aquinas, *On Being and Essence*, trans. Armand Mauer, C.S.B. (Toronto: Pontifical Institute of Medieval Studies, 1968), p. 47.

49. Rand, *IOE*, pp. 41–42. Some emphasis added.

50. Ibid., pp. 49.

51. Ibid., pp. 49–50.

2
Rand
on
Concepts

Wallace Matson

CARDS ON THE TABLE

The Fountainhead was my introduction to Ayn Rand. I was an undergraduate with friends in the school of architecture, among whom the novel made a stir. One friend, who aspired to be a Howard Roark (and succeeded pretty well, happily without recourse to dynamite), gave me a copy. It had a great impact, all to the good: not a pretty picture of the world, but an antidote to juvenile relativism and cynicism, saying that creative integrity was not necessarily doomed to frustration. And the blowing up of Cortlandt Homes remains one of the powerful images of modern fiction. I still enjoy wandering around the Berkeley campus of the University of California in a Walter Mitty mood calculating what charges, where put, would demolish the dozen Cortlandts disgracing a location that once almost became what it was planned to be, the noblest educational site in the land.

However, for many years I read no more Rand, until another friend—this one a graduate student of philosophy with heretical ideas—thrust on me a copy of the *Introduction to Objectivist Epistemology*. My reaction was mixed. On the one hand, the leading ideas struck me as both important and neglected; on the other, the luminous and vigorous style only brought to the fore a number of questionable argumentative moves, and the many shafts directed at "modern philosophy" seemed to miss their mark. But on the whole, I thought it deserved more serious attention from the so-called professional philosophers than it was getting—which as far as I knew was none at all. I casually made a remark to this effect, one thing led to another, and now I have been invited to contribute to this volume.

The misgivings I felt in accepting the invitation have intensified. For one thing, the more careful readings I have been obliged to give to the *Introduction to Objectivist Epistemology* (on which this study is solely based) have shown up more difficulties than I had noticed at first. For another, I have been given to understand that Ayn Rand (whom I never met or corresponded with) expressed disapproval of the very idea of this book—academic discussion of her work. One is reluctant to offer criticism when it is not only unsolicited but explicitly rejected in advance.

Nevertheless I shall go ahead. In the first place, I promised. In the second, I think a book like this would have been good for Miss Rand, whether she thought so or not. This is not said arrogantly. As Sir Karl Popper—a "modern philosopher" with whom Rand has much in common—has taught us, intellectual progress is inextricably bound up with critical give-and-take, a fact the importance of which is not diminished by the insufferability of particular critics. Like organic evolution, critical dialogue is wasteful, inefficient, and violent, but the only alternative is stagnation. Rand is too interesting a thinker to be left to herself. The mainstream of thought needs her contribution.

At any rate, my intentions, like those of Major-General Stanley's daughters, are well meant. As a materialist and essentialist in philosophy, and (small-*l*) libertarian in politics, surely I qualify as being on Rand's side and ought not to be dismissed summarily just on account of association with "linguistic analysts" and assent to some of the things Wittgenstein and others have said.

In the section "In Praise of Objectivism" I shall point out what I take to be both right and important in the *Introduction to Objectivist Epistemology* (*IOE*).[1] In "Objections to Objectivism" I shall discuss those aspects that do not seem entirely satisfactory as they stand and that I had hoped would be modified or at any rate defended in the promised "future book on Objectivism" (p. 7).

IN PRAISE OF OBJECTIVISM

1. *Objectivism is objective.* Perhaps the most fundamental of all divisions in philosophy is between inside-out philosophers on the one hand, such as Descartes, Hume, and Kant, who take as their starting point the (alleged) data of consciousness— "impressions," "ideas," "the sensuous manifold"—and ask, "How can we get from these data to a world independent of the data?"; and the outside-inners on the other hand, the likes of Aristotle and Spinoza, who, beginning with a world out there as given at least in its most general features, conceive their task to be one of systematic explanation, in which consciousness, the culmination of natural phenomena, is the last topic to come up for consideration. Inside-outism has often seemed inescapable; for, after all, where *can* we begin knowledge but with our thoughts? But Hume showed that if we start inside and do not cheat, we can never get outside; and since Kant failed to rebut him, the latter-day partisans of this approach, notably the logical positivists, have been obliged either to lapse into skepticism or else to develop strange doctrines implying that the Andromeda galaxy is a logical construction out of astronomers' glimpses, to the great glee of preachers and other apostles of unreason.

Rand will have none of this. "Existence" is an "axiomatic concept," she tells us (p. 52); and "Existence exists" is a "formal axiom" (p. 55). (I take her to mean by this that there are things independent of our thinking about them.) Existence is "implicit in every state of awareness" (p. 52); and although "one cannot analyze or 'prove' existence as such, it cannot be denied without being covertly affirmed (pp. 54−55).[2]

Our knowledge of existence is contained in our concepts, to the theory of which the book is almost entirely devoted. Although our awareness, our faculty of concept formation, is active and not passive (p. 31), concepts are not subjective or arbitrary but are dictated by the nature of things. Rand explains lucidly how this can be so without having to postulate either Platonic ideas or Aristotelian forms. Hers is a similarity account of concept formation:

Similarity is the relationship between two or more existents which possess the same characteristic(s), but in different measure or degree.

The process of concept-formation consists of mentally isolating two or more existents by means of their distinguishing characteristic, and retaining this characteristic while omitting their particular measurements—on the principle that these measurements must exist in *some* quantity, but may exist in *any* quantity. A concept is a mental integration of two or more units possessing the same distinguishing characteristic(s), with their particular measurements omitted. [P. 75.]

The notion of apprehending the particulars subsumed under a concept as its "units," which is "man's distinctive method of cognition" (p. 8), and of measurement (in a very broad sense) as implicit in the unit, are of great interest and an improvement on other similarity theories, inasmuch as by this means the temptation to explain similarity itself in terms of identity of parts can be successfully resisted. Rand displays much ingenuity in showing how the question How much? can be meaningfully raised in initially unpromising cases, such as those concerning love and furniture.

2. *Essence as an epistemological notion.* The chapter on definitions is particularly illuminating. "A definition," Rand writes, "is a statement that identifies the nature of the units subsumed under a concept" (p. 40). Being a statement, a definition is true (if correct). Furthermore, Rand insists, all definitions are contextual in the sense that what will suffice to identify the nature of the units depends on the range of the user's knowledge and his particular degree of sophistication. Thus a child's definition of man might be "A living being that speaks and does things no other living beings can do" (p. 43). But when the child grows up, he will prefer to define man as "A rational animal," because he will have come to grasp the fact that the rational faculty is the characteristic of man that serves to explain the facts that he can speak and do so many other wonderful things. It supersedes the previous definitions without falsifying them. Possession of the rational faculty is to be preferred to other characteristics that all and only men have, such as laughter, featherless bipedality, or even language, because of this greater explanatory scope, which warrants its designation as the *essence* of man— essence, not as a metaphysical ingredient apprehended by a mysterious special cognitive faculty, but as an epistemological

notion. (However, I doubt whether Rand is as far from Aristotle here as she thinks she is.)

Rand does not explicitly discuss the philosophy of science in this book, but I think her notion of a sophisticated definition ("a condensation of a vast body of observations," p. 46) makes it equivalent to a *theory*; and recognition of this fact can provide support for her opposition to the "dogma that a 'necessarily' true proposition cannot be factual" (p. 68). I shall try to explain my meaning with the aid of an example I have used elsewhere.[3]

At a prescientific stage, *sulphur* will be defined as (say) a yellow powdery substance that burns with an acrid odor and kills fleas. As knowledge of its chemistry accumulates, it will be redefined as a nonmetallic element with the atomic weight of 32.06. It is to be observed that at this stage no reason is given why there should not be a variety of sulphur (yellow, nonmetallic, elementary) that has some other atomic weight ("heavy" sulphur, we might call it if we came across it), so the statement of atomic weight is not regarded as necessarily true. With still further advances, however, the periodic table of the elements is developed, on which sulphur appears as Number 16, the sixth element in the third row—meaning that its atom consists of a nucleus enveloped by two completed electron shells and a third or valence shell containing six electrons. *Sulphur* can now be defined as "Element No. 16"—a statement that, in Rand's words, "stands for chains and paragraphs and pages of *explicit* propositions referring to complex factual data" (p. 46)—but, more than that, embeds sulphur in an elegant conceptual schematism which is such that from it the various previously noted properties of sulphur can be deductively derived.

Yet it is not quite accurate to say that this definition, which indeed does enunciate the essence, even the Lockean *real* essence of sulphur, is a statement of "the fundamental *characteristic*" of sulphur. It is better than that. Being Element No. 16 is no characteristic of sulphur—it is what sulphur *is*. It is, we might say, a redescription of sulphur in the technical terminology of an articulated theory, in which—ideally at any rate—everything is formally derivable from definitions. And if, as we assume is the case, the smelly yellow powder found around volcanoes instantiates one of these definitions, the truths about that yellow powder partake of the necessity of the formal derivations. The fact that the identity of the powder with No. 16 had to be established in the laboratory and not just on the blackboard does not alter the logical picture.

The attainability of truth that is at once factual and necessary paves the way to the proof of the "validity of scientific induction" mentioned by Rand (p. 8) as a desideratum but not pursued in this book. The alleged problem of induction arises because, so it is held, the statement "The course of nature will continue uniformly the same" is not a necessary truth—"we can at least conceive of a change in the course of nature"—so, if proved at all, it must be proved inductively, which would obviously be a circular procedure.

However, the truth is that we *cannot* conceive a change in the course of nature. We *cannot* conceive that sulphur, which is Element No. 16, should continue to be sulphur but cease to be Element No. 16, i.e., cease to exhibit the behavior that the theory assigns to Element No. 16. To do so would involve contradiction. If it is replied that, granted Element No. 16 must remain Element No. 16, it is nevertheless conceivable that Element No. 16 should begin tomorrow to exhibit quite novel behavior—combining with helium, e.g., to form helium sulphide—the reply is that the purported conceivability of this mishap presupposes an untenable distinction between what a thing *is* and what it *does*, fostered by the ruinous metaphor of *law of nature*. Citizen Jones can remain Jones even while going berserk and flouting all the laws of civilized society, but sulphur cannot remain Element No. 16 (which *is*, among other things, the having of exactly six electrons in the valence shell) and combine with Element No. 2 (which *is* the having of no valence shell at all), chemical combination *being* the sharing of valence electrons. Helium sulphide is just as straightforwardly contradictory as the round square.

(The foregoing is a sketch of how to show that the problem of induction rests on a mistake, so that once the mistake has been pointed out the problem does not arise. I take it that this fills Ayn Rand's bill for "proving the validity of scientific induction." If, however, she means to show that induction by simple enumeration—a procedure some writers mistakenly believe to be employed in the natural sciences—is valid or at least reliable, I have not shown that; neither can it be shown, since it is false.)

1. *The question of foundations.* (This is not really an objection but a pointing to something that ought to be taken up in a more comprehensive treatment of Rand's philosophy.) Rand rightly denounces the subjectivists, the inside-outers as I call them, but in *IOE* she does not rebut their arguments, which, however perverse, are often presented with great rhetorical effect. From Descartes to Russell and Ayer, these people have convincingly commended themselves as having overcome vulgar prejudice (that is the theme, for example, of Descartes's "First Meditation") to penetrate right down to the very bedrock of all knowledge. Do I *know* it's not all just a dream? can be made to sound like the profound question of the humble but candid truth-seeker, and the insinuation is hard to resist that one who answers affirmatively is under obligation to provide an argument from unshakable premises—more certain than that he is awake—in support of his "opinion."

It is not generally conceded to be sufficient to enunciate an "axiom" to the effect that "Existence exists" and "to sweep one's arm around and say: 'I mean *this*'" (p. 41). The subjectivists are not so obliging as to deny existence outright. Neither is it sufficient just to accuse them of "the fallacy of the 'stolen concept,'" "the act of using a concept while ignoring, contradicting, or denying the validity of the concepts on which it logically and genetically depends" (p. 9). The argument based on the stolen concept is transcendental: His argument against p depends crucially on concept C. But it is impossible that he should have concept C unless p were true. Therefore, etc. If such an argument is to go through, it must be established beyond doubt that the second premise is true, i.e., that there is no possible route to the possession of concept C other than via p. This amounts to proof of a universal negative, a task of formidable difficulty. (Consider Plato's unconvincing attempt to show that we could not have the concept of equality unless our souls existed before we were born. Or consider the Kantian philosophy, so emphatically rejected by Rand.)

What then can be done to overcome this initial rhetorical advantage of the inside-out philosophy? If there is some luminous general principle to which we can appeal, some self-evident truth that is incompatible with the Cartesian approach, I do not know what it is, and apparently no one else does either, inasmuch as three and a half centuries have failed to turn it up.

However, this does not mean that subjectivism is impregnable. If one trumpet blast will not knock over the walls, they may nevertheless fall after a million shovelings have undermined them. Two philosophers have demonstrated an effective technique: Thomas Reid in the eighteenth century, and—dare I mention his name?—J. L. Austin in our day. It consists in shifting the burden of proof from the shoulders of the objectivist back to those of the subjectivist where it belongs; of querying, at each step, the subjectivist's argument purporting to show that our awareness of the world is indirect and therefore problematic; the strategy, in short, of "dismantling the whole doctrine before it gets off the ground."[4]

2. *Is objectivism objective enough?* Despite its title, the key notion in *IOE* is not *knowledge* but *concept*. And the major concern of objectivism is "the validity of concepts": that concepts should "correspond to something that is to be found in reality" (p. 7). And what is a concept? As we shall see, the answer to this question is not entirely clear; however, the official definition is "a mental integration of two or more units which are isolated according to a specific characteristic(s) and united by a specific definition" (p. 15). Concepts are "produced by man's consciousness in accordance with the facts of reality, as mental integrations of factual data computed by man—as the products of a cognitive method of classification whose processes must be performed by man, but whose content is dictated by reality" (p. 31).

Now despite the references to "units" (which are out there in the real world), "the facts of reality," and "factual data," I have a fear that the phrases *mental integration* and *produced by man's consciousness* bear within them the seeds of subjectivism. In the absence of an explicit definition of *mental*, which Rand does not provide, I do not know how to construe them otherwise than as signifying that according to Rand a concept is something whose habitat is the mind, something not itself a bit of the objective reality, but at best "corresponding" to it. But if this is so, the fundamental notion of Rand's philosophy seems to have all the characteristics of a Cartesian or Lockean "idea"—and we know what *that* leads to!

Concepts, we are told, are "neither revealed nor invented, but . . . produced" (p. 31). What, exactly, *is* it that is produced when I "mentally integrate" my friends and acquaintances? What is it that is described farther on in the same sentence as a "product of a cognitive method of classification"? Not, evidently, something we can lay on a table. It must be some "state of mind." (Compare the definition of *knowledge* as "a mental grasp of a fact(s) of reality," p. 35.) So knowing that *p* consists in being in a certain state of mind, grasping the concept C is being in another.

The familiar problems now raise their heads. How do I know whether you know that *p*? By knowing whether you are in the appropriate state of mind. But how can I find that out? I cannot, if your state of mind is something knowable only by introspection, as it presumably is. How indeed can *I* know whether *I* know that *p*? Granting that I can know my own state of mind, how do I know that it is the right one for knowing that *p*? Because it corresponds to the fact that *p*? How am I going to find out whether it does? How am I going to compare a state of mind with something that is not a state of mind? What, indeed, does it mean to talk of doing so? Let us go no farther down this well-worn slide into the crocodile pit of solipsism, but study rather to avoid getting onto it.

3. *Who needs concepts?* The trouble arises because the concept is conceived to be the vehicle of objective knowledge, and the concept is something mental. Perhaps things could be fixed up by retracting the word *mental* or by defining it in some way so as to render it harmless. But I shall suggest a more radical procedure: that of rejecting the notion of the concept altogether.

I hasten to add that the operation envisaged will not interfere with Rand's saying what I take her to *want* to say but, on the contrary, will facilitate it.

It is perhaps worth pointing out as a preliminary that the word *concept*, in our time enjoying such a vogue both in and out of philosophical contexts, is almost a neologism; and its pedigree ought to have made Rand particularly suspicious of it. The works of Plato and Aristotle can be translated without its help. It does not occur in the King James Bible. It is, in fact, a bit of Schoolmen's Latin that hardly made an appearance in English before being pressed into service to render Kant's *Begriff*. Only within living memory has it leaked from academic lingo via educators and high-toned journalists into the fairly ordinary white-collar vocabulary. (Still not blue-collar: Archie Bunker's son-in-law would talk about concepts, but not Archie.) And it is not altogether clear in what ways it is supposed to be an improvement over its predecessors *notion*, *idea*, and *conception*. Dictionaries are unhelpful on this point.

To point out that *concept* is jargon is not, of course, to prove that we can get along without it. It is possible that *concept* is exactly the word to express the nature of the vehicle of knowledge even though no one *said* so until comparatively recently. But we ought at least to be stimulated to consider whether the word really is indispensable. We might try the experiment of getting along without it. I do not mean to suggest that we use *notion*, *idea*, or *conception* instead; of course we could do that, but not so trivially that we dispense with the very *concept* of the concept.

My suggestion is that we try to make do with just *words*. If it turns out to be possible to do so, we will evidently gain in objectivity. Words, unlike concepts, are plainly not mental entities. They *can* be laid on a table; more to the point, they can be bound in books, recorded on tapes and discs, tossed around, taken back, and even eaten. There is no problem about my knowing what words you are using or about whether or not you understand a certain word. There are plenty of objective tests available, of which the successful enunciation of a formal definition is one—*only* one, and not the most reliable without corroboration. You certainly understand the word *heliotrope* if you have a 100 percent success rate in picking out heliotrope-colored yarns from a miscellaneous collection. You probably understand it if you can recite the official definition (whatever it is) or specify the wavelength of heliotrope light; but then again you may not. And, while we may grant that you can pick out the right yarn *because* something is "going on in your mind"—and retina and optic nerve—we do not know and do not need to know what that something may be. Suppose we *did* somehow know that you were properly "mentally integrating" the "units" of heliotrope: that would make no difference to our verdict as to whether or not you understood the word, unless we had also established a perfect correlation between such integrations and successes at, for example, picking out yarns.

The world is full of a number of things, some of which are alike in having a color that the inventors of the English language signified by the noise or mark *heliotrope*. At a certain point in the education of a child in an English-speaking community, he learns to discriminate this shade and to apply this vocable to it. This is no different in principle from his concurrent learning to play "Yankee Doodle" on the kazoo. If one wishes to call them "forming concepts" of heliotrope and "Yankee Doodle" respectively, that *could* be all right, but it is rather likely to lead to irrelevant mystification about mental processes. To eliminate such references is to gain "objectivity," surely, and just as surely without descending to "a parrot's psycho-epistemology" (p. 24). The parrot may enunciate the vocable, but it cannot pass the tests of using it to talk about things. If a parrot were produced that could really talk—i.e., use language in the multifarious ways in which a human being uses it—then advocates of concepts would be forced to admit that the bird had "formed the relevant concepts." Which shows, incidentally, that there is a *conceptual* link between concept-talk and talk about ability to use language. Whatever we have solid objective reasons to say about concepts, we can say equally well in the idiom of words and their uses. The surplus (if any), those things we can say in the concept-vocabulary but not in the word-vocabulary, have to do only with occult processes, which—it seems obvious to me at any rate—an objectivist would wish to eliminate.

The official objectivist doctrine on the relation of words to concepts is as follows: "A word is merely a visual-auditory symbol used to represent a concept; a word has no meaning other than that of the concept it symbolizes, and the meaning of a concept consists of its units. It is not words, but concepts that man defines—by specifying their referents" (p. 26). This is puzzling as it stands, for if "a word has no meaning other than that of the concept it symbolizes," it evidently follows that a word *does*, as such, have a meaning after all, namely, "that of the concept it symbolizes." So a word, e.g., *man*, and a concept, e.g., whatever it is that is symbolized by the word *man*, have the *same* meaning. One is tempted to conclude that words and concepts therefore *are* the same—at any rate with respect to meaning, which would seem to be all that matters.

There are other passages where concepts and words grow close together, e.g., where the learning of concepts and words, on the one hand, is contrasted with the learning of "strings of sound" on the other (p. 24); and where reference is made to "methods of organizing words (concepts) into sentences" (p. 37). Nevertheless, I believe Rand's conception of the difference and relation between words and concepts is given in the first part of the first sentence of the quotation, before the semicolon: a word is a noise or mark *used* as a *symbol* to *represent* a concept (which, it will be remembered, is a "mental integration"). If we speak of the meaning of a word, we do so derivatively, by metonymy: the full expression should be "the meaning of the concept which the word symbolizes." (Compare "the money in my checkbook," which of course is short and loose for "the money in the bank indicated by the last figure in my checkbook.")

So the word *man* symbolizes the concept *man*. It is the concept, the mental integration, that alone has meaning. Its meaning consists of Adam, Eve, Cain, Abel, and so forth.

Now what I primarily want to suggest is that we bypass the concept and speak more objectively and directly of the use of words to mean things. But before I can do that, something must be said about the conception of meaning here embodied, namely, that meaning is the same as reference. I wish there were grounds on which to hold that Rand did not mean that concepts are *defined* by specifying their *referents*, but I fear there are not. The doctrine is held quite consistently throughout *IOE*, e.g., where denoting a concept is said to be the same as standing for "an unlimited number of concretes of a certain kind" (p. 15); and where grasping meanings is said to be the same as "grasping the *referents* of words, the kinds of existents that words denote in reality" (p. 23).

This can at best be only a partial account of meaning. For if the meaning of concept *C* is all its units, i.e., all the particulars subsumed, then if there are no such particulars, the concept must be without meaning. So *ghost, witch, dodo, centaur,* and so on are meaningless. Meaning must include, also, the sense, "the nature of the units," or their "*essential* characteristics" as identified in the definition (pp. 40–41). I suppose Rand would assent to this; perhaps in her terminology the concept itself is the carrier of what I (following Frege) have called the sense. (There remains a difficulty about units, of which there are supposed to be "two or more" before you can have a concept [p. 13].)

Thus amended, the doctrine would be that a word (noise or mark) symbolizes a concept that is a mental state, the consequence of a mental process called integration, which "isolated" "two or more units" "according to a specific characteristic(s) and united" them "by a specific definition" (p. 13), which in turn "is a statement that identifies the nature of the units subsumed under the concept" (p. 40). This mental state, then, is the sense of the concept; the units subsumed are the reference.

If that is the theory, one more quite small amendment should transform it into as objective an account of meaning as we can wish for. We need only substitute for the troublesome (because subjective) mental state component the notion of an ability.

Let us say the definition of a word is a statement identifying the essential characteristic(s) of the units to which the word is to apply. The test of a person's understanding of (the meaning of) a word is that he applies it to the right units—the ones referred to by the definition—and, moreover, has the ability to do this as a causal consequence of his having recognized that just these units possess the essential characteristic(s) mentioned in the definition. (If no units exist, he applies the word to nothing.) Note that this definition (of understanding) does not require that in order to understand a word a person must be able to state its definition explicitly. That would be an unrealistically stringent requirement. On the other hand, it goes farther than the mere ability to get the reference right.

I offer this account in the belief that it preserves what is of value in Rand's treatment—the notion of the unit, the essential characteristic "out there," and recognition of that essential characteristic by the user of the word—while avoiding the mysterious and subjective, namely, the concept as a third entity between word and thing, and the mental state in which it allegedly lurks. Perhaps it will be said that recognitions and abilities are mental too. Yes, they are, but harmlessly so; they can be detected by means other than introspection.

While this account will work for most nouns, adjectives, and verbs, and some other words, it is, I admit, insufficiently general. But, unless I am mistaken, its deficiencies in this respect are shared by Rand's original version; and my aim here is not to produce what I consider to be the correct theory of meaning (which I think must begin by recognizing that it is not concepts, nor even words or sentences, but *people* that mean), but only to suggest how Rand's theory could be changed to accord better with what I take to be the spirit of objectivism.

By way of illustration, I will append a few specimens of leading sentences from *IOE*, in Rand's version (left column) and also as they would read if my proposal for revision were accepted (right column):

"A *concept* is a mental integration of two or more units which are isolated according to a specific characteristic(s) and united by a specific definition" (p. 15).	A *word* is a symbol that is used to refer to two or more units which are isolated according to a specific characteristic(s) and united by a specific definition.
"Every word we use (with the exception of proper names) is a symbol that denotes a concept, i.e., that stands for an unlimited number of concretes of a certain kind" (p. 15).	Every word we use (with the exception of proper names) is a symbol that refers to an indefinite number (including zero) of concretes of a certain kind.

"The first concepts a child forms are concepts of perceptual entities; the first words he learns are words designating them" (p. 23).	The first words a child learns are words designating perceptual entities.
"It is often said that definitions state the meaning of words. This is true; but it is not exact" (p. 40).	It is often said that definitions state the meaning of words. This is true.
"An invalid concept invalidates every proposition or process of thought in which it is used as a cognitive assertion" (p. 47).	A misused word invalidates every sentence or process of thought in which it is misused as a cognitive assertion.

CONCLUSION

The foregoing is not, and is not presented as, anything more than a preliminary study of *IOE*. Much more needs to be said on all the topics I have mentioned both in praise and in criticism; and I have omitted consideration of many questions that might be of interest, e.g.:

1. Can the notion of "omitted measurements" be carried through a complete account of abstraction? (Even in Rand's presentation it gets a bit artificial-sounding when we come to prepositions and the like; and there are special problems concerning abstraction at higher levels: for instance, if particular measurements—presumably spatial—are omitted to get the concept "house," what is left over to discard in forming the concept "edifice"?)

2. Did Rand succumb to the computer model of reasoning—that thinking is nothing but the adding and subtracting of concepts? (I am afraid she did.)

3. Do we have to hold that *all* definitions admit of truth and falsity? (I think some do and some do not, and it is important to distinguish between them.)

4. Under just what conditions can a statement of fact be deemed necessarily true?

Readers of *IOE* will have noted that all the remarks in it about "modern philosophers" are contemptuous. Many are obscure, at least to me; I cannot divine exactly what doctrines are being attacked or who is supposed to hold them. But when Rand labels her enemies, they are most frequently called "the nominalists of modern philosophy, particularly the logical positivists and linguistic analysts" (p. 46); and when she names names, they are Wittgenstein and Russell. The sole quotation from an opponent is Wittgenstein's "Don't look for the meaning, look for the use" (p. 62), grossly misinterpreted as calling for Gallup polls to discover the meaning of concepts, which is itself a stock calumny of the procedure of some "linguistic analysts."

I wonder whether Rand stopped reading philosophy about 1945. One still seeking to slay the jabberwock of logical positivism could hardly have been *au courant* in 1966. Moreover, the reader will have noticed that none of the lines of criticism that I made in the third part of this paper are original with me; they all derive from well-known works by such people as Ryle, Austin, and Wittgenstein (of *Philosophical Investigations*). Perhaps Rand studied all these writers and rejected them advisedly, but it seems more likely that because of understandable disgust with the logical positivists she saw no point in familiarizing herself with the work of people widely regarded as their epigones. But, if so, it was a great pity. She ought to have known that *these people were on her side*—that Ryle exorcised the remaining ghosts from philosophy, that Austin was chief mongoose to the positivist cobra, and that Wittgenstein's remark about looking for the use of linguistic expressions (rather than some mysterious entity labeled "meaning") expressed an insight that Rand herself had: "the use (i.e., the meaning and the application) of concepts" (p. 59).

This separation from the mainstream was an unfortunate consequence of what was most admirable about Rand: her long-continued defense of important truths, acceptance of which was customarily looked upon for nearly half a century, especially in academic circles, as putting one not just into a minority but quite outside the pale.

But is it not written: "The voice of the intellect is a soft one, but it does not rest until it has gained a hearing. Ultimately, after endlessly repeated rebuffs, it succeeds. This is one of the few points in which one may be optimistic about the future of mankind"?[5]

NOTES

1. Ayn Rand, *Introduction to Objectivist Epistemology* (New York: The Objectivist, 1966), p. 7. All further references to this work appear within parentheses in the text.

2. Cf. Aristotle's defense of the principle of noncontradiction.

3. Wallace Matson, *Sentience* (Berkeley: University of California Press, 1976), ch. 2.

4. J. L. Austin, *Sense and Sensibilia* (London: Oxford University Press, 1964), p. 142.

5. Sigmund Freud, *The Future of an Illusion* (New York: Doubleday, 1957), p. 96.

3
Ayn Rand's
Epistemology
in
Historical
Perspective

ᘛ

Robert Hollinger

INTRODUCTION

There are three main topics that relate to Ayn Rand's theory of knowledge: (1) her theory of concept formation, (2) her interpretation of the philosophical tradition, and (3) the axiomatic foundations she offers for her objectivist metaphysics and epistemology. It will be my aim here to show that her view on what is wrong with the tradition deserves to be taken seriously but that her philosophical axioms, while understandable in light of her criticisms of the tradition, cannot bear all the weight she places upon them. This is so for two reasons: (1) they are philosophically banal, and (2) their acceptance is compatible with the rejection of specific philosophical doctrines Rand would wish to maintain.

I am not going to discuss Rand's theory of concept formation, although I realize this is a crucial feature of her view. I want to take a broader, more fundamental look at her philosophy in light of the tradition.

The following is a representative example of Rand's interpretation of the tradition and the impact of the tradition on modern culture:

Mankind could not expect to remain unscathed after decades of exposure to the radiation of intellectual fission-debris, such as: "Reason is impotent to know things as they are—reality is unknowable—certainty is impossible—knowledge is mere probability—truth is that which works—mind is a superstition—logic is a social convention—ethics is a matter of subjective commitment to an arbitrary postulate" and the consequent mutations are those distorted young creatures who scream, in chronic terror, that they know nothing and want to rule everything.[1]

Rand goes on to embellish these remarks. She maintains that the philosophical tradition, from Descartes to Kant and down through varieties of twentieth-century Anglo-American and continental philosophies, are so many variants on "epistemological agnosticism, avowed irrationalism, ethical subjectivism." In particular: (1) Kant divorced reason from reality. (2) Pragmatism makes expediency a criterion of knowledge and morality, and social consensus a benchmark of rationality. (3) Logical positivism and linguistic analysis elevate social consensus to final arbiters in metaphysics, epistemology, and ethics via the appeal to linguistic conventions and ordinary language. (4) Existentialism is the most dramatic form of nihilism and irrationalism, of the appeal to faith and emotions, as opposed to reason and objectivity.

The upshot of these and other developments, according to Rand, is a situation in which the knowability, indeed the very concept, of an objective reality is denied. Hence, the ability of the individual mind to discover (at least part of) the nature of this reality is taken to be an illusion. Faith, belief, and social consensus are substituted for reason, knowledge, and the activities of the rational person's consciousness.

Finally, while some philosophers in the tradition were, in Rand's view, legitimately skeptical of unproved assertion and of supernatural criteria of knowledge (e.g., ideals of knowledge such as those put forward by Plato and Descartes), other philosophers went even further and denied that anything is knowable or that any epistemological standards could be defended.[2]

On the face of it, many of these claims about the tradition ring true, although there is little, if any, defensible support for them to be found in Rand's writings. At the same time, a lot of Rand's claims, together with the vociferous manner in which they are put forward, are of a piece with, say, the view of Heidegger that all of western philosophy since Parmenides is a falling away from Being.[3] At the very least, Rand's interpreta-

39

tion of the tradition requires careful unpacking and elaboration. Even writers who are quite sympathetic toward Rand make remarks such as: "there is no question that often Rand's style of philosophy is literary, hyperbolic and emotional. This always makes interpreting her difficult and troublesome. . . . Nevertheless, . . . there is a meaningful philosophic doctrine underlying Rand's seemingly merely ideological points, . . . and patience and sensitivity can bring that doctrine out."[4]

I believe there is a grain of truth in Rand's attack on the tradition, just as there is a grain of truth in the similar attacks of Heidegger and Husserl, whose views will be mentioned later. It is for this reason that I shall seriously try to assess the merits and demerits of Rand's remarks on the tradition in the sequel.

The following theses[5] capture the basics of Rand's philosophy:

    1. Existence exists.

        a. Whatever one perceives exists. (Berkeley and Meinong would advocate this, too!)

        b. Consciousness is the faculty that perceives what exists.

    2. A is A. A thing is itself. Existence is identity; all things have a specific nature. Consciousness (via the process of concept formation) is the only faculty that can tell us *what*, e.g., a thing is. (Perception tells us *that* it is.)

    3. Reason is the only instrument for acquiring knowledge and thus the only means for survival qua man.

    4. Reason tells us what the nature of a thing is. Logic is the art of noncontradictory identification.

Unfortunately, because Rand maintains what Popper calls the idea that truth is manifest and thus the idea of the conspiratorial theory of ignorance, her response to those who would deny her axioms[6] would be: they are irrational or immoral, or both! This clearly will not do. Unless Rand's philosophy can be supported by more than the four axioms cited above, or until it can be shown that these axioms support only her philosophy, it will be difficult to take her views seriously. That is, she must show that her remarks are not merely the banalities they seem to be.

It is only by understanding her views on the tradition and by seeing her doctrines as an attempt to overcome what she thinks of as the main errors of the tradition that one can make sense out of what she is doing. It may be that what seems to be philosophical naïvete is directly a result of her basic understanding or misunderstanding of the tradition. Let us see if this is so.

RAND AND THE TRADITION

It turns out, I think, that there is a saner and more defensible gloss on what Rand says; and, though by no means original with her (Husserl, Heidegger, Popper, Blanshard, and Leo Strauss have put forward similar interpretations), this saner interpretation raises some crucial issues about the nature of philosophy and the reasons for what Husserl calls "the crisis of western reason."

It will be convenient to first sketch two interpretations of the philosophical tradition that have been alluded to more than once already: those of Husserl and Heidegger.[7] This might strike devotees of Rand's philosophy as analogous to starting off a treatment of Rand's political philosophy by discussing the views of John Kenneth Galbraith; but there are actually very close parallels between the views of Rand and the other two philosophers mentioned, on the topic at hand—although, needless to say, *only* on the topic at hand!

Both Husserl and Heidegger believe that European culture is in a crisis period, largely owing to the impact of western philosophy. For Heidegger, the history of metaphysics from Plato onward represents a continuous falling away from Being (the attention on "things," e.g., substance ontologies, is a hallmark of this falling away). Technological civilization is the nadir of this development, albeit the final culmination of an historical dialectic that begins with Plato and runs through Nietzsche. Western philosophy is dominated by subjectivism; Plato's theory of forms, no less than Descartes' epistemology, Nietzsche's will to power, and technological man's emphasis on manipulation and control as criteria of knowledge and praxis are expressions of this subjectivism, according to Heidegger, for they all are attempts to define Being in terms of what human beings can get a handle on, i.e., manipulate and control through thought and action. Thus, for Heidegger as for Rand, western philosophy is thoroughly subjectivistic, although their "solutions" to this predicament are, of course, vastly different.

For Husserl the crisis of the "European Sciences" represents the loss of the western *telos*. This mission, with its quasi-religious overtones, begins with Plato and Socrates. Perhaps the clearest statement of this mission is the *Republic*'s program for an ideal state, and the connected ideal of knowledge as dialectic in the image of the divided line. The highest form of knowledge—the dialectic—is required to bring out the telos and logos of Being, and accounts for the layers of knowledge and being—including science (which is a relatively low form of knowledge). This ideal provides at once the basis for Husserl's critique of modern science and philosophy, and the point to which we must return if we are to renew our efforts to fulfill the telos of western culture.

The falling away, on Husserl's view, comes with the advent of modern science. Galilean science is characterized by an attempt to make science the touchstone of all knowledge and reality; it represents the loss of telos and thus the loss of true knowledge as defined by Plato. (The "good" as the highest form is at once logos and telos.) Understanding of the order of Being is thrown overboard in favor of the idea that reality and knowledge are confined to what can be controlled and manipulated: the domination of man and nature (e.g., Bacon's view that knowledge is power) leads straight to the nihilism of our age, whether this is in the form of behaviorism or scientism, or of Romanticism and irrationalism. It is only by returning to the roots of our tradition that we can find salvation. For until this is done, the impact of this mechanization and devaluation of life and Being will persist; for Husserl, too, the crisis of our civilization (including World War I) is directly rooted in bad philosophy.

Now, whatever the merits and shortcomings of these views—and my crude sketch of them should not detract from their significance—there can be little doubt that Rand's view of the tradition, its historical mission, its falling away, and its negative cultural impact are of a piece with the views of Heidegger and Husserl.

Rand sometimes divides up the tradition between rationalists, who seek to deduce knowledge from concepts "inside their heads," and empiricists, who never move beyond the level of percepts. In other words, rationalists "abandon reality," "while empiricists cling to reality—by abandoning their mind."[8] For the rationalist, sensory experience plays no role; and for the empiricists, reality is limited to percepts. Both are equally mistaken, according to Rand.

Although remarks of this sort pervade Rand's writings, the most sustained discussions of these themes occur in the following works: "For the New Intellectual" and "This is John Galt Speaking,"[9] "The Cashing In: The Student Rebellion,"[10] *Introduction to Objectivist Epistemology,*[11] and "The Objectivist Ethics."[12] Since, as far as I can see, these works express variations on the same basic themes, I shall focus in what follows on the first two essays just cited, although other material will be referred to whenever appropriate. I shall first summarize Rand's key points, make explicit the claims and controversies she takes up, and go on to give my own gloss and evaluation of her stance toward the tradition, in the hope of preserving what I think is correct and valuable in her discussion.

Rand begins her article "For the New Intellectual" with the following remarks:

What are the intellectual values or resources offered to us by the present guardians of our culture? In philosophy we are taught that man's *mind is impotent*, and *reality is unknowable*, that *knowledge is an illusion*, and *reason a superstition.*[13]

[Moreover, these same thinkers have no answer to give to] those voices out of the Dark Ages who gloat that *freedom* and *reason* have had their chance and have failed, and that the future belongs once more to *faith* and *force.*[14]

This passage captures crucial features of Rand's own philosophy, as well as the gist of her critique of modern epistemology and metaphysics. (Ironically, Heidegger and Husserl attribute the crisis in western culture to precisely that philosophy whose loss Rand here bemoans!) Let us now try to decipher these remarks and begin the critical phase of this investigation.

"In philosophy we are taught that man's mind is impotent, that reality is unknowable, that knowledge is an illusion, and reason is a superstition." The obvious place to begin is here: *which* philosophers and *what* philosophical doctrines and theories does Rand have in mind? Unfortunately, this point of departure is of little help, since Rand's answer is: *all* philosophers (with the exception of Aristotle and, to a lesser degree, Aquinas) and *all* philosophies (except Aristotelianism). Rand may be right; at least, as I shall later argue, there's a grain of truth in her view. But, for exegetical purposes, it would be helpful to have more to go on. Suppose, then, we turn to each charge, one by one, and consider who and what Rand has in mind. (Textual evidence does indicate that the chief villains in her story are Plato, Hume, Kant, and Descartes; we shall get to them in due course.)

(a) *Man's mind is impotent.* What, precisely, is this supposed to mean? Clearly, it means that, according to Rand, philosophers hold that (b) *reality is unknowable*, and thus (c) *knowledge is an illusion*—because (d) *reason is a superstition.*

Now, in order to deal with these charges adequately one should have a quite detailed look at the history of philosophy. Nevertheless, this much can be said about them: *if* one defines the scope and limits of reason and knowledge, and the concept of reality, in the way that Plato, Aristotle—and the majority of the tradition—accept, then it *will* turn out that reality does become (more or less) unknowable or unknown. Thus it will turn out that knowledge, if not an illusion, is at best a regulative ideal, and that reason is an empty abstraction.

But it is at this point that the issues become joined. Perhaps the correct inference to draw is that there is something wrong with the conceptions of reality, knowledge, and reason embedded within the tradition—a tradition that gives rise both to classical rationalism and to classical skepticism, and that produces the oscillation between dogmatism and skepticism Rand correctly attacks. In short, her analysis of the situation is basically correct; but there may be other morals drawn. The inference I just drew is no less warranted than the moral Rand draws from the history of modern philosophy: viz, that any philosophy which fails to do justice to these conceptions of reality, knowledge, and reason is ipso facto wrongheaded, pernicious, irrationalist, and so forth. Indeed, her view—which I share—that existentialism, nihilism, behaviorism and certain simpleminded formulations of pragmatism, utilitarianism, and analytic philosophy are in part the outgrowth of this failure of the classical tradition, is not carried through far enough. For all these views are at bottom just the other side of the classical rationalist coin and thus stand or fall with it. Nihilism and subjectivism, for example, accept the concepts of knowledge that Rand attributes to the tradition. Of course, recognizing this point leaves us with the task of articulating plausible models of knowledge, reality, and reason.

It just won't do to say, as Rand does, that the choice is between freedom and reason on the one hand and faith and force on the other; for these contrasts and their alleged contradictory nature are themselves part of the rationalist-skepticist dispute and are in any case not self-evidently clear. It is more accurate to say that a certain paradigm of freedom and reason has failed and that those—including Rand—who take this failure as tantamount to a victory of faith and force, and as a defeat of freedom and reason, are not just mistaken but have also fallen prey to the paradigm that gives rise to both rationalism and skepticism. Rand herself still operates under the assumption that faith and force are the only alternatives to reason and freedom, just as whim is the only alternative to rationality.[15] But these assumptions are at least open to serious question and cannot be taken as unquestionable Archimedean standards for the evaluation of alternative points of view.

Thus, a basic problem Rand ignores, or at least takes to be unproblematic, has to do with the question of whether the pair of distinctions reason/freedom and faith/force are mutually incompatible and internally incompatible. First, Rand's overly narrow application of the laws of thought, e.g., the principle of contradiction and the law of excluded middle, lead her to assume that these pairs are contradictory. Here she is prone to the same dichotomy used by other classical liberals, notably Popper.[16]

Indeed, Rand stands doubly guilty on this count, since as a presumably serious Aristotelian, she could at least have considered whether these pairs are actually contrary or perhaps subcontrary rather than contradictory. If one of these relations should turn out to be the actual logical relationship between freedom and force, reason and faith, so that, say, reason and faith are not mutually exclusive, would that mean we should be committed to nihilism, irrationalism, subjectivism, or what have you?

An open question remains. One might as well hold, as Rand does, that the only alternative to the view that the truth is manifest is that man must act on whim! In fact, both of these Randian bits of rhetoric stem from the same source: they are manifestations of her allegiance to the view that the truth is manifest.

It might be objected at this point that this part of my discussion suffers from two basic defects: (1) it does not take the idea of axiom systems seriously enough; and (2) by denying a sharp distinction between faith and reason, it fosters irrationalism or subjectivism.

As a consequence of (1), what I say about the banality of Rand's axioms misses the point: axioms *should* be banal, because they are obviously true. To this charge I plead guilty, but I think the objection misses *my* point. I am not claiming that Rand's axioms are false or unimportant. What I am claiming is that they are philosophically unhelpful for several reasons. First, recent work by Quine, Wittgenstein, and others, to whom I shall refer in more detail later, shows that such axioms are so vague that they are unhelpful in specific cases (e.g., "*Is* a contradiction in the offing?"). As Feyerabend puts it, they are so vague that just about anything can be made consistent with them, which is why (he thinks) those who endorse such claims as having any real bite are driven, in effect, to maintain "anything goes." Second, no one in their right mind would reject these axioms. Since such people advocate doctrines that are incompatible with Rand's, the question naturally arises: who is right? Such questions must, *ex hypothesi*, be answered independently of the axioms. At the very least, one must make a case that non-Randian doctrines are incompatible with the axioms, but this brings us back to my first point.

With respect to objection (2), my view is not that there is a sharp faith/reason distinction with many things thought to fall under the reason side of the dichotomy actually falling under the faith side. Those who subscribe to this view, such as existentialists, actually maintain basically the same view of reason as does Rand: "If God is dead, everything is permitted." My view is that it is difficult to make a clear distinction between faith and reason or rationality and irrationality, and that the traditional (i.e., Cartesian-Kantian) way of making such a distinction—which Rand evidently endorses—is misleading at best. Recent philosophers who have taken this line—Quine, Kuhn, Wittgenstein, Rorty, and Feyerabend—are not "irrationalists" except by the tendentious standard Rand endorses. Indeed, the very charges of irrationalism and subjectivism take for granted the very idea of rationality that Rand endorses and these authors combat. Hence, at the very least, such accusations beg the issue.

A second, related problem has to do with the relationship *within* each pair of the above distinctions, viz, freedom and reason, faith and force (or at least ignorance and coercion, to be somewhat more accurate). One thing in common between Rand and much of the tradition she abhors is the assumption that freedom and reason are directly rather than inversely proportional. Yet, it does not require much thought to realize that this assumption may be nothing more than a blind bit of enlightenment faith. Writers such as Skinner may well be right: the more knowledge we have, the more we see that we are *not* free.

Indeed, according to the view Rand accepts, the ideally rational person (i.e., one with all the relevant information) would not have any freedom—save the freedom to be irrational, since he would see that reason, knowledge, and truth force the right view upon him; for the freedom to decide is, in this view, directly proportional to the amount of ignorance one is under at the time! It is thus no coincidence that Rand, despite all her talk of freedom in the ethical, political, and epistemological realm, claims that a rational person has only one choice: to think or not to think! So much for freedom *and* reason!

Those familiar with Dostoevsky's *Notes from the Underground* may find it amusing that Rand sees reality in precisely the terms of the underground man: as a stone wall, which one can either obey or futilely bang against. That is to say, one can either be a fatalist or an irrationalist. The fact that Rand and the underground man both see the choice between either the stone wall of reality and reason or irrationality and freedom gives us additional evidence that the dichotomy between rationalism and nihilism is not all that sharp and that the standard view of the relation between freedom and reason needs some rethinking.

At this point let me return to my main line of discussion. Rand's next move in the account of the tradition developed in "For the New Intellectual" is the introduction of two philosophical archetypes: Attila and the Witch Doctor. According to Rand, they "embody two variants of a certain view of man and of existence." She says:

> The essential characteristic of these two remain the same in all ages: Attila, the man who rules by brute force, acts on the range of the moment, is concerned with nothing but the physical reality immediately before him, respects nothing but man's muscles, and regards a fist, a club or a gun as the only answer to any problem—and the *Witch Doctor*, the man who dreads physical reality, dreads the necessity of practical action, and escapes into his emotions, into visions of some mystic realm where his wishes enjoy a supernatural power unlimited by the absolute of nature.[17]

Let me take up some of the issues raised by these remarks.

1. The witch doctor, i.e., the traditional philosopher (as an ideal type) is "the man who dreads physical reality, dreads the necessity of practical action, and escapes into his emotions, into visions of some practical realm where his wishes enjoy a supernatural power unlimited by the absolute of nature." This quasi-Nietzschean remark suggests the idea that Plato and others maintain a utopian ideal of knowledge. So their response to Attila—e.g., the sophists or the seventeenth-century skeptic—is itself rooted in a kind of skepticism, since it postulates an otherworldly set of standards as the only alternative to skepticism. As a result, for Plato, Descartes, and Kant (a) knowledge is impossible and (b) rational action and the justification of our practices, both epistemic and (broadly speaking) normative, becomes impossible.[18]

2. The witch doctor and Attila have (in effect) a "consciousness held down to the perceptual method of functioning, an awareness that does not choose to extend beyond the automatic, the immediate, the given, the involuntary, which means:

an animal's epistemology, or as near to it as a human consciousness can come." This may be true of Hume or Nietzsche, but is
it true of Plato? Perhaps if, as Rand and Husserl believe, Hume
and Plato are just developing variations on the same idea: either
accept utopian standards (i.e., rationalism) or face nihilism. (For
Heidegger both Plato and Nietzsche are "subjectivists.")

3. In sum: "It is against the faculty of *reason* that Attila and
the Witch Doctor rebel. The key to both their souls is the long-
ing for the effortless, irresponsible, automatic consciousness of
an animal. Both dread the necessity, the risk and the responsibility of rational cognition. Both dread the fact that 'nature, to
be commanded, must be obeyed.' Both seek to exist, not by conquering nature, but by adjusting to the given, the immediate, the
known." [19]

If the absolute of nature is a given, how can we fail to obey it,
and how can we succeed in conquering it? Why is it not a fact
about human nature, as Hume believed, that we do and must
survive by animal instinct and not reason? Why is Descartes not
right in claiming that the ideal state of knowledge consists in the
availability of an algorithm for deducing "automatic," "uncon-
scious" theorems from a body of axioms expressing facts about
the given (passively forced upon the rational mind) via the use
of deductive logic? Why is Bacon correct in asserting that to understand nature we must conquer it, rather than submit to it or
develop contemplative relationships to it?

As I understand her, Rand is raising some very crucial issues
in these passages, regardless of whether her own views are ultimately supportable. According to Rand, rationalism is an attempt to define reality, reason, and knowledge in subjective
terms and then project these onto objective reality to satisfy certain irrational sorts of infantile cravings. According to this
Nietzschean interpretation of rationalism, truth, knowledge, reality, and reason are redefined by the rationalist so as to make
one's own wishes, whims, and ideas the very criteria of reality.
The result of this is:

The damnation of this earth as a realm where nothing is possible
to man but pain, disaster and defeat, a realm inferior to another,
"higher" reality; . . . the damnation of reason as a "limited," decep-

tive, unreliable, impotent faculty, incapable of perceiving the "real" reality, and the "true" truth; the split of man in two, the splitting of his consciousness against his body, and his moral values against his own interest.[20]

There are many issues, both exegetical and analytic, raised here. But the key issues are these:

1. Much of philosophy (e.g., Descartes, Plato, and Kant) is governed by a utopian ideal of knowledge and an otherworldly conception of reality, together with a superhuman or nonhuman ideal of reason. The result of this is a continuous oscillation between dogmatism and skepticism, which are equally false and pernicious.

2. The ever widening gulf between reason and practice, between the "vulgar" views of common sense and the philosophical standards of theory (including, I would add, science) is largely responsible for the nihilism and irrationalism of the modern age.

3. The root of this paradigm is a kind of theology, a kind of mysticism, which, by ignoring the conditions of human existence and those of nature, makes it appear that we cannot know anything because what we claim to know is limited by just these conditions![21]

THE ISSUE OF RATIONALITY

It will be helpful to provide a gloss on what Rand is saying by focusing on the issue of rationality. A convenient point of departure is D. Pole's "The Concept of Reason." According to Pole:

The rational . . . is the objective; thinkers who think rationally think alike—at least unimpeded, and given the same data, they think alike. . . . We oppose the objective to the arbitrary—the arbitrary, that can know of no right or wrong. Reason, then, presupposes evaluation, the difference of better and worse, of ideal and actual, and unless we are to rest content with arbitrary differences which . . . the very concept (of rationality) forbids, it commits us further to the ideal possibility of the non-arbitrary agreement among thinkers—whom it is then only tautological to call "rational." It relates to truth, too, inasmuch as the approach to true beliefs, both non-accidental and self-authenticating, is and must be by way of Reason, that is, the non-arbitrary assessment of evidence, observation, and the like.

We expect rational minds to think alike; they "see" what there is to be "seen." (When we "genuinely disagree" . . . "one of us is right or at least wrong" . . . which yields a . . . definition of objectivity.) Reason is the sole route to truth; or the only non-arbitrary road to truth.[22]

Universality and necessity serve reason as obligatory ideals. This, in a nutshell, captures both the Cartesian theory of rationality and its connection with the Cartesian program that underlies modern epistemology and theories of scientific method. It will be helpful at this point to elaborate on both of these items in some detail.

First, what Pole calls the rationality principle must be clearly formulated, since its status (i.e., its acceptability) underlies the debates I want to evaluate here. The principle states: "It is impossible that two equally rational people, i.e., two people in possession of the (same) data, having equal facility in (deductive) logic, should disagree with each other about what conclusions or interpretations rationality requires. To think otherwise is to call into question such 'obligatory ideals' as Objectivity, Truth, Knowledge (universality and necessity) and Methodological Objectivity/Justification." To appreciate how this principle must stand or fall with the entire Cartesian program, several key features of the latter must be mentioned.

1. Objectivity/realism. The world consists of things (events, processes) that have a fixed intelligible structure, i.e., a *logos* and a *telos*, which is causally and conceptually independent of human activity.

2. Knowledge. Knowledge consists in the fact that the human knower has discerned the universal and necessary essence of the objective structure of the world.

3. Truth. There is one truth about this world, and this one truth must be construed teleologically, i.e., the truth is objective—fixed in accordance with the world's logos and telos—and progress toward the truth, i.e., the growth of knowledge, of objective/rational methods of inquiry and practice, is also teleological (although not necessarily progressive).

4. Rationality. Rationality consists in adopting the most

(only?) efficient means for promoting the discovery of objective truth, i.e., for the acquisition of knowledge. One must develop reason, i.e., the faculty for discovering truth, by articulating a program (Cartesianism), à la Descartes, Russell, Carnap, or whomever; the only alternative to such a procedure—which must provide an algorithm for discovering that truth—is Humean skepticism, nihilism, irrationalism, relativism, and so forth. Deductive inference, self-certifying intuitions or experiences concerning "first truths," must constitute the core of this program. The program can then be employed on an ever increasing body of hard facts or data so as to yield an objective picture of the world that approximates the truth, or at least approaches it asymptotically. All beliefs, actions, theories, and methods—in science and ethics—must be certified as rational by these criteria or else must be committed to the flames as sophistry and illusion, that is, must be seen as so many subjective interpretations or projections onto the world. Since the truth is one, disagreements must imply that one or both parties to a disagreement have erred, either because of faulty reasoning, ignorance of the facts, or premature judgment. All rational persons are essentially identical.

5. Methodological Objectivity. From the point of view of formulating rules for discovering and justifying objective truth (methodology), the rational thing to do is to look at the world from an objective, neutral, God's-eye perspective. That is, the rational inquirer must ape the stance of God, who alone perceives the world objectively, i.e., *sub species aeternitatis*. Methodological objectivity requires that rational inquirers look at the hard facts in ways that do not distort them. Since all interpretations and value judgments are distorting (they are subjective and idiosyncratic—and assimilated to secondary qualities), rationality requires the stance of an ideal (Laplacean) observer or computer, who passively takes in the facts and uses the self-certifying machinery of deductive logic in accordance with the rules laid down by the Cartesian program. All subjective factors—historical, psychological, sociological, nonlogical—must be eliminated, being at best irrelevant and at worst detrimental to the rational search for truth. Just as all persons are essentially

alike *in abstracto* (when stripped of everything but the faculty of reason), all objective methodologies are essentially alike (when stripped of all accidental, i.e., nonlogical, features). Rational inquiry and, thus, rational agents proceed in a logical vacuum in which a pure (Cartesian) ego operates as a data-processing machine that insures complete objectivity.

If I am right, the ideal of rationality embedded in Cartesianism is untenable because it is incoherent. If rationality requires that we take a quasi-divine stance toward the world, if we must place ourselves outside the world to act rationally and objectively so as to discover truth, we are in effect being told that rationality requires us to act in nonhuman or superhuman fashion.[23] It is no wonder that classical philosophy oscillates between dogmatism and skepticism, for even skeptics (such as Hume, Sartre, Nietzsche, and Kierkegaard) tacitly accept that the only choice open to us is between some variant of Cartesianism or total nihilism. Classical skepticism accepts exactly the same models of objectivity, knowledge, truth, and rationality that rationalists accept; in effect, it generates a *reductio* of them so that skeptical conclusions are drawn. In short, virtually all of philosophy consists of so many variations on the Cartesian paradigm. Obviously, this is not the place to pursue these matters in depth. However, several general remarks are in order.

Rand is surely right, it seems to me, that the tradition at issue must oscillate between nihilism and an otherworldly ideal of knowledge. In fact, as F. Will[24] and others—including Heidegger and Husserl—show, nihilism, Platonism, and the like are but sides of the same coin—variants of the same mistaken paradigm. At the very least, the one thing we are not entitled to do is use this paradigm as an unproblematic Archimedean reference point for judging the plausibility of new proposals regarding the ideas of knowledge, objectivity, and rationality.

However, Rand's strategy sometimes falls victim to this very criticism: we cannot use the philosophical standards of Aristotelianism as such a reference point either, if only because slogans such as Don't evade reality, or Always use reason, are quite empty, unless you have already solved the substantive difficulties at issue. Although Rand does emphasize the basic weaknesses in this tradition, e.g., the utopian idea of knowledge, she often talks as though any philosophical doctrines that do not advocate a kind of naïve realism about objectivity, knowledge, and reason are bound to be nihilistic. At other points, her development of Aristotelian doctrines, e.g., the contextualism put forward at the beginning of the *Nicomachean Ethics*, are more promising. But what Rand failed to realize is that the modern heirs to Aristotle include authors such as Quine and Dewey as well as various Oxonians, who are all anathema to Rand. By the same token, there are elements in Aristotelianism that are themselves infused with the Platonic, Cartesian, Kantian paradigm Rand is at pains to attack.

To summarize this stage of the discussion, I have provided an interpretation of some key developments in modern epistemology that I take to be supportive of some of Rand's views about the tradition. While this interpretation is not original to me òr Rand and was arrived at independent of my readings in Rand, it is at least congruent with what she says, up to a point. There are, however, some residual difficulties for Rand's philosophy if my interpretation of the Cartesian paradigm is right. These difficulties stem from two factors.

1. Rand's own views contain remnants of the Cartesian paradigm she tries to attack. She clearly accepts the rationality principle and the idea of knowledge, objectivity, and reality embodied in Cartesianism—these going back, of course, to Plato and Aristotle. She does reject, to some degree, the "utopian" element in the Cartesian model; but her own epistemology is no less rationalistic in just the ways that seem—for well-known and not altogether incorrect reasons—to make classical rationalism problematic for most contemporary thinkers. Indeed, many of the views she rejects thus come to be embodied, although in different forms, in her own philosophy, e.g., the idea that whim is the only alternative to rational choice, as this is conceived on the Cartesian model.

2. By the same token, many views that Rand attacks have, on some variations, closer affinities with some of her key doctrines and assumptions than she is either able or willing to recognize. For instance, her views on the relation between consciousness,

volition, and knowledge are compatible with certain well-known expressions of pragmatism and certain formulations of empiricism. (Knowledge is routed in praxis; knowledge is contextual and not judged by reference to a context-free absolute standard.) There are, that is to say, more and less acceptable formulations of such doctrines. Rand's oversimplification of such views misses this basic point and thus prevents her from making use of ideas that fit in with her own philosophy and might enhance them.

A case in point is her allegiance to Aristotle's well-known principle that one should not expect more certainty in methods or results than the nature of the subject matter allows; another is her view that knowledge has practical roots.[25] Clearly, Rand's attack on the utopian elements in the Cartesianism that eventuates in wholesale nihilism is based upon these sound and sensible principles, as is her discussion of the relation between business and knowledge (cf. Plato and Aristotle on *Poesis*, *Techne*, *Episteme*, and *Praxis* versus the otherworldliness of "pure" reason).

But what Rand fails to see is that many of the doctrines and philosophers she attacks (at least by implication), such as Quine, Wittgenstein, and Dewey are Aristotelians in this respect. In fact, Quine's notion of a "naturalistic epistemology" is quite compatible with Rand's epistemology so far as the motivation behind it is concerned; although Quine's version of empiricism, if such it be, is quite different from Rand's. Thus, Rand's view that one does not have to be omniscient to possess knowledge is compatible with a number of views that she may or may not like. The task is, then, either to show why those of her doctrines which grow out of this principle are better than rival doctrines that are equally compatible with it or else to make use of doctrines which might enhance Rand's program, even if they come from the pens of people whom Rand would consider anathema.

To put this point quite bluntly, there is a sense in which Oxford philosophers, pragmatists such as Dewey, Quine, and Rorty and those in the Hermeneutic tradition of Wittgenstein, Kuhn, and Gadamer are just as much the legitimate heirs of Aristotle as is Rand. To be sure, they may take Aristotle's important writings to consist of the early parts of the *Nicomachean Ethics*, *Categories*, and the *Topics*, while for Rand the *Metaphysics* and similar writings express the best in Aristotle. But the point remains: there are large chunks of Aristotle that Rand does in fact make use of and that are also at the core of movements such as pragmatism and ordinary language philosophy. So, either Rand's philosophy is not the only one compatible with a high regard for Aristotle, or her scatter-gun attacks on pragmatism, ordinary language philosophy, and so forth, neglect the fact that some of her own doctrines are of a piece with theirs, at least insofar as their common Aristotelian element goes.

Finally, to reiterate a point made at the outset, the articulation and defense of the sort of philosophy Rand seems to favor cannot ignore all the water that has gone under the bridge since Aristotle. Neither can one ignore all the difficulties such a view must face: the problem of underdetermination; problems about radical indeterminacy and ontological relativity made known by Quine, Goodman, and others; doctrines about the relations between language, thought, and cognition and their impact on epistemological theories; issues involving translation, incommensurability, and so on. These issues will not go away, and realists (e.g., Kripke, Putnam, Harré, and Chomsky)[26] who see the need to deal with them are ipso facto one step ahead of Rand.

Yet, the conclusion of this essay is this: Rand, writing at a time when it was unfashionable to be a realist or rationalist, managed, despite herself, to pinpoint some basic difficulties in our philosophical tradition; and, again, despite herself, managed to suggest some potentially fruitful directions for the realist to explore. Her blend of commonsense realism, coupled with a staunch advocacy of a free, open society and an unremitting attack on the practical ramifications of bad philosophy (especially those epistemologies that lead to nihilism and a closed society) have earned her (as they have earned Popper, whose thought parallels hers on these points) a lasting debt of gratitude. But gratitude for the sort of achievements mentioned should not be mistaken for gratitude for something Rand never has done: develop her good sense for the rights and wrongs of the issues into a defensible and workable theory of knowledge.

NOTES

1. Ayn Rand, *Capitalism: The Unknown Ideal* (New York: Signet Books, 1966), pp. 246–47.

2. Ayn Rand, *For the New Intellectual* (New York: Signet Books, 1961), p. 157. Hereafter cited as *FNI*.

3. See E. Husserl, *The Crisis of European Science and Transcendental Phenomenology*, trans. D. Carr (Evanston: Northwestern University Press, 1970); M. Heidegger, *Being and Time* (New York: Harper, 1962). See also the writings of Karl Popper, esp. "On the Sources of Knowledge and Ignorance" and "Three Views Concerning Human Knowledge" in *Conjectures and Refutations* (New York: Basic Books, 1962).

4. Douglas Den Uyl and Douglas Rasmussen, "Nozick on the Randian Argument," *The Personalist*, April 1978, p. 203.

5. Rand, *FNI*, pp. 124–27. Cf. Ayn Rand, "The Objectivist Ethics," in *The Virtue of Selfishness* (New York: Signet Books, 1964), pp. 18–22.

6. Cf., e.g., W. V. Quine, "On What There Is," in *From a Logical Point of View* (New York: Harper, 1961).

7. Heidegger, *Being and Time*; Husserl, *Crisis of European Science*. See also M. Natanson, *Edmund Husserl: Philosopher of Infinite Tasks* (Evanston: Northwestern University Press, 1973); A. Gurvitsch, "The Last Work of Edmund Husserl," in *Studies in Phenomenology and Philosophy* (Evanston: Northwestern University Press, 1966); H. Marcuse, "Science and Phenomenology," in J. Gould and W. Truitt, eds., *Existentialist Philosophy* (Encino, Calif.: Dickenson, 1973). Rand, like Husserl, Heidegger, and Popper, assigns tremendous importance to philosophy as a cause of cultural, political, and social developments. She holds that humankind cannot survive without a rational philosophy; yet she also holds that most of modern history has been dominated by irrational philosophies. One may thus conclude, I suppose, either that Hume and Nietzsche were right and it is instinct and not reason that promotes survival, i.e., utility is no guide to truth, or else that Rand is wrong to suppose that more than a few people need to be rational for humankind to survive!

8. Ayn Rand, "Kant vs. Sullivan," *The Objectivist*, March 1970, p. 1.

9. Rand, *FNI*.

10. Rand, *Capitalism*.

11. Ayn Rand, *Introduction to Objectivist Epistemology* (New York: The Objectivist, 1966).

12. Ayn Rand, "The Objectivist Ethics," in *The Virtue of Selfishness* (New York: Signet Books, 1964).

13. Rand, *FNI*, pp. 10–11. Emphasis added.

14. Ibid., p. 12.

15. One of the main dichotomies Rand draws is between those who are in favor of reason and those who act on whim, as if these are the only alternatives. This is, of course, to accept the Cartesian idea expressed by Sartre that if

God is dead everything is permitted. Aside from debatable figures such as Dostoevsky's underground man, no one, including Sartre, Nietzsche, Kierkegaard, Ayer, Carnap, or any other skeptic, has ever put forward a view defending whims. On the other hand, as Feyerabend likes to say, one who defends a view of rationality such as Rand's is, by virtue of the *uselessness* of these standards, committed to the idea that anything goes.

16. See R. Edgley, "Reason and Violence: A Fragment of the Liberal Ideology," in S. Korner, ed., *Practical Reason* (New Haven: Yale University Press, 1976).

17. Rand, *FNI*, p. 14.

18. Ibid.

19. Ibid., p. 15.

20. Ibid., pp. 17, 18, 19.

21. Cf. the remarks of Rand about Kant's philosophy, ibid., pp. 31–32. For more on the issues raised on this score, see T. Nagel, "What is it like to be a Bat," *Philosophical Review* (1974), pp. 435–51.

22. D. Pole, "The Concept of Reason," in R. Dearden, R. Hirst, and R. Peters, eds., *Reason* (London: Routledge, 1973), pp. 1–26, at pp. 4, 7, 21.

23. See S. Hampshire, *Thought and Action* (New York: Viking, 1959), ch. 1; N. Maxwell, *What's Wrong with Science?* (Hayes, England: Bran's Head Books, 1975); D. Hamlyn, "Objectivity," in Dearden, et al., *Reason*, pp. 96–111; T. Nagel, "The Absurd," *Journal of Philosophy* 59:716–27.

24. F. Will, *Induction and Justification* (Ithaca: Cornell University Press, 1974). Ironically this is a driving force behind the later views of Wittgenstein, as well as pragmatists such as Dewey and Quine.

25. Rand, *FNI*, p. 55. Rand develops the line of argument implicit in this principle in *Introduction to Objectivist Epistemology*. While this account suffers from the same shortcomings I have detailed in this essay, the defense of a theory of knowledge based upon this principle seems to me not just the best feature of the work of Rand—and Dewey—but a desideratum for any serious theory of knowledge. Devotees of Rand would be well advised to look at the recent work of Quine (as well as to rethink their view on Dewey). For instance, see W. V. Quine, "Epistemology Naturalized," in *Ontological Relativity and Other Essays* (New York: Columbia University Press, 1970). On the relation between capitalism and pragmatism, see Joseph W. McGuire, *Business and Society* (New York: McGraw-Hill, 1963).

26. See Robert Hollinger, "Natural Kinds, Family Resemblances and Conceptual Change," *The Personalist* (Autumn 1974), pp. 323–33; id., "A Defense of Essentialism," ibid. (Autumn 1976), pp. 327–43; id., "The Philosophical Significance of the Duhemian Argument," ibid. (Summer 1978), pp. 421–40. See also Robert Hollinger, "Aspects of the Theory of Classification," *Philosophy and Phenomenological Research* (March 1976), pp. 319–38; id., "Two Kinds of Fictionalism," *Monist* (October 1977), pp. 555–66; id., "The Role of Aspect Seeing in Wittenstein's Later Thought," *Cultural Hermeneutics* (November 1974), pp. 229–43. My own thoughts have been greatly influenced by the realists just mentioned. One key part of my own

strategy in defense of realism against the sort of doctrines mentioned is to distinguish between theory-free knowledge and theory-invariant knowledge. The latter is all the realist requires, and the skeptical doctrines mentioned above touch only the validity of the former idea. Advocates of these skeptical doctrines usually miss this point and take the refutation of the first idea as tantamount to rejection of the second. This is simply a mistake.

II

Ethics

4

Life,
Teleology,
and Eudaimonia
in the
Ethics
of
Ayn Rand

⊙

Douglas J. Den Uyl
and
Douglas B. Rasmussen

Ayn Rand's approach to ethics is one that does not begin by assuming any particular moral viewpoint. She is much more concerned with the foundation of ethics than most ethicians. Rand begins her ethics with what we have called a "transcendental" question. She asks: what makes values possible? By this question she means not just what makes interests, wants, and pleasures, *as opposed to* rights, obligations, and duties possible. Rather, she is concerned with what gets the entire normative enterprise—both theories of goodness and theories of right—off the ground. Why, in other words, are there things that are considered good or actions one is obligated to perform *in the first place*? In a way, Rand is like Plato. She feels the threat of the ethical nihilist who denies the existence of moral knowledge. Rand is concerned about the person who does not want to play the moral game. She considers the response offered by many contemporary ethicians, "because it is right," to be weak and responsible for the dangerous separation of morality from human living. Rand rejects the Kantian starting point in ethics.

She does not consider universalizability, in any of its formulations, as sufficient to ground ethics.

Rand's starting point in ethics comes from a much different ethical paradigm—the Aristotelian one. When she asks "Why are there values?" she is asking "Why is there end-oriented behavior?" *Value* for Rand is a morally neutral term. It can be best understood to refer to an object of an action, an end or goal—as Aristotle would say, "that-for-the-sake-of-which something is done." Rand puts it simply: "A value is that which one acts to gain and/or keep."[1] Jack Wheeler's essay explores this similarity, and many others, between Rand's ethics and Aristotle's ethics and shows that Rand's ethics is clearly in the classical Greek tradition.

A value considered as an end can be the object of either a purposive or nonpurposive action. Rand regards insentient living things as attaining values in the sense that the automatic functions of the organism result in the attainment of an end.[2] As David Lowenthal has recently put the issue:

Living things develop from an immature to a mature stage: at any given point they can be healthy or unhealthy: some of their activities involve striving for something needed, in the main unconsciously. . . . Try to understand [the process of maturation] only in terms of itself or its preceding conditions at any given moment, and you will miss the main feature of the development. . . . With the proper sustenance, internal causes proceed to guide the organism's growth according to the kind of thing it is. Such biological development is analogous to purposive human action toward some end, except that it is lacking in conscious awareness.[3]

Valuation, then, is present in any living thing: it is the process of acting for an end, be it purposive or nonpurposive. Such processes Rand takes to be one of the facts of the world. Yet she does not consider this end-oriented behavior to imply the existence of an immaterial conscious agency at work throughout nature. Again, as Lowenthal has put the issue, to maintain a place for end-oriented behavior in nature is *not* "to prove the existence of God, to make any statement whatsoever about the kind of process by which living things first appeared. It is simply to notice the facts of the case—empirical facts—rather than to provide an explanation of their origin."[4] Rand concurs with this analysis of end-oriented behavior and, moreover, does not consider such behavior to be exhibited throughout nature. Rather, she considers teleological explanation to be applicable only to beings of a particular type: living beings. It is only to living things that considerations of ends or goals are appropriate. Thus, teleological explanation must be considered when dealing with the behavior of living things but not with nonliving things. Rand rejects any single-science approach, be it an attempt to universalize teleology or an attempt to universalize mechanism.

To claim that end-oriented behavior is exhibited in the behavior of living things is certainly not novel; yet it is not so common to state that such behavior is confined to a particular class of entities—that is, to say that *only* living beings engage in end-oriented behavior.[5] To say the latter, one has to have discovered what it is that makes such behavior possible. Just what does the nature of such behavior imply? Rand would argue for the following three general theses:

1. End-oriented behavior implies that there is an alternative present. If there were no question of achieving an end, if an end's achievement were guaranteed—then there would be no necessity to act for an end. End-oriented behavior demands the existence of an alternative.

2. End-oriented behavior requires the existence of an entity of a certain type—namely, it must be an entity whose actions could achieve or fail to achieve an end. If success or failure with respect to some end were not conditional on the entity itself—in other words, if it were not at least possible for some of the entity's actions to achieve an end—then *it* could have no ends.

3. End-oriented behavior requires that the alternative faced by an entity be capable of making a difference, having an effect or consequence upon the entity. If the result of failing to achieve some end were ultimately no different than the result of achieving that same end, there would be no significance to either achieving it or not achieving it. Hence no *alternative* would be faced by the entity. An alternative must be capable of making a difference to the entity which faces it.

These three general conditions must exist if there is to be end-oriented behavior. All three of these conditions are present only in a single class of entities—living things. Rand puts the matter as follows: "There is only one fundamental alternative in the universe: existence or non-existence—and it pertains to a single class of entities: to living organisms. The existence of inanimate matter is unconditional, the existence of life is not: it depends on a specific course of action."[6] If failure or success with respect to some end could not ultimately be differentiated at the level of existence for some entity, there would be no difference between failure or success metaphysically speaking. Any difference offered between the two would be strictly illusory: for, really, there would be no necessity for an entity to act, since there would be no real alternative. Nothing would actually matter.

Rand's grounding of teleology in the very nature of living things is a novel and important addition to the Aristotelian tradition. Recently, however, Alan Gotthelf has argued in "Aristotle's Conception of Final Causality" that such a view of teleology is indeed Aristotle's own. He states that the primary use of "for the sake of" is in regard to the development of a living organism and that all other uses of "for the sake of" are understood by Aristotle to be definable in terms of this primary use.[7] In other words, final causation in Aristotle should not be interpreted in terms of some "immaterial agency" present in all of nature or in an "as if" mechanical fashion, but as an irreducible potential for form that characterizes organic development.[8]

Teleology, then, is found in the universe because the very nature of living things involves the development toward the form of the mature organism, and this means that life is the ontological basis for end-oriented behavior. Nonliving beings face no alternative of existence or nonexistence. A nonliving thing, e.g., a sofa or a boulder, may be open to the possibility of nonexistence. The sofa could be reconstructed into something else—say a bed—and a boulder could be smashed into a million pieces so that it becomes gravel or sand; but neither of these is an alternative that the sofa or boulder faces. They may be respective possibilities open to the sofa or boulder, but they are not alternatives faced by them. The sofa or boulder does not achieve or fail to achieve its existence as a result of its actions. *Their existence is not an object, a result, or an end of their actions.* The basic "stuff" of the world may change or evolve toward increasing complexity or simplicity, but it cannot cease to be—its existence is conditional on nothing. Thus, nonliving beings face no alternatives and hence cannot perform end-oriented actions. Only living things can do so.[9] Rand's insight that life is the necessary and sufficient condition for end-oriented behavior certainly conforms to Gotthelf's interpretation of final causality and shows how much she is within this Aristotelian naturalist tradition.

Putting Rand's insights regarding the nature of end-oriented behavior in different but related language, we can say that the reason there are natural functions is because life is just the type of being that is inherently functional. Eric Mack's work, both in this volume and elsewhere,[10] explores this issue in much greater detail.

Rand holds that an ultimate value is "that final goal or end to which all lesser goals are evaluated."[11] Given that there is valuation in the world, given that end-oriented behavior exists, there must be something that constitutes the final cause of such behavior. Rand accepts the necessity of there being something that explains such behavior and considers the answer to be provided by the nature of living being. Life is the ultimate value or end. Rand states:

Without an ultimate goal or end, there can be no lesser goals or means: a series of means going off into an infinite progression toward a non-existent end is a metaphysical and epistemological impossibility. . . . Metaphysically, *life* is the only phenomenon that is an end in itself: a value gained and kept by a constant process of action. Epistemologically, the concept of "value" is genetically dependent upon and derived from the antecedent concept of "life."[12]

All end-oriented behavior ultimately aims at life, but life as such, in the abstract, does not exist. For any given living being, then, it is life as the *kind* of thing it is that constitutes its ultimate end or value. In fact, it is the nature of the living entity, the kind of thing it is, that determines whether the life of the entity is achieved. Rand states that "the fact that a living entity *is* determines what it *ought* to do."[13] In other words, living beings are the source of values in the world. For Rand there is no chasm between facts and values, not because all facts are values or all values are facts, but because some facts are inherently value laden. Considered metaphysically, life is a value. Rand does not believe, however, that it is an *intrinsic* value, that is, a value that is not the object of some entity's actions. Rather, a living being acts to live. All the actions that a living being takes for various ends—no matter what the level—constitute its life. The success at being the sort of living thing it is is determined by reference to its nature; but the value of the entity's life consists in the relationship between the entity's actions and the objects it pursues. As Rand states, "life is an end in itself: a value gained and kept by a constant process of action." [14]

In the case of human life, the standard Rand offers for evaluating the ends chosen by a human being is man's life qua man. "That which is proper to the life of a rational being is the good." [15] That is to say, man's life qua man is the *totum bonum*, the ultimate moral value. It is the end toward which all human choices implicitly aim, [16] and it is thus the standard by which moral goodness is determined.

Though Rand does not explicitly use the following terms, she does seem to be committed to the idea that a good *x* is one that conforms to its nature or fulfills its natural function. In this regard she is adopting much from the Greek ethical tradition but is still making her own important contribution; for fulfilling a natural function or conforming to one's nature are only occurrences for living things. Thus, although Rand denies intrinsic value, she can still hold that good and value exist in nature. There are good oaks, good horses, and good men precisely because the natural order contains end-oriented action.

We have already noted that it is not enough to speak only of life in the abstract. We must, therefore, consider the question of *what sort* of living thing a human being is. The attempt to answer this question will necessarily lead to discussions about the specific values appropriate to the particular kind of thing under consideration. Were we to change our object of consideration from one kind of thing to another, the particular list of values associated with one kind of thing would not be applicable to the other kind.

Since we are concerned with Rand's ethics, our attention must be directed toward human nature. And if we look to human nature, we must distinguish those characteristics of human nature that are relevant for the determination of ethical norms. In Rand's eyes, the most fundamental fact about human nature appropriate to a theory of ethics is that human beings have no automatic means of survival.[17]

Man has no automatic code of survival. He has no automatic course of action, no automatic set of values. His senses do not tell him automatically what is good for him or evil, what will benefit his life or endanger it, what goals he should pursue and what means will achieve them, what *values* his life depends on, what course of action it requires. His own consciousness has to discover the answers to all these questions—but his consciousness will not function automatically.[18]

The various elements of this passage constitute the central themes for the foundations of Rand's ethics. Indeed, she elaborates on each of them in her essay "The Objectivist Ethics." Although we cannot detail each of the points made above, we can safely summarize those points by saying that man is a living being essentially characterized by choice and rationality.

If we have no automatic mode of survival, then we must choose among alternative courses of action just to maintain our very existence. Yet to do even this much it is necessary that we approach reality with full conceptual awareness; for, as Rand tells us, "no percepts and no 'instincts' will tell him how to light a fire, how to weave a cloth, how to forge tools."[19] The conceptual apparatus we possess as human beings is itself volitional. That is to say, we must *direct* our consciousness toward reality in an effort to gain any clarity at all about how to deal with that reality. Rationality and choice are thus not two separate faculties, but rather distinct aspects of the same cognitive contact with the world. The preceding point is best expressed in the following words of Tibor Machan:

Man's rationality must involve the capacity to choose. Conceptual awareness could not occur without the freedom to engage in such action, without man's *power* to initiate the act of forming concepts. . . . While sensory and perceptual awareness may be produced in animals by those features of the world that possess sensible qualities, there is nothing in nature that produces concepts; there is nothing in nature that forces generalizations, classifications, theories, and ideas upon us.[20]

Notice that our passages from Rand and Machan offer descriptions of essential features of human nature. Therefore, whether the issue is our mere survival (how do I obtain food) or more sublime pursuits (how do I satisfy my aesthetic needs), the fact remains that the only way human beings can accomplish their ends is by exercising choice and rationality.

The foregoing facts about man's nature[21] serve to distinguish man from other creatures, such that what is properly called morality can be seen as applicable only to human beings. What, therefore, distinguishes the morally good action from the types of good found in other living creatures is that the morally good action is dependent upon the existence of choice.[22] To put the matter more precisely, one's actions are subject to moral evaluation only if those actions are chosen. The morally good action is an action chosen for its appropriateness to human life, while the morally evil action is a chosen action that is detrimental to human life. Finally, because our consciousness is itself volitional, rationality will become the basic virtue for Rand.

The necessity for a code of conduct is dictated both by the fact that there is no automatic course of action given to men and because our particular mode of apprehending reality is conceptualization. In the former case, the lack of an automatic course of action demands that we develop a substitute—namely, rules or norms that serve to guide our action. Without these guidelines the significance of each event would have to be completely reevaluated with the consequent result of a complete paralysis of action. With respect to the latter case (rationality), the act of conceptualization is an act of integrating data and formulating mental units that extend to a large number of specific individuals. In the realm of action, concepts are formulated conceptions about which courses of action are life-enhancing by integrating various types of cases that are then expressed as a rule or principle of action. A code of conduct is thus demanded by both the volitional and the rational aspects of our nature. Rand concludes:

Ethics is *not* a mystic fantasy—nor a social convention—nor a dispensible, subjective luxury, to be switched or discarded in any emergency. Ethics is an *objective, metaphysical necessity of man's survival*—not by the grace of the supernatural nor of your neighbors nor of your whims, but by the grace of reality and the nature of life.[23]

We should pause at this point and note that those features of a moral code required by contemporary moralists—e.g., universality, necessity, and consistency—are also features of Rand's ethics. However, Rand neither draws these criteria from some mysterious noumenal self, nor does she say they are the formal properties of our moral language or of our action.[24] The universality of moral principles derives, instead, from the common human nature to which those principles refer. The same thing may be said for necessity and consistency, with the addition that the identities of things in the world also determine which courses of action will be successful. The moral "must" results from the fact that our identity, taken together with the identities of things around us, demands certain courses of action and excludes others. Consistency is also required because things have natures and must therefore be treated similarly over time, if we are to deal successfully with them. These "formal" features of morality, although found in Rand, do not take on the significance they do in contemporary neo-Kantian ethics; for Rand does not try to construct a theory of obligation out of those formal features alone.[25] She instead sees those formal features in terms of their role in a realist metaphysics—that is, as aspects of, rather than categories for, the very nature of things.

Rand's conception of human nature is more extensive than our previous comments may have suggested. It is true that man must use his reason in order to achieve his physical survival. But mere physical survival is not what Rand means when she speaks of living a good human life: "'Man's survival *qua* man' means the terms, methods, conditions and goals required for the survival of a rational being through the whole of his lifespan—in all those aspects of existence which are open to his choice."[26] This passage is sufficient to render inaccurate any interpretation of Rand's egoism which sees that egoism to be advancing the pursuit of momentary gain. Beyond this mistaken interpretation, however, the issues become complicated as to the correct interpretation of Rand's picture of human nature and the phrase *man's life qua man*. We shall have to restrict ourselves, however, to a mere sketch of her views. Some interesting and more detailed comments, though, are made on this and related issues in both the Mack and Wheeler essays.

We are able to gain an insight into what Rand considers to be necessary for living a proper human life (a life qua man), if we look to the central virtues of her ethical theory. There are three central virtues paired with three central values.[27] The three central values of Rand's system are reason, purpose, and self-esteem. These represent fundamental ends, the achievement of which constitutes living a proper human life. Notice that rationality is both a means and an end for Rand. Not only is reason the appropriate tool for guiding our actions, but the exercise of reason is also a value in its own right. The value of reason for Rand can be compared to Aristotle's defense of the role of reason in a proper human life. Henry B. Veatch, commenting on Aristotle, states:

As Aristotle sees it, for a man to live intelligently is not merely an affair of what he calls in his technical language, "intellectual virtue"—the virtues of skill and know-how when it comes to determining what needs to be done or ought to be done. No less is it an affair of so-called "moral virtue"—such being the virtues of choice, through the acquisition and possession of which a man may come consistently to want and prefer just those courses of action which reason dictates as requisite and needing to be done.[28]

The values of purpose and self-esteem are meant to indicate that a proper human life will be organized around an integrating plan with the concomitant experience of worth that results from the fulfillment of the plan. In a sense, these latter two values follow from the first. Rational action requires the construction of plans and goals, and self-esteem is the experience of efficacy that comes from the rational pursuit of one's purposes. The three values must be taken as a whole, for the drift of Rand's argument is that none of the three values can be obtained without the others.[29]

Now the corresponding virtues that Rand links to the aforementioned values are rationality, productiveness, and pride. The second virtue is the most controversial, as we shall see in Charles

King's essay. We suspect, however, that each of the virtues could be controversial, so we shall rest contented with a brief description of each and not enter the debate.

Rationality is the most basic virtue and "the source of all man's other virtues."[30] If values are the ends to be sought, then virtues will be those actions appropriate to the achievement of those ends.[31] The act of rationality means the act of "the fullest perception of reality within one's power and to the constant, active expansion of one's knowledge."[32] Rationality, in other words, is an active commitment to guide all of one's actions by reason. Wishes, desires, moods, emotions, and whims may, in some cases, serve as motives or springs for action; but they must never be considered as substitutes for the guidance reason provides. The decision to guide one's life by reason reflects the recognition that reason is, in fact, the only appropriate tool we possess for the achievement of a successful life; for, as we have already noted, man's conceptual faculty is his special mode of cognizing reality—the one that offers the best (and often the only) chance of reaching his goals. It is not that one will necessarily perish or even *appear* unsuccessful if one ignores this virtue.[33] Rather, Rand's claim is that the degree to which one ignores the virtue of rationality is the degree to which one's life is less than what it could have been. And the outer limit of ignoring this virtue (assuming one could rely on others to maintain his existence) is what Plato referred to as a soul out of harmony, an existence of internal conflict.

The last point leads us to the second virtue, productiveness, which is an extension of the virtue of rationality. Just as purpose is dependent on reason, so too is productiveness dependent on rationality. Productive work constitutes the material expression of rationality. On the lowest levels, productive work is an implementation of those judgments about how to sustain one's existence. On a more elevated plane, productive work should be considered not only as a means to one's livelihood, but, more important, as an exercise of one's fullest potential—a potential that, given man's nature, can only be realized by the full use of one's mind.

It is important to recognize that for Rand productivity does not mean merely having a job. Instead, productivity means being devoted to what it is currently fashionable to call a career. Moreover, productivity does not require one to produce "consumer goods." An intellectual can be just as productive as a business man, even though the former's product may not be as widely used and appreciated. So long as one's endeavors are rational (i.e., contributory to human well-being); and provided reason is one's guide, any occupation is permissible. Finally, and here Rand makes an advance over Aristotle, "it is not the degree of a man's ability nor the scale of his work that is ethically relevant here, but the fullest and most purposeful use of his mind." [34] That is to say, if one's abilities, circumstances, and mental capacity can be exercised to their fullest as a carpenter, then an individual who realizes his potential in this line of work is of equal moral worth to a brilliant scientist whose achievements are more widely acclaimed. [35]

The final central virtue of Rand's ethics is pride. Succinctly put, pride is the act of earning one's own self-respect. One popular misconception of egoism is the supposition that people necessarily esteem and love themselves. Rand points out, however, that man "is a being of self-made soul." [36] We all know what is necessary in order to gain the meaningful respect of others. The same process must be employed to gain self-respect, except that with self-respect it is much more difficult to cheat. A man of self-respect never compromises his values nor claims more than he has earned. He is a person of integrity, and his integrity stems from the fact that he neither evades reality nor haphazardly drifts through life. We take pride in ourselves when we recognize that our accomplishments are the result of our own choice to purposefully seek to achieve our highest potential. Since the virtue of pride cannot be a part of one's life without a prior commitment to the other two virtues and since those other virtues are the morally proper acts for human beings, one can readily see why Rand takes pride as "moral ambitiousness." [37]

Although rationality, productiveness, and pride constitute the core of the Randian virtues, she also mentions other virtues: independence, integrity, honesty, and justice. [38] It is not always clear in Rand just where one virtue leaves off and the other begins. In some sense, however, Rand's list of virtues must be considered as distinct but not separate, as a continuum. Given her architectonic—that is, given that all the virtues flow from the virtue of rationality—there could be no radical separation or disparity between the various virtues. But to enter this area further would take us too far afield.

Rand's theory of happiness must be our next topic of discussion, for virtuous action and happiness are closely connected. The importance Rand attaches to happiness cannot be overstated, since Rand argues that the achievement of happiness is "man's highest moral purpose."[39]

Rand defines happiness as a "state of non-contradictory joy."[40] She goes further to claim that the maintenance of one's life and the pursuit of happiness are not separate issues.[41] Holding one's life as the ultimate value and regarding happiness as one's highest goal are "two aspects of the same achievement."[42] These statements show both that the value of life is not merely biological survival and that happiness is not merely repeated pleasures. In the former case, mere biological survival is obviously no guarantee of happiness, since there are many living but miserable men. We are thus directed to a fuller conception of human nature if we are to appreciate Rand's remarks. In the latter case, happiness is not merely repeated pleasure, because Rand demands that one's joy be the result of an integrated set of values—something that is only possible to an actively rational mind.

In "Nozick on the Randian Argument," we contend that Rand's conception of happiness is a classical one[43]—one that is perhaps best regarded to be a eudaimonistic theory. The recent work of David Norton captures in more detail the substance of the doctrine that Rand struggled to express.[44] Norton argues that eudaimonia is the wholehearted commitment to self-actualization.[45] The whole person is put into each act. The integrated sense of values connects both past and future acts to present ones, since values are guided by the logos of a given purpose.[46] The phrase *noncontradictory joy* in Rand's definition is a cryptic expression of Norton's more developed insights; for both Norton and Rand wish to make clear that happiness is inextricably bound to the existence of an integrated self. This is why we believe that the following passage from Norton's book can also serve as a summation of Rand's view of happiness.

The eudaimonic individual experiences the whole of his life in every act, and he experiences parts and whole together as necessary, such that he can will that nothing be changed. But the necessity here introduced is moral necessity, deriving from his choice. Hence we may say of him interchangeably, "He is where he wants to be, doing what he wants to do," or "He is where he must be, doing what he must do." [47]

If our description of Rand's ethics has been at all accurate, there remains a question to be considered, namely, Why refer to Rand's ethics as an egoism? Surely this is an inappropriate label. Rand considers this very question in the introduction to her book, *The Virtue of Selfishness*.

The title of this book may evoke the kind of question that I hear once in a while: "Why do you use the word 'selfishness' to denote virtuous qualities of character, when that word antagonizes so many people to whom it does not mean the things you mean?" To those who ask it, my answer is: "For the reason that makes you afraid of it." [48]

Now this response is neither antagonistic nor defensive, but rather profound. It emphasizes the fundamental basis for our ethical concerns—the fact that life—more precisely the life of an individual human being—is the sole reason we speak of virtue at all. Our concern for ethical matters cannot be idle and unrelated to the lives of individuals. If we realize that morality is intimately related to our very person, that whether we make a success or shambles of our lives is the matter of ethics, then morality cannot be placed apart from the beneficiary of its teaching, apart from the individual. The one who asks the question at issue has not yet realized that ethics, properly conceived, is not a set of demands imposed from the outside (by others or God). Ethics is, rather, a set of principles discovered as being to one's own direct benefit as a human being. The responsibility of being a human being, of facing life boldly and directly and making all one can of oneself is to be faced squarely by each person. Rand realizes that this fact is something some people seek to avoid. Her response to the question of why call her ethics an egoism was an attempt to direct her audience to this realization.

For Rand the purpose of ethics is the achievement of human happiness. This is what Tibor Machan has called *classical egoism*,[49] and it seems to us that this label is appropriate. Rand's view of the self is neither Kantian (some *ding an sich* totally unrelated to life) nor Hobbesian (some bundle of passions and urges), but Aristotelian.[50] The ego or the I of Rand's ethical egoism is similar to Strawson's conception of the *unity* of persons, rather than of persons conceived as some combination of elements (e.g., of a body and a mind). Once again David Norton is instructive on this issue.

To conclude, our analysis of the person comprises three fundamental elements. Two of these elements are the distinct modalities of being—actuality and possibilities—while the third is a relation between the two that gives rise to an existential process, namely, the relation of potentiality. Every person is both his empirical actuality and his ideal possibility, or daimon.[51]

If one correctly understands Rand's doctrine of the self, her defense of individualism is also clarified. Just as her view of the self is not Hobbesian, so also is her individualism not Hobbesian. Human beings are not atomistic units in pursuit of desire after desire. One's life can become the sort envisioned by Hobbes, but that is not its essential nature.[52] Apart from its political manifestations, to be discussed in our essay that opens the next section of this book, Rand's defense of individualism is simply a defense of personal integrity. Consider the following:

The basic independence of the individualist consists of his loyalty to his own mind; it is his perception of the *facts of reality*, his understanding, his *judgment*, that he refuses to sacrifice to the unproved assertions of others. That is the meaning of intellectual independence—and that is the essence of an individualist.[53]

Rand applies the term *social metaphysician* to one whose self-esteem or source of values is primarily dependent on the opinions or attitudes of others.[54] Her attack on the type of mentality exhibited by the social metaphysician is really a defense of this reformulation of a truth noted by the ancient Greeks: "the individual's acknowledgment of the worth of others is his confident sense of his own self-worth." [55]

Rand's contribution to ethics consists not only in her impassioned defense of many classical values—a defense that has affected the large number of readers of her books—but also in her efforts to ground such values more thoroughly in human nature itself. If we can but leave the shadow of Kant for a moment, we may find that an ancient light still shines to show us the way. It is our view that Rand's ethical teaching has given renewed fuel to a light once thought to be flickering for the last time.

NOTES

1. Ayn Rand, "The Objectivist Ethics," in *The Virtue of Selfishness* (New York: New American Library, 1964), p. 15. *The Virtue of Selfishness* is hereafter cited as *VOS*.

2. Ibid., p. 16.

3. David Lowenthal, "The Case for Teleology," *Independent Journal of Philosophy* 2 (1978):97.

4. Ibid.

5. The contention that robots, machines, computers, and the like act for ends is considered and rebutted in Douglas Den Uyl and Douglas Rasmussen, "Nozick on the Randian Argument," *The Personalist*, April 1978, pp. 186–87.

6. Rand, "Objectivist Ethics," p. 15.

7. Allan Gotthelf, "Aristotle's Conception of Final Causality," *Review of Metaphysics*, October 1976, p. 237n.

8. Ibid., p. 253: "The notion of an irreducible potential for form supplies the proper content to the awareness that for Aristotle organic development is actually *directive*, without implying (as the 'immaterial agency' interpretation does) that it is *directed*; and it identifies the ontological basis of the awareness that the existence of stages of a development can be understood only in terms of its end—by establishing that the *identity* of the development is its being *irreducibly* a development to that end, irreducibly the actualization of a potential for form."

9. We cannot understand what living things are or how they function except insofar as we understand functioning as ordered to the maintenance of the entity's life, which for any particular living thing is understood as the living entity's development to maturation or even, in more explicit Aristotelian terms, the actuation of the particular living thing's form. *And* we do not need to view the actions of nonliving things in terms of an end in order to understand their behavior.

10. Eric Mack, "How to Derive Ethical Egoism," *The Personalist*, Autumn 1971.

11. Rand, "Objectivist Ethics," p. 17.

12. Ibid.

13. Ibid.

14. Ibid.

15. Ibid., p. 23.

16. Cf. discussion of this issue in Den Uyl and Rasmussen, "Nozick on the Randian Argument," sec. 1.

17. We know which features of human nature are fundamental for ethics and which are not, according to their respective contributions to the existence and necessity for norm-governed action. If Rand is right in concluding that human beings need an ethical code, then those features of human nature which are essential (as opposed to accidental) will be the features most fundamental to the science of ethics; for the necessity of an ethical code is itself a function of the *necessary* features of human nature.

18. Rand, "Objectivist Ethics," p. 19.

19. Ibid., p. 21.

20. Tibor Machan, *Human Rights and Human Liberties* (Chicago: Nelson Hall, 1975), p. 74.

21. It is worth noting at this stage a point made in Den Uyl and Rasmussen, "Nozick on the Randian Argument" (p. 193): "Since 'nature' is not a special metaphysical constituent for Rand as it appears to be for Aristotle, there is no bifurcation of an entity. Rand would argue that her entities are through and through 'one' or 'whole'."

22. Rand, "Objectivist Ethics," p. 23.

23. Ibid., p. 23. It should be noted that, for Rand, morality is just as necessary for a man on a desert island as it is for one in society. A code of values is necessary for both situations because the reason for the existence of a code of values is dependent on human nature and not on the number of human beings.

24. For a discussion of the problems with starting from the formal features of action, cf. Douglas Den Uyl, "Ethical Egoism and Gewirth's PCC," *The Personalist*, Autumn 1975.

25. Veatch may be right to suppose that a full return to Kant may be the only salvation for contemporary attempts to ground ethics on formal conditions alone. Cf. Henry Veatch, *For an Ontology of Morals* (Evanston: Northwestern University Press, 1971), pp. 165–66.

26. Rand, "Objectivist Ethics," p. 24.

27. Ibid., pp. 25–27.

28. Henry Veatch, *Aristotle: A Contemporary Appreciation* (Bloomington: Indiana University Press, 1974), pp. 108–9.

29. The hierarchy of values is ascertained from Rand's discussion of the hierarchy of virtues. The basic virtue is rationality, and thus the basic value is reason. The commitment to reason will result in a commitment to the other values, but the reverse does not hold. We cannot, for example, seek self-esteem and ignore reason and purpose, since the latter are each necessary (and together sufficient) conditions for the former.

30. Rand, "Objectivist Ethics," p. 25.

31. Ibid.

32. Ibid.

33. Ibid., p. 24.

34. Ibid., pp. 26–27.

35. This is not to say, however, that the objective merits of their respective achievements should be given equal weight.

36. Rand, "Objectivist Ethics," p. 27.

37. Nathaniel Branden, "Psychotherapy and the Objectivist Ethics," a paper delivered before the Michigan Society of Consulting Psychologists on November 24, 1965, and before the Psychiatric Division of the San Mateo County Medical Society and the San Mateo County Health Department on January 24, 1966.

38. Rand, "Objectivist Ethics," p. 26.

39. Ibid., p. 27.

40. Ibid., p. 29.

41. Ibid.

42. Ibid. Rand does argue, however, that while happiness can be the goal of one's life, it cannot be the standard. She seems to mean by this distinction that one cannot simply commit oneself to happiness, but must rather commit oneself to those virtues and values mentioned above. Yet the problem that arises here is that these values are both standards and ends—that is, standards by the very fact that they are our proper ends. Happiness, we believe, should be conceived the same way; and we think that the complete context of Rand's remarks indicate the connection between standard and purpose as well. The separation she makes (pp. 29–30) is primarily for the purpose of refuting hedonism.

43. Den Uyl and Rasmussen, "Nozick on the Randian Argument," p. 201.

44. David Norton, *Personal Destinies* (Princeton: Princeton University Press, 1976), ch. 7.

45. Ibid., pp. 195, 222.

46. This is why Norton states that "eudaimonism is not reserved to the conclusion of the process of self-actualization, but in full measure attends to every step of the process" (ibid., p. 236).

47. Ibid., p. 222.

48. Rand, *VOS*, p. vii.

49. Tibor Machan, "Some Recent Work in Ethical Egoism," *American Philosophical Quarterly* (January 1979).

50. Veatch, *For an Ontology of Morals*, pp. 66–93.

51. Norton, *Personal Destinies*, p. 16.

52. Rand, "Counterfeit Individualism," *VOS*, p. 136.

53. Ibid.

54. Rand, "The Argument from Intimidation," *VOS*, p. 141.

55. Norton, *Personal Destinies*, p. 11.

5

Rand
and Aristotle:
A Comparison
of Objectivist
and
Aristotelian
Ethics

ଵ

Jack Wheeler

Throughout her writings, Ayn Rand has very little to say about Aristotle's ethics. While she reveres Aristotle as the greatest of all philosophers,[1] she explicitly says this is not because of his ethics: "Not to leave you with the impression that Aristotle's ethics or politics are his greatest achievement" (she says in response to Randall's claim that they are[2]), "I want to stress very emphatically that Aristotle's greatest achievement lies in the field of epistemology."[3] The only substantive comment Rand makes regarding Aristotle's ethics in all of her writings is contained in her lecture "The Objectivist Ethics," and it is negative: "Aristotle did not regard ethics as an exact science; he based his ethical system on observations of what the noble and wise men of his time chose to do, leaving unanswered the questions of: *why* they chose to do it and *why* he evaluated them as noble and wise."[4] This is a doubly troubling statement. First, it is grossly inaccurate and tempts one to conclude that Rand's knowledge of Aristotle's ethics is quite slim. Indeed, one wonders whether Rand has read Aristotle at all when one sees her denouncing Randall for asserting that Aristotle advocated a "welfare state," claiming instead that "an Aristotelian statist is a contradiction in terms."[5]

Clearly, Rand has never read books 7 and 8 of the *Politics*. At the beginning of book 8, for example, Aristotle states: "We ought not to think that any of the citizens belongs to himself; rather, they all belong to the state, for each is a μόριον [small piece or portion] of the state."[6] While the collectivist tone of these books may be vitiated by the fact that they (together with books 2 and 3) were written in the forties of the fourth century B.C., when the Platonic influence upon Aristotle had not yet diminished, this does not excuse Rand's ignorance. (The remainder [*Politics* 1, 4, 5, 6], which is anticollectivist, was written in the twenties, contemporary with the writing of the *Nicomachean Ethics*.)[7]

Again, Rand's criticism that Aristotle did not regard ethics as an "exact science" is equally odd, for this has nothing to do with "observing wise men," but rather, as Aristotle notes: "It is the mark of an educated mind to expect that amount of exactness in each kind which the nature of the particular subject admits."[8] Or does Rand really wish to claim that one can have mathematical precision for ethics on a par with physics?

What is doubly puzzling about all of this is that, upon close examination, there are extraordinary similarities between objectivist and Aristotelian ethics in both metaethical and normative categories. Thus we find the strange situation of Rand praising Aristotle above all other philosophers on the one hand and ignorantly criticizing his ethics on the other. At the same time she presents an ethical system of her own that she claims is original yet that is in many ways strikingly Aristotelian.

It is not, however, the purpose of this essay to speculate on the source of this similarity but, rather, to demonstrate it. We shall begin with both Rand and Aristotle's basic metaethical concepts.

THE MEANING OF GOOD

The primary metaethical concept for Aristotle is ἀγαθόν (good). At the very start of the *Nicomachean Ethics*,[9] Aristotle notes, "It has been well said that the *agathon* is that at which all things ἐφίεται [aim];[10] and a few chapters later he says clearly, "We may define [*agathon*] as that for the sake of which everything else is done, ἢ οὗ χάριν τὰ λοιπὰ πράττεται."[11]

Nicomachean Ethics 1.6, however, is devoted to refuting Plato's Idea of Good, the notion that *good* refers to a single identical predicate (the arguments of *Ethics* 1.6 thus apply ipso facto to, e.g., Moore's notion of *goodness* as a simple un-analyzable quality). Therefore, as Stewart notes, "different things are called good" for Aristotle, "not because they all contribute well to *one* end, but because they all contribute to *their respective ends.*"[12]

Aristotle places, then, agathon primarily in the category of *relation*; it denotes for him a certain proportion, ἀναλογίαν. "When different things are called good," Rackham explains, "it means they each bear the same relation to—viz, contribute to the welfare of—certain other things, not all to the same thing."[13]

For Hardie, however, this is only "part of Aristotle's answer," for it embraces the goodness of means or instrumental goods only; it does not take into consideration the goodness of ends or intrinsic goods. "Aristotle certainly thinks that ends, 'goods that are pursued and loved for themselves' (1096b10–11), are good, and not only the means by which these ends are achieved."[14] "Now Aristotle does make this distinction: Let us then separate things good in themselves, καθ᾽αὑτά, from things useful as means, ὠφελίμων, and consider whether the former are called good because they fall under a single Idea."[15] Hardie at this point accuses Aristotle of failing to find an answer.[16] But the examples Aristotle proceeds to give of things good (*kath hauto*)—φρονεῖν, wisdom; ὁρᾶν, sight; ἡδοναί τινες καὶ τιμαί, certain pleasures and honors—make his meaning of kath hauto clear: to be kath hauto is to perform a certain kind of *function*, i.e., it is the final means by which the mark aimed at in goal-directed activity is struck and the goal thereby achieved. Obtaining a good kath hauto is sufficient in itself to achieve the goal.[17]

Aristotle's agathon, then, while standing for no single predicate—or, to use Kalin's terminology, while all referents of agathon are not *materially* the same—does have a single, consistent meaning, all applications of it being *formally* the same.[18]

In all applications the agathon is the goal of an activity (formally the same), but the specific goal will vary according to the nature of the activity (materially different).

This thoroughly teleological metaethics makes it clear that for Aristotle the only things that could possess values or goods, *agatha*, are individual, goal-pursuing entities. *Good* means *good for*, and has meaning only insofar as it refers to what is good for the individual moral agent. An egoism is thus necessarily built into Aristotle's basic metaethics, forcing him to consider as literally unintelligible any nonegoistic metaethics, e.g., the notion of a "common" good that has no relevance to the individual interests of human beings and toward which individuals must sacrifice their own interests. An Aristotelian analysis uncovers an egoism lying at the basis of the very meaning of the fundamental metaethical concept.[19]

Those readers familiar with Rand's views may see already striking similarities between this analysis and the objectivist position. For Rand the primary metaethical concept, corresponding to Aristotle's agathon, is *value*. Her metaethics begin with the well-known statement in Galt's speech:

There is only one fundamental alternative in the universe: existence or nonexistence—and it pertains to a single class of entities: to living organisms. . . . It is only a living organism that faces a constant alternative: the issue of life or death. Life is a process of self-sustaining and self-generated action. If an organism fails in that action, it dies; its chemical elements remain, but its life goes out of existence. It is only the concept of "Life" that makes the concept of "Value" possible. It is only to a living entity that things can be good or evil.[20]

Both Rand and Aristotle propose, then, a metaethics that is nonrelativist and nonsubjectivist but, rather, objectivist—naturalistically objectivist and not religiously or supernaturally so. There are no appeals to God or a cosmic supernatural power in either theory to give ethics its binding legitimacy, but rather an appeal to the very objective nature of things. The good is what is *good for*: goal-directed, purposefully acting entities for Aristotle; living, organic entities for Rand.[21]

In fact, it really should come as little surprise that Aristotle, whom Rand lauds for advocating an objectivist metaphysics paralleling her own, should advocate an objectivist metaethics (paralleling her own). Furthermore, both offer the same solution to the *is/ought* problem. Ross notes that Aristotle's teleology is an "immanent" teleology, that the end and good of "each species is internal to the species." He brings the egoism of Aristotle's teleology into clear focus when he comments:

Only once, perhaps, does Aristotle suggest—and only doubtfully— that a characteristic of one species may be designed for the benefit of another: sharks have their mouths on their under surface in order that, while they turn to bite, their prey may escape—but also to keep them from over-eating! (*Parts of Animals* 696b24–32.)[22]

Aristotle does not, of course, discuss the is/ought problem, since the issue is of modern origin. But when Rand discusses the problem, she does so utilizing the same immanent teleology:

In answer to those philosophers who claim that no relation can be established between ultimate ends or values and the facts of reality, let me stress that the fact that living entities exist and function necessitates the existence of values and of an ultimate value which for any given living entity is its own life. Thus the validation of value judgments is to be achieved by reference to the facts of reality. The fact that a living entity *is*, determines what it *ought* to do.[23]

THE GOOD FOR MAN

Once Aristotle grounds the intelligibility of the good in what is good for the particular entities in question, he then asks, What is good for man? His first question is:

If there be something which is the τέλος of all the things done by human action, this will be the practical *agathon* . . . if there be some one thing alone which is τέλειον [final and complete]—or if there be several final ends, the one among them which is most *teleion*—this will be the ἄριστον [the supreme good or best of all *agatha* which we are seeking].[24]

He continues to explain:

In speaking of degrees of finality, we mean that a thing pursued as an end in itself is more final than one pursued as a means to something else, and that a thing never chosen as a means to anything else is more final than things chosen both as ends in themselves and as means to that thing; accordingly, a thing chosen always as an end and never as a means we call absolutely final.[25]

He concludes: "Now εὐδαιμονία above all else appears to be such a thing, since we always choose it for its own sake and never as a means to something else."[26]

Further, *eudaimonia* is αὔταρκες, self-sufficient, a thing that "merely standing by itself alone renders life desirable and lacking in nothing."[27] Thus, "*Eudaimonia*, being found to be something final and complete, and self-sufficient, is the *telos* [the goal] at which all (human) actions aim."[28] Aristotle's analysis continues with an examination of the nature of human *eudaimonia*. This entails for him an examination of the nature and function, ἔργον, of man.[29] To see why this is so, we must go outside the *Nicomachean Ethics*.

In the *Metaphysics* Aristotle explains that the formal cause, the εἶδος of a thing, is its essence or identity or nature, the "that which it is to be such-and-such," τὸ τί ἦν εἶναι, which is to be understood in terms of that thing's final cause, ἕνεκα, or end, τέλος. The formal and final cause or essence and end of any given existent are for Aristotle one and the same.[30] And in *Parts of Animals*, we learn that the nature of living organisms is such that their formal cause lies in the functional unity of parts, i.e., the unity of parts of an organic entity cannot be understood or explained apart from the function of that unity—the function being the maintenance of its existence, to sustain the organism's life and to sustain it in a certain optimal way, which we designate as health.[31]

Thus, since each species of living thing possesses a particular unity and will function characteristically according to that unity, we must examine the nature of man and the particular way in which his parts function such that he achieves his end or final cause, optimal survival. And since the end or final cause of any organism is agathon, the good, and βέλτιστον, the greatest good, of that organism,[32] when we know the particular function of man, we can know what will constitute his genuine well-being.

Now the nature of man is such that he survives in a different way from plants and other animals; the former survive via nutrition and growth, the latter via sentience; and while these are necessary for man's proper functioning, he does not survive by means of them alone.[33] It is purposeful conduct, the result or active exercise of man's capacity for ratiocinative thought, that separates man from all other living organisms and provides him with his distinctive function and means of survival.[34]

The ἔργον of man is, then, "the active exercise of his ψυχή in conformity with λόγος, reason."[35] And just as the function of, e.g., a harper is to play the harp, so a good harper qua harper is one who plays the harp εὖ, well. Similarly, the good man will be he who likewise performs his function qua man eu. The good man will thus exhibit virtue or excellence, ἀρετή, in performing his proper human function. Agathon/eudaimonia for man can thus be defined as activity of one's *psuche*[36] in conformity with *arete*, the excellent and superior performance of one's proper *ergon*.[37]

It is crucial to note here that eudaimonia is an activity and not merely a state of mind. This is why *happiness* is an inadequate translation of the term. Rackham prefers *well-being* or *prosperity*, and Austin opts for *success*.[38] Austin's suggestion is quite helpful not only in its accuracy, but also in its felicitous contrast with modern Christian/Kantian values.

"He is a successful businessman" is a common expression. But if one were to say of someone instead, "He is a successful human being," it would sound odd to our modern ears. Yet for Aristotle one can, indeed, be a success as a human being: this is what eudaimonia is; it is the basic standpoint of Aristotle's ethical theory. Furthermore eudaimonia, as an activity and not as a passive state, is literally an *end in itself*. It requires a conscious effort of rational thought and purposive conduct to achieve and sustain the continued existence of one's eudaimonia.

All nonrandom activities, by definition, have a goal, and the purpose or function of an activity is to reach its goal. The activity of eudaimonia, then, has no goal beyond itself: its goal is nothing other than the continuance of its own existence. Here is an egoism of such purity, clarity, and depth that it is difficult to see how it might be exceeded.

The parallels continue. Corresponding to Aristotelian eudaimonia is Rand's *happiness*, which she describes as "that state of consciousness which proceeds from the achievement of one's values,"[39] and "a state of non-contradictory joy."[40] Just as Aristotle equates *agathon* with *eudaimonia*, so Rand views the primary value for man as happiness. "Every man is an end in himself; he exists for his own sake, and the achievement of his own happiness is his highest moral purpose."[41] Rand sees happiness as "the successful state of life."[42]

Furthermore, just as for Aristotle one's eudaimonia is achieved through the active exercise of man's distinctive capacity, *logos*, so also Rand claims that "rationality is man's basic virtue, the source of all his other virtues,"[43] that "the moral is the rational."[44] "Happiness is possible only to a rational man, the man who desires nothing but rational goals, seeks nothing but rational values, and finds his joy in nothing but rational actions."[45]

For both Aristotle and Rand, then, rationality is man's distinctive capacity and "basic means of survival."[46] And it is through the active and continuous exercise of reason that man achieves happiness and moral virtue. For Rand reason must be exercised "in all of one's waking hours,"[47] "in the context and terms of a lifetime,"[48] and "through the whole of one's lifespan."[49] For Aristotle, its activity "must occupy a complete lifetime—for one swallow does not make a spring, nor one fine day; and similarly one day or a brief period of happiness does not make a man μακάριον [blissful] and *eudaimona*."[50]

REASON AND ETHICAL CONDUCT

Both Rand and Aristotle generate specific virtues, concrete normative conduct, from the primary virtue of rationality. For Aristotle, since eudaimonia is an *energeia*, activity, of one's psuche in conformity with arete, arete will be differentiated according to the parts of the psuche: for the psuche is not one simple thing but is itself a functional unity of parts, each part with its own ergon, and thus its own arete.

Aristotle divides the psuche into two basic parts, one without a principle or reason, ἄλογος, and one with such a plan or principle, λόγος. The part that is *alogos* has itself two divisions, the first of which is omitted from consideration, since it exhibits no specifically human excellence.[51] (This is the vegetative or nutritive part, and its study is more appropriate to a physician than to an ethical and political philosopher.) The second division, the appetitive and desiring part, is, however, capable of obeying a rational principal, and such obedience is its proper ergon. The virtues this part of the soul exhibits are then called the virtues of character, ἠθικαί.

The proper ergon of the part possessing *logos* is the capacity to understand a rational principle, to engage in a process of rational thought or reasoning, and to construct a logical plan. Thus the virtues of this part are called virtues of intellect, διανοητικαί.[52]

An arete of character will be a ἕξις, a disposition, permanent condition or habit, which can be formed correctly only if one engages in their corresponding activities neither excessively nor deficiently, but rather to the appropriate degree. (It is important to understand here that *appropriate* means *appropriate to the individual* in the context of that individual's own particular identity as a human being. In elucidating his famous doctrine of the mean, Aristotle carefully explains that the mean is relative to the individual, and is not the same for everyone.[53] Again, the good has formal, but not material, identity for all human beings.) The standard by which one chooses the appropriate mean and avoids excess and deficiency relative to oneself Aristotle calls the ὀρθὸς λόγος, the correct principle. That part of the psuche capable of learning and understanding the *orthos logos* is the rational part; thus grasping and specifying the orthos logos, such that the appetitive part of the psuche can obey it and act in accordance with it, is a virtue of the intellect.

The principal ergon of the rational part of the psuche is the attainment of truth or knowledge of reality; it performs this function via five basic intellectual dispositions, which correspond to five basic types of knowledge. These dispositions are: τέχνη, art or technical skill; ἐπιστήμη, scientific knowledge of that which is invariable in nature (truths of mathematics and what we would call "laws of nature"); νοῦς, rational insight regarding the truth of basic metaphysical principles (such as the principle of noncontradiction); σοφία, wisdom, the combination of *episteme* and *nous*; and φρόνησις, practical wisdom or prudence.[54]

The purely egoistic nature of *phronesis* is stated straightforwardly:

It is the mark of the *phronimos* to be able to deliberate well about what are *agatha* and *sumpheronta* [good and advantageous] for himself, not in one department, for instance what is good for his health or strength, but what is advantageous for the *eu zen* [the good life] in general.[55]

Phronesis is, then, a truth-attaining rational disposition of the psuche of the individual and is concerned with action, purposive conduct, regarding things that are good and bad for human beings in general and the individual himself in particular. Thus he who possesses phronesis is "one who can discern his own particular welfare."[56] This is why, Aristotle explains, men like Anaxagoras and Thales were known as *sophos*, wise, but not phronimos: because they had an ignorance of τὰ συμφέροντα ἑαυτοῖς, their own interests.[57]

Since the ergon of the rational part of the psuche is to attain knowledge of reality and that of phronesis is to attain the knowledge of what actions are most conducive to the attainment and maintenance of one's own genuine eudaimonia, it is phronesis which determines the orthos logos.[58]

In other words, (1) the proper function of every individual human being qua human being is to live happily, successfully, and well; (2) one achieves personal happiness and success through purposive rational conduct; (3) this conduct has two bases: (a) a settled disposition of character, or the appetitive part of one's soul, determining the choice, προαίρεσις, of one's actions, which consist essentially in the observance of a mean of behavior relative to one's particular identity; (b) a disposition of the intellect, or rational part of one's soul, to know what actions are most conducive to the attainment of one's happiness and well-being, and to specify, on the basis of this knowledge, the standard determining the appropriate mean.[59]

For Rand, as we have seen, "rationality is man's basic virtue, the source of all his other virtues," while "man's basic vice" is irrationality.[60] The various virtues of conduct that she specifies, such as independence, integrity, honesty, justice, productivity, and pride, are such because they are specific applications of acting rationally.[61] Rationality for Rand "is the recognition of the fact that existence exists, that nothing can alter the truth and nothing can take precedence over the act of perceiving it, which is thinking—that (one's own) mind is one's only judge of values and one's only guide to action."[62]

While Rand offers nothing really corresponding to the doctrine of the mean and her list of specific virtues differs in places from Aristotle's, there is one place where they do merge quite dramatically: the virtue of pride. Aristotle's famous description of the man of *megalopsuchia*—greatness of soul, proper pride, or self-respect[63]—lies in *Nicomachean Ethics* 4.3. Pride in oneself is, of course, one of Christianity's seven deadly sins; and when Aristotle praises the man who has pride in himself and refers to pride in oneself as "a crown of the virtues,"[64] it is thus perhaps more amusing than surprising to observe that it causes Bertrand Russell to shudder.[65] Megalopsuchia is the mean between vanity, unearned pride, and *micropsuchia*, unwarranted humility. It is proper, earned, warranted pride in oneself—for it cannot exist without possession of the other virtues, without καλοκἀγαϑία, moral nobility.[66]

Since moral perfection for Aristotle means (1) willfully exercising phronesis to understand and acknowledge that orthos logos which in any given situation specifies the conduct most conducive to the achievement of one's own eudaimonia, (2) willfully choosing to act in accordance with the conduct specified by the orthos logos such that one's genuine eudaimonia will best be achieved, and (3) developing both (1) and (2) to the point where one characteristically exercises phronesis and acts in accordance with the orthos logos as a matter of habit[67]—moral perfection being, therefore, to always act in accordance with one's own best interests—the crown of virtues for Aristotle, the final proof of one's own moral perfection, is *pride in being egoistic.* One is morally perfect to the extent one is perfectly egoistic and vice versa. To take pride in being morally/egoistically perfect is for Aristotle the ultimate moral achievement for man.

Aristotle and his man of megalopsuchia have thus ascended the very pinnacle of egoism. None have climbed higher. Only Ayn Rand has made an ascension equal to Aristotle's:

Pride is the recognition of the fact that you are your own highest value and, like all of man's values, it has to be earned . . . that the first precondition of self-esteem is that radiant selfishness of soul which desires the best in all things, in values of matter and spirit, a soul that seeks above all else to achieve its own moral perfection, valuing nothing higher than itself—and that the proof of an achieved self-esteem is your soul's shudder of contempt and rebellion against the role of a sacrificial animal, against the vile impertinence of any creed that proposes to immolate the irreplaceable value which is your consciousness and the incomparable glory which is your existence to the blind evasions and stagnant decay of others.[68]

LOVE AND FRIENDSHIP

Books 8 and 9 of the *Nicomachean Ethics* are devoted to a discussion of φιλία, normally rendered as *friendship*; but as Ross notes, it refers to "any mutual attraction between two human beings."[69] Aristotle quickly moves to establish the egoistic basis of the virtuous aspect of this attraction, viz, that *philia* is a necessary condition for the achievement of one's eudaimonia: "For no one would choose to live without friends, even though he possessed all the other *agatha*."[70] But it is only a very specific type of philia that fulfills this condition. Since there are only three things that are lovable—the ἀγαθόν, good; the ἡδύ, pleasant; and the χρήσιμον, useful—there are only three types of corresponding philia: philia of virtue, of pleasure, and of utility. It is the first type that fulfills the condition: "The type of *philia* that is perfect, τελεία, is that between the good, and those who resemble each other in *arete*."[71] For while "*Philia* based on pleasure has a similarity to *philia* based on virtue, for good men are pleasant to one another; and the same is true of *philia* based on utility, for good men are useful to each other,[72] . . . . only good men can be friends for what they are in themselves.[73]

That all philia has an egoistic basis is made clear. "The forms which friendly feeling for our neighbors takes and the marks by which the different forms of *philia* are defined, seem to be de-

rived from the feelings of regard which we entertain for ourselves."[74] In particular, "in loving a friend, men love what is
good for themselves, for the good man in becoming a friend becomes a good to his friend."[75] Perfect friendship, Ross concludes, is for Aristotle "based on the love of the good man for
himself."[76]

The essence of Aristotelian philia is, then, *moral admiration—*
and, unless one morally admires himself and takes pride in his
own moral worth, he can neither love himself nor (in the perfect
sense) love others. Clearly, Randian love has the same basis: "To
love is to value. Only a rationally selfish man, a man of *self-
esteem*, is capable of love. . . . The man who does not value
himself cannot value anything or anyone."[77] Or compare "Love,
friendship, respect, admiration are the emotional response of
one man to the virtues of another, the spiritual *payment* given
in exchange for the personal, selfish pleasure which one man derives from the virtues of another man's character"[78] with

If happiness consists in life and activity, and the activity of the good
man is good and so pleasant in itself, and if the sense that a thing is our
own is also pleasant, yet we are better able to contemplate our neighbors than ourselves, and their actions than our own, and thus good
men find pleasure in the actions of other good men who are their
friends; since those actions possess both these essentially pleasant
qualities, it therefore follows that the supremely happy man will require good friends, insomuch as he desires to contemplate actions that
are good and that are his own, and the actions of a good man that is
his friend are such.[79]

Aristotle would strongly disagree with Rand's position that
the primary values and benefits to be gained by the individual
from living in a human society are but knowledge and trade.[80]
He would say that Rand has little understanding of the fact that
the φύσις, the nature or identity, of man is such that he is "a
πολιτικὸν, a social being, and is *designed by nature to live in a
group with others, συζῆν πεφυκός.*"[81] A social life in a community is thus for Aristotle a necessary condition for complete personal eudaimonia. For him, a community is, or ought to be, a
partnership, κοινωνία, of free men, ἐλευθέρων, which exists for
the good life, the εὖ ζῆν,[82] and possesses a sense of community

between good men, or ὁμόνοια, concord, friendship between citizens.[83]

Aristotle's mature position is that the state exists for the good of the individual: "A political association . . . should exist for the *sumpherontos*, advantage, of its members."[84] He looks upon egoistic moral admiration as the proper foundation for a community:

It is the consciousness of oneself as *agathon* that makes existence desirable, and such consciousness is pleasant in itself.[85] Therefore [cf. supra, n. 78], a man ought also to share his friend's consciousness of his existence, and this is attained by their living together, and by conversing and communicating their thoughts to one another: for this is the meaning of living together as applied to human beings; it does not mean merely feeding in the same place as it does when applied to cattle.[86]

Although Rand does not discuss man's inherent need for a community, her portrait of the ideal society—Galt's Gulch in *Atlas Shrugged*—has much in common with Aristotle's community of concord between good men; and it indicates that she may, indeed, be aware of it.

We have seen that for both Rand and Aristotle genuine friendship and love for others are based on love for and pride in oneself and one's own moral worth. But to what extent do the parallels continue, i.e., between Randian *selfishness* and Aristotelian φιλαυτία, self-love? The question for Aristotle is whether one ought to love most oneself or someone else.[87] He reminds us that "All feelings that constitute *philia* for others are an extension of regard for self."[88] And since "We admit that one should love one's best friend most; (and) the best friend is he that, when he wishes a person's good, wishes it for that person's own sake, even though nobody will ever know of it; and this condition is most fully realized in a man's regard for himself,"[89] he concludes that "A man is his own best friend. Therefore he ought to love himself the most."[90]

What Aristotelian *philautia* and Randian selfishness have most in common is that both, in the same way, bear little resemblance to the ordinary meaning of the English word *selfish*. The entries for *selfish* and *selfishness* in the *Oxford English Dictionary* are: "devoted to or connected with one's own advantage or welfare *to the exclusion of regard for others*" and "regard for one's own interest or happiness *to the disregard of the well-being of others*" (emphasis added), and there is no term in the English language corresponding to these entries with the words in italics deleted. Rand has Galt declare that rational selfishness entails that: "I do not seek to derive my happiness from the injury of others, but earn it by my own achievement. Just as I do not consider the pleasure of others as the goal of my life, so I do not consider my pleasure as the goal of the lives of others."[91] And for Aristotle, the love of the *agathos* for himself has precious little to do with the so-called self-love exhibited by the *phaulos*, the immoral man, who exceeds the mean of just behavior and indulges the irrational part of his soul.[92] Genuine self-love is, rather, that pride-filled striving of the man of megalopsuchia to attain a life of moral beauty. Most people, however, through ignorance or incontinence have neither the understanding of what genuine eudaimonia is nor the ability and will to achieve it. Thus,

If a man were always bent on outdoing everybody else in acting justly or temperately or in displaying any other of the virtues, and in general were always trying to secure for himself the *kalon*, moral beauty and nobility, no one will charge him with love of self nor find any fault with him. Yet as a matter of fact such a man might be held to be a lover of self in an exceptional degree, for he takes for himself the things that are noblest and most truly good.[93]

HEROIC EGOISM

This essay has attempted to demonstrate the near identity that exists at many points between Randian and Aristotelian metaethics.[94] But beyond that, in terms of normative conduct, it is submitted here that what Rand and Aristotle have most in common is a similar version of the ideal man. A comparision of Rand's principal characters—Roark, Rearden, Dagny, D'Anconia, and Galt—with Aristotle's agathos, the good man, should persuade one that both Rand and Aristotle have a fundamentally *heroic attitude toward life*. The Aristotelian agathos and the Randian hero are *morally heroic* and *heroically rational*. It is this vision of *heroic egoism* that they both hold up to mankind as an inspiring and thrilling ethical ideal.

None of the foregoing should be construed as diminishing Rand's achievements in and contributions to the field of moral philosophy. The author must admit that he so often finds the stately elegance, the extraordinary depth of courteous analysis, and most especially the profound *temperament* of reason exhibited on every page of the *Nicomachean Ethics* a welcome relief to the incessant bombast and continuous venting of Randian rage. Nonetheless, the author considers the objectivist ethics a most immense achievement, the study of which is vastly more fruitful than any other in contemporary thought. It is suggested, however, that this study may be aided substantially by a concomitant study of the ethics of Aristotle.

In many ways, Ayn Rand stands higher and sees farther than any other thinker of our day. She does so because she stands, not just metaphysically and epistemologically (as she would admit), but ethically (as she would not admit), on the shoulders of Aristotle.

NOTES

1. Ayn Rand, *The Virtue of Selfishness* (New York: New American Library, 1964), p. 14. This work is hereafter cited as *VOS*.

2. J. Randall, *Aristotle* (New York: Columbia University Press, 1962), p. 243.

3. Ayn Rand, from remarks made at the close of the *Ayn Rand Program* in 1963 on radio station WKCR (Columbia University) in New York. The broadcast was devoted to a review of *Aristotle*, by J. Randall, that appeared in the *Objectivist Newsletter* in May 1963. The author has a tape of the broadcast.

4. Rand, *VOS*, p. 14.

5. Ayn Rand, *Objectivist Newsletter*, 4 vols. (1962–65), reprint in 1 vol. (New York: The Objectivist, 1965), 2:19.

6. Aristotle *Politics* 8. 1337a28–30. The Bekker pagination will be used in citing the Aristotelian corpus.

7. W. Jaeger, *Aristotle*, trans. R. Robinson (London: Oxford University Press, 1962), pp. 282, 284, with 264–66.

8. Aristotle *Nicomachean Ethics*, trans. and ed. H. Rackham (Cambridge, Mass.: Harvard University Press, Loeb Classical Library, 1934), 1094b24.

9. Following Rackham and Hardie, we shall view the *Ethics* as the authoritative statement of Aristotle's ethical theory. Ibid., p. xiii. W. Hardie,

Aristotle's Ethical Theory (London: Oxford University Press, 1968), pp. 4–5. Hardie notes that the *Ethics* "has always over the centuries been so regarded."

10. Aristotle *Ethics* 1094a2–3.

11. Ibid., 1097a18–19.

12. J. Stewart, *Notes on the Nicomachean Ethics of Aristotle* (London: Oxford University Press, 1892), p. 88.

13. Aristotle *Ethics* 1096b28.

14. Hardie, *Aristotle's Ethical Theory*, p. 66.

15. Aristotle *Ethics* 1096b14–16.

16. Hardie, *Aristotle's Ethical Theory*, p. 67.

17. Aristotle *Ethics* 1096b17–18.

18. The distinction between the *material* concept of value, the position that "there is *one* set of values which is or ought to be *common* to everyone," and the *formal* conception of value, the position that "ultimate value for different people . . . is the same *kind* of good but not the same particular instance of it," is made by J. Kalin, "In Defense of Egoism," in *Morality and Rational Self-Interest*, ed. D. Gauthier (Englewood Cliffs, N.J.: Prentice-Hall, 1970), p. 77. Kalin takes the position that the good can be formally the same but materially different for each individual moral agent. This view effectively counters Moore's view that the good must be materially the same for every moral agent. See G. E. Moore, *Principia Ethica* (Cambridge: Cambridge University Press, 1903), secs. 58–61, 63.

19. It may seem anachronistic to view Aristotle's position as one of egoism. In a certain real sense, no Greek can be labeled an egoist any more than an altruist. The whole issue of egoism and altruism is modern. Indeed, the entire project of attempting to reconcile one's own interests with benevolence or the interests of society as a whole seems clearly to start with Hobbes and the Hobbesian view of man. Hobbes applied the Galilean resoluto-compositive method of explanation to a study of man in society: to explain, on this method, is to resolve a complex whole into its individual parts and then to show how the parts must be combined to reconstruct the whole. With individual men in a complex society, Hobbes assumed the existence of *presocial* individuals who by *definition* (i.e., by Hobbes's arbitrary stipulation) lack those characteristics which belong to the "compromises" of social life. The individual governed by these presocial drives—which Hobbes decided were essentially nonsocial or antisocial, competitive and aggressive—surrendered to an unchecked, unthinking lust to achieve his immediate, mostly bodily, desires. In a state of nature, the necessary result was a "war of all against all." Cf. A. MacIntyre, "Egoism and Altruism," *Encyclopedia of Philosophy* (New York: Macmillan, 1972), 2:462.

Once this view of the essential nature of the individual human being became accepted—which it was, for it fit in well with the basic position of Christianity that man is intrinsically evil by nature through original sin—it is little wonder that a problem arose as to how to reconcile this view with life in society and a benevolence toward others.

This view was the a priori, nonempirical invention of Hobbes and was quite alien to Greek thought. As MacIntyre notes, "In neither Plato nor Aristotle does altruistic benevolence appear in the list of virtues, and consequently the problem of how human nature, constituted as it is, can possibly exhibit this virtue cannot arise." (Ibid.)

Granted, however, that the Greeks possessed no consciously and explicitly formulated concepts of post-Hobbesian and post-Kantian egoism, benevolence, or altruism, it is still possible that they held ethical positions, which, similar to the "materialism" of the Ionians, would *now* be conceptually categorized as egoism or something very much like it, *if* such a position were put forth today.

It is in this sense that a Greek, such as Aristotle, may be said to advocate ethical egoism, i.e., the conviction, however poorly or clearly articulated in the minds of its holders, that there is some sort of necessary connection, if not outright identity, between morally virtuous action and action conducive to the interests and happiness of the individual moral agent.

For a thorough review of contemporary thought on ethical egoism, see T. R. Machan, "Recent Work in Ethical Egoism," *American Philosophical Quarterly* 16 (1979): 1–15. Machan's own definition, of egoism, it should be noted, is strikingly, if perhaps unknowingly, Aristotelian: "We want an answer to 'How should I conduct myself?' Egoism answers by saying that one should conduct one's life so as to achieve, in one's particular case, excellence as the kind of being one is" (p. 13).

20. Ayn Rand, *Atlas Shrugged* (New York: Random House, 1957), pp. 1012–13. This quote is excerpted from Galt's speech, the principal statement of Ayn Rand's philosophy (pp. 1009–69), which is reprinted in its entirety in Ayn Rand, *For the New Intellectual* (New York: New American Library, 1961), hereafter cited as *FNI*.

21. Rand explicitly excludes all entities save for individual living organisms from the category of goal-directed entities: "Only a *living* entity can have goals or can originate them" (*VOS*, p. 16). Aristotle, however, makes no such explicit exclusion and also refers to the πόλις, the city-state, as being a goal-directed entity capable of having a good. The telos and agathon of the *polis* is made clear, though, when he says that it exists for the συμφέρον, advantage, of its members (*Ethics*, 1160a12). Many, however, would regard Rand's explicitness to be a definite improvement on the theory.

22. D. Ross, *Aristotle* (London: Methuen, 1923), p. 126. It may be asked if this species view is applicable to egoism. Yes, it is—for Aristotle is here discussing the conditions for proper survival of an organism, and such discussion can only take place epistemologically within the context of a given organism's species, i.e., the specific *kind* (species) of organism it is and the specific way in which this kind of organism survives.

Rand generates her theory of rights from this starting point. All human beings have the same conditions for proper survival. But while there are, for Rand, no genuine and rational conflicts of interest between human beings because of this fact, there may easily be such between human beings and members of other species, whose conditions for survival are different from man's. Thus, while no human being has the right to violate the rights of another fellow human being, he may violate the "rights" of a member of another species if their interests are in genuine conflict.

23. Rand, *VOS*, p. 17.

24. Aristotle *Ethics* 1097a22–30.

25. Ibid., 1097a30–34.

26. Ibid., 1097a34–b1.

27. Ibid., 1097b16–17.

28. Ibid., 1097b20–21.

29. Ibid., 1097b24–25.

30. Aristotle *Metaphysics* H4. 1044a36–1044b2.

31. Aristotle *Parts of Animals* 640b–645a. Cf. Ross, *Aristotle*, pp. 123–26.

32. Aristotle *Metaphysics* 2.1013b26–28.

33. Aristotle *Ethics*, 1097b34–1098a3.

34. Ibid., 1098a3–7. πρακτική "for Aristotle denotes purposeful conduct, of which only rational beings are capable."

35. Ibid., 1098a7–8.

36. "Literally 'activity of soul'; ψυχή however has a wider connotation than either 'soul' or 'mind,' and includes the whole of the vitality of any living creature." Ibid., 1098a7.

37. Ibid., 1098a7–19.

38. Ibid., 1095a20; J. Austin, "*Agathon* and Εὐδαιμονία in the *Ethics* of Aristotle," in J. Moravcsik, ed., *Aristotle: A Collection of Critical Essays* (New York: Doubleday, 1967), p. 281. Austin observes that " 'success' is not a moral notion for us . . . *eudaimonia* is certainly quite an unchristian ideal." In addition, by sticking to what Aristotle actually says and not indulging in Prichard's habit of saying, "what Aristotle should have said is . . ." or "what Aristotle really meant is . . . ," Austin is able to expose Prichard's "unquestioned assumption" that Aristotelian eudaimonia simply means pleasure or feeling pleased, a state of mind (p. 273)—thus relegating Prichard's accusations of inconsistency in the *Ethics* to irrelevance. Cf. H. Prichard, "The Meaning of Ἀγαθον in the *Ethics* of Aristotle," ibid., pp. 241–60.

39. Rand, *FNI*, p. 123.

40. Ibid., p. 132.

41. Ibid., p. 123. Note the emphasis on happiness as an achievement, necessitating activity.

42. Ibid.

43. Rand, *VOS*, p. 27.

44. Rand, *FNI*, p. 128.

45. Ibid., p. 132.

46. Rand, *VOS*, p. 23.

47. Ibid., p. 25.

48. Ibid., p. 24.

49. Ibid.

50. Aristotle *Ethics* 1098a18–20.

51. Ibid., 1102b11–12.

52. Ibid., 1103a4–5.

53. Ibid., 1106a32.

54. Ibid., 1139b14–17.

55. Ibid., 1140a25–28.

56. Ibid., 1141a25–26 with 1140b6–7.

57. Ibid., 1141b4–6.

58. Ibid., 1144b28. "I.e., prudence is the knowledge of right principle, the presence of the ὀρθὸς λόγος in the ψυχή of the φρόνιμος."

59. Cf. ibid., 1106b36–1107a3.

60. Rand, VOS, p. 25.

61. Ibid., pp. 25–26.

62. Rand, FNI, p. 128.

63. Ross, *Aristotle*, p. 208.

64. Aristotle *Ethics* 1124a1. The word Aristotle uses is κόσμος, adornment, crowning ornament. We can see that the merging of Aristotelian and Randian pride is virtually complete when we witness Rand declaring in Galt's speech that "pride is the *sum* of all virtues." Rand, FNI, p. 179.

65. Bertrand Russell, *A History of Western Philosophy* (New York: Simon & Schuster, 1946), p. 176.

66. Aristotle *Ethics* 1124a1–4. The *kalon* is a uniquely Greek concept for which there is no correspondence in Rand's thought. It is at once an ethical and an aesthetic concept—and involves performing a moral act with grace and balance (balance being another concept of crucial significance to the Greek mind, and Aristotle's mean must be understood in this context), doing the right thing, on the right occasion, toward the right people, for the right purpose, and in the right manner, the performance and witnessing of which is *aesthetically* satisfying. Thus the *kalon* can best be translated as either the *morally noble* or the *morally beautiful*.

67. I.e., so that one is beyond the point of moral temptation and struggle; thus, when one is faced with a moral choice (e.g., to be honest or to lie/cheat/steal), the thought of choosing the immoral alternative does not even occur: one has become "naturally" honest. It is interesting to note that it may well be impossible for any nonegoistic ethic to reach beyond this point, for it seems an inherent tendency in these to define moral behavior in terms of moral struggle, e.g., overcoming one's selfish/immoral desires and doing one's duty instead. But once one thoroughly understands that moral behavior *is* behavior that is in one's best interest and knows in what genuine happiness consists and how it is best achieved, the possibility of moral struggle within oneself dissolves.

68. Rand, FNI, p. 131.

69. Ross, *Aristotle*, p. 230.

70. Aristotle *Ethics* 1155a5.

71. Ibid., 1156b7.

72. Ibid., 1157a2–3.

73. Ibid., 1157a18.
74. Ibid., 1166a1–2.
75. Ibid., 1157b32–34.
76. Ross, *Aristotle*, p. 231.
77. Rand, VOS, p. 32. Rand's emphasis.
78. Ibid., p. 31. Rand's emphasis.
79. Aristotle *Ethics* 1169b31–1170a4.
80. Rand, VOS, p. 32.
81. Aristotle *Ethics* 1169b18–19.
82. Aristotle *Politics* 1252b28–31, 1279a22.
83. Aristotle *Ethics* 1167b2.
84. Ibid., 1160a11–12.
85. Note how diametrically Aristotle is opposed here to traditional Christian morality. It is the consciousness of oneself as sinful, as evil by nature and requiring God's arbitrary grace for salvation, that provides the core of Christian psychology. One is driven to conclude that Aristotle would approve of Rand's condemning the concept of original sin as "monstrous," "a feat of evil" that singlehandedly destroys "morality, nature, justice, and reason." Rand, *FNI*, pp. 136–37.
86. Aristotle *Ethics* 1170b9–13.
87. Ibid., 1168a28.
88. Ibid., 1168b6.
89. Ibid., 1168a34–35.
90. Ibid., 1168b10.
91. Rand, *FNI*, p. 132.
92. Aristotle *Ethics* 1168b15–23.
93. Ibid., 1168b25–31.
94. My purpose has been to discuss the basic parallels between Aristotelian and Randian ethics. One principal feature of Aristotle's ethics, however, has no parallel in Rand's thought: the supreme value of ϑεωρία, the contemplative life. It is therefore not discussed. However, it does have a Randian nature, for it consists of experiencing and contemplating the rationality of the world as the most intensely satisfying conceptual aesthetic experience possible to man. For a fuller discussion of this and of the egoism of Aristotle's ethics in general, see C. J. Wheeler, *Ethical Egoism in Hellenic Thought* (Los Angeles: University of Southern California, Doheny Library, 1976), pp. 231–39.

6
Life and the Theory of Value: The Randian Argument Reconsidered

◖◗

J. Charles King

There is no doubt that Ayn Rand's novels and philosophical writings have played an extremely important role in the recent resurgence of individualist and libertarian thought in the United States. Because Rand has written both fiction and philosophical essays, her influence has been felt in very different ways. For some she has provided an inspiring vision of a society of liberty and individualism through her fiction, particularly *Atlas Shrugged*. For others she has provided the main thrust of a philosophical justification for the advocacy of liberty and individualism.

While I acknowledge with gratitude the inspiration I have received from Ayn Rand's novels, I have never found the main line of her philosophical argument convincing. On the other hand, many persons whom I respect find it the most convincing line of argument concerning moral and political questions they have encountered. I thought that my own skepticism concerning Rand's basic ethical argument had been very well developed in Robert Nozick's article, "On the Randian Argument," and never, therefore, undertook further written criticism of it.[1]

However, in light of the reply to Nozick's paper published by Douglas Den Uyl and Douglas Rasmussen as "Nozick on the Randian Argument," it is clear that the Randian argument is in need of reconsideration.[2] Rather than reconstruct here the extensive disagreements between Nozick and Den Uyl and Rasmussen, I shall attempt a new examination of the Randian argument, stating it as I understand it and then subjecting it to those criticisms which lead me to believe it is inadequate. I shall do all of this, however, with the benefit of having read the essays already mentioned and shall, when appropriate, refer to these earlier essays.

THE RANDIAN ARGUMENT

Ayn Rand holds that *morality* or *ethics* is a code of values to guide man's choices and actions.[3] Ethics as a science she takes to be the discovery and definition of such a code. Her basic strategy for this discovery is to ask first what values are and why men need them. She believes that when these questions are answered, one then has the key to discover what is the *proper* code of values for human beings. Let us, therefore, examine her answers to these questions in turn.

Rand states that value is that which one acts to gain and/or keep. I take this to mean that whatever is the object of a goal-directed action is a value for that actor. In this connection we may do well to remember that one usually distinguishes between the *valued* and the *valuable*. The valued is whatever is actually sought by any individual, the valuable is what is worthy of being sought or what ought to be sought. Now I take it that Rand's is a characterization of the valued. Thus, she can reasonably say that the valued is what one acts to gain or keep. In a later step of the argument she provides us with the transition from the valued to the valuable.

She further holds that value is not a primitive concept but a concept that has at least two crucial presuppositions: (1) the existence of an entity that can act to achieve a goal, and (2) alternatives facing that entity. Den Uyl and Rasmussen suggest that these alternatives must make a difference to the entity in question.[4] This point is perhaps reinforced by Rand's use of the example of the indestructible robot. For the present, however, I will assume that this is merely unpacking what is meant by saying that an entity really faces alternatives in the first place.

Before going on to the important implications of these two points, we should also notice one other position about value that Rand advances. She characterizes an ultimate value as that final goal or end to which all lesser goals are the means. Further, she holds that without an ultimate value there can be no lesser goals or means, since a series of means going off into an infinite progression toward a nonexistent end is impossible. She says explicitly, "It is only an ultimate goal, an *end in itself*, that makes the existence of values possible" (OE, p. 17).

From the two presuppositions of value already explained, Rand argues that only living beings can have values, for only living beings are capable of meeting the two conditions at issue. Only living beings face genuine alternatives, because only living beings can cease to exist. Mere matter does not cease to exist. Its form may change but the matter remains. Life, however, is a process of self-generating and self-sustaining action. Living beings, thus, may be destroyed completely. They may die and simply cease to be the kind of thing they were. Thus, only living beings face this most basic alternative of existence or nonexistence. Living beings are thus the only things that are capable of goal-directed behavior. Rand seems, indeed, to make a connection here between the fact that living beings face the alternative of existence or nonexistence and the very possibility of goal-directed behavior. I find her explanation of the connection unclear, but the following reconstruction by Den Uyl and Rasmussen seems to be a reasonable one.

There is a result that comes from achieving a goal and a result that comes from failing to achieve a goal (even if there is a lack of positive result). The difference in the result to the being who acted to achieve the goal determines, tells us, if the goal is achieved. What differentiates the results of goal-directed behavior? The most fundamental difference possible is the difference between existence and non-existence. If such a difference did not exist, if some being were not conditional, if an action could not result in the existence or non-existence of the entity that acted to achieve a goal, then there would be no differences in the results of achieving a goal or failing to. If there were no difference in result with respect to an entity existing or not existing, then what other differences could there be? What could make results differ if there were not this basic difference? None. Thus, it is the difference between a living being existing or not existing that creates all the other alternatives a living being faces, and it is because life is something that must be maintained that there are goals in the first place.[5]

The life of all organisms, Rand holds, depends upon two factors: (1) obtaining enough fuel for survival and (2) their own actions in the proper use of that fuel. In some living organisms these processes are more or less automatic. Human beings, however, are beings of volitional consciousness. Human beings must choose how they are to act. They do not automatically act in accordance with their nature. But because human beings must choose how to act, they need a code of values to guide them in their choices. Thus, I take it that we have been provided with Rand's answers to the two questions she originally suggested.

But if all of this is granted, then Rand holds that for any living being there can be only one possible ultimate value, namely the organism's life. The very continuation of its life depends upon what is required for its life as the kind of organism it is; thus, its life is its standard of value. But, as a being of volitional consciousness, man needs to choose the standard. What is automatic in other animals must be chosen by man. If a man asks about the proper choice, the answer is the same, his life. Man's life is therefore the ultimate value, that final goal toward which all other goals are directed. This ultimate value provides the standard of value of the objectivist ethics. For each individual human being, his own life will be the purpose of his life, that is, his own adaptation of the pursuit of the standard in his own individual case. As I understand her, Rand asserts that there is nothing arbitrary or due to man's choice in this fact that man's life is the ultimate standard of value. One may, of course, as has already been pointed out, choose to reject the standard; but in doing so, one rejects what is nevertheless necessarily one's own appropriate standard of value because of one's very nature as a human being.

If we ask why man's life must be taken as the standard of value, one understanding of the answer is simply that if one would survive, doing those things required by one's nature for survival is the only way to act. Notice that this answer seems contingent upon one's taking survival as a goal. At least in Galt's speech this seems to me clearly to be the implication of what Rand says.[6] Den Uyl and Rasmussen, on the other hand, argue that one must necessarily choose life as an end.[7] It is not clear to me (especially in Galt's speech) that Rand takes this line, but the Den Uyl and Rasmussen interpretation is worth noting. They claim that:

Given that life is a necessary condition for valuation, there is no other way we can value something without also (implicitly at least) valuing that which makes valuation possible. Paradoxically perhaps, we could value not living any longer, but in making such a value we must nevertheless value life. Death, a living thing not-being, does not require any actions for its maintenance. Death is not a positive way of being. Rather, it is a negation—the absence of being a living thing. It has no required actions; it has no needs. Death cannot be an ultimate value, then, simply because it does not require any actions and thus cannot be the reason or cause of goal-directed behavior. Therefore, we cannot "suppose" death or anything else (other than life) as the ultimate value, for the very activity of "holding something as a value," let alone as an ultimate one, depends on life being the ultimate value in the sense of "ultimate" discussed earlier. Thus there is an inconsistency in the request, "Prove life is valuable." The very meaning of "valuable" presupposes the value of life.[8]

Whichever interpretation one chooses here, it is clear that Rand holds there is only one appropriate standard of value for human beings—only one thing ultimately valuable, namely, man's life. But this standard requires further explanation. Rand makes it very clear that by valuing life a person does not simply hold onto life at any price; rather, one values one's life as the kind of thing a human being is, that is, a rational being. Survival as a man, then, means the survival of a rational being in those choices and alternatives open to such a being throughout a lifetime. The crucial point to understand here is that the standard of man's life implies the standard of a rational being. Reason, according to Rand, is the faculty that identifies and integrates the material provided by the senses. It is the faculty of reason and its process, thinking, that makes possible the survival of human beings. Human beings do not automatically use this faculty, which makes it possible for them to continue their life. It is a faculty one must choose to use. Nonetheless it is the defining faculty of human beings. The process of employing concepts to deal with reality is the process that makes human life possible. It is the process that defines what it is to survive as a human being. Thus it gives us the key to understanding what is meant in the objectivist standard, which holds that man's life is the ultimate value.

In the essay "The Objectivist Ethics," Rand goes on to employ this standard of value to explain the resulting view of the virtues and of the foundations of rights. I shall examine her views on those two topics in the final section of this essay. For the present, however, I wish to concentrate on that portion of the argument already presented, since the argument to the conclusion that life is the ultimate standard of value is the portion of the argument to which I want to direct primary critical attention.

DESIRE AND THE THEORY OF VALUE

In this section I want to state as clearly, precisely, and concisely as possible my reasons for finding the Randian argument unconvincing. To do so I must first call attention to a confusion that exists in Rand's terminology as well as in the terminology of Den Uyl and Rasmussen.[9] Rand says explicitly, "It is only an ultimate goal, *an end in itself*, that makes existence of values possible" (OE, p. 17). The argument she goes on to present to show that there must be an ultimate value depends upon the same identification of "ultimate value" with "end in itself." But the concept of ultimate value should be distinguished from the concept of an end in itself. To be sure, if there is in any system of values an ultimate value, then that ultimate value will be an end in itself. But there may be in a system of values no ultimate value whatever, while there are any number of ends in themselves. Simply put, an end in itself is something that is desired for its own sake, not merely as a means to something else.

It is true that any system of values must contain at least one end in itself. It might well be, for example, that I value health as an end in itself, that I value pleasant companionship as an end in itself, that I value pride as an end in itself. The point is just this, I may well take any number of things as ends in themselves without having to admit thereby that any one of them is the ultimate value, that is, the one value in terms of which the value of all others can be explained. My valuing of health as an end in itself might simply be unrelated to my valuing pride as an end in itself.

If I am to reach rational decisions, I will need to have some kind of ranking order between values; but from the fact that something is an end in itself, it does not follow that it cannot be more or less valued than another thing that is also an end in itself. Thus, the organization of a code of values, while it may depend upon the existence of ends in themselves, does not depend upon the existence of an ultimate value. The claim that there must be an ultimate value, if there is to be any value at all, is therefore mistaken.

There may be in a particular system of values an ultimate value. It might happen that a system of values is so arranged as to lead to one final end in itself, one thing toward which all other values are aimed. But it does not follow that there *must* be an ultimate value if there is to be any value at all, as both Rand and Den Uyl and Rasmussen suppose. We do not, therefore, in choosing a code of values, face the choice of choosing life or else some other thing as the ultimate value. A code of values may admit of any number of ends in themselves and may not be organized so that one particular value plays the role that Rand assigned to ultimate value.

With this objection as background, I can—I think—make clear my next and chief objection to Rand's account concerning life and value. This requires a return to the point of the connection Rand seems to make between the fact that living beings face the alternative of existence and nonexistence and the very possibility of goal-directed behavior. In the passage quoted earlier, Den Uyl and Rasmussen say explicitly that if there were no difference in result with respect to an entity's existing or nonexisting, there could be no other differences. This does seem to be a fair interpretation of Rand's invitation to imagine an immortal and indestructible robot in order to make clear the point that it is only to a living entity that things can be good or evil (OE, p. 16). She invites us to suppose that the robot cannot be affected by anything, cannot be changed in any respect, cannot be damaged, injured, or destroyed.

The robot example is ambiguous in just the following way. If we take the Den Uyl–Rasmussen interpretation, the crucial point is that the robot cannot be destroyed. If we take Rand's words literally, however, perhaps we are to think that the robot is not affected in *any way whatever*. The example is plausible if, in thinking the robot cannot be affected in any way whatever, we mean that the robot either does not *know* or does not *care* what happens to things around it. But, of course, if the robot neither knows nor cares, the example seems uninteresting.

Den Uyl and Rasmussen are simply mistaken in supposing that alternatives could not make a difference to an entity that did not face the difference between existing and not existing. Simply imagine that one suddenly finds, through whatever means, that one has been made immortal. One cannot be destroyed no matter what. Perhaps one's body has been impregnated with a chemical from a strange planet that renders one's tissues impervious to disruption of their structure from any force existing in the universe. There is no reason in supposing this hypothesis of indestructibility that we would then lose all interest in what is going on around us. Even if we knew that we were ourselves indestructible, we might still find some persons sexually attractive; we might still like to eat (to be sure, on the hypothesis that even if we didn't eat, we would still survive; but we might, after all, simply enjoy the taste of a good steak); we might still enjoy the pleasures of the bottle; we might still enjoy the association of friends; we might still be interested in philosophical problems and so on ad infinitum. The mere removal of the possibility of destruction would not remove a whole range of the interests or desires of ordinary human life. Thus, it would be quite possible for one who is totally indestructible, nevertheless, to have a very rich system of values.

Now I emphasize that these aforementioned values would be values on Rand's own view in that these would be things the being would act to gain or keep. If we return then to the robot example, we see why the example as given in "The Objectivist

Ethics" is confusing, for the inclusion of the provision that the robot is not affected by anything might lead one to believe that the robot feels no desires, feels no satisfaction or pleasure, simply does not care about anything. In that case, of course, one cannot imagine that the robot would have any values. But even though the robot is indestructible, as soon as we suppose the robot might have preferences or desires, or, to put it another way, might care about one thing or another, whatever it may be (perhaps simply admires a particular landscape and would like to preserve it or simply sit and look at it), then the robot can view things as for and against him and can in fact have values. Strictly speaking, then, the question of destructibility or indestructibility is irrelevant as to whether a being can have values.

What a being must have to have value is, rather, the capacity for desire or preference or interest or caring. Any of the number of terms can be chosen. For convenience I shall refer simply to the capacity for desire.[10] Thus, if the being is able to desire some circumstances rather than others, that being is able to have values. To be sure, the only beings we know of that we are certain to have these capacities are living beings. In that respect then, it is perfectly true to say that in our experience the activity of valuing presupposes a living being and thus presupposes life.

But, of course, it cannot follow from those mere facts that life will be the standard of value itself. Once one sees it is the possibility of desiring that is crucial for a being to be able to value, then one sees that, while life may be one among other values a being holds, it need have no privileged place. Of course, to most of us life is very high on our ordering of preferences and is, indeed, among the various things we want for their own sakes. But history records many individuals who, even if they could have continued to live what might be called a rational existence in Rand's terms, would nevertheless have preferred to sacrifice their own life to bring about some greater value. The point of this is simply that value finds its beginning in desire, not merely in the process of life that in our experience gives rise to desire. Desire enables one to value even things that transcend, in one way or another, one's own span of life.

Den Uyl and Rasmussen will apparently want to argue that the point of view just presented is in some way internally inconsistent, because they hold that since life is a necessary condition for the activity of valuation there is no way that one can value anything without also, implicitly at least, valuing that which makes valuation possible. It is important to note that, even were this argument acceptable, it would only succeed in showing that life was always a value as a *means*, not that life was always an end in itself or certainly not that life was always an ultimate end. When one sees this, one may then grant to Den Uyl and Rasmussen that at the time one is placing a value on something one must admit that to the extent one valued having placed a value on that thing, then one valued life as a means, since it was the condition that enabled one to place a value on the thing at all. But, of course, all of this would only show that life was grudgingly acknowledged to be valuable as a means to an end; and it would be, after all, the end one was valuing. This object of one's desire would be what made life itself a value.

Thus, the Den Uyl and Rasmussen version of the argument connecting the fact of the destructibility of human beings with their having to take life as an ultimate value does not work. But one may take the other possible version, namely, that life has to be the standard of value if one wishes life to continue (which may or may not be the version contained in Galt's speech). There is, however, no particular reason for me to have to deny this version save for this: once again one would thereby admit only that life was an instrumental value. If what makes me want to stay alive is to play golf as often as possible, it is the fact that I take playing golf as an end in itself and an ultimate value that leads me to place a value on life, not the other way around. The mere fact that I must be alive to play golf makes life only an instrumental value not an ultimate value or an end in itself.

Thus, no matter which of the two interpretations one takes, Rand neither succeeds in proving that life is the ultimate value nor proves that man's life is the objective standard of value for all men. Her argument fails because of a confusion about ultimate value and ends in themselves and because she has not seen correctly the connection between desire and the possibility of value.

In making these claims I would not be misunderstood. I am not in any sense arguing that death is a value, that I myself do not place a high value on my own life, that I do not think other persons should place high values on their lives, or that I disagree with Rand when she points out the strictures of reality facing the choices of each and every human being. She is, of course, quite right in pointing out that various conditions are necessary for human life to continue. To live we must have food and, in many climates, shelter, as well as various other essentials. These do not grow on trees; they must be earned through productive work. If one does not do the work oneself, one can, of course, survive only by profiting from the efforts of others. On all these points, which Rand makes with great clarity and force, I agree that she is entirely right. Nonetheless, one may admit these points and take them as important in developing moral theory and social theory without accepting Rand's main argument in the theory of value. My criticism is directed only at the claim that she shows life to be the appropriate standard of value for all human beings. That argument I have shown to be mistaken.

I should like to turn now to a further criticism of the next step in Rand's argument, namely, the claim that the kind of life that provides the standard for human beings is life as a rational being, not mere survival. I turn to this because someone might suppose that in arguing against the Den Uyl and Rasmussen interpretation of the importance of survival, however well substantiated in Rand's text, I have not argued against Rand's most important argument. My previous comments have been directed at her general claim that for organisms of all kinds, including man, life would be the standard of value. The most specific question of the appropriate standard for human beings is, of course, answered by her to be the standard of man's life as a rational being. I wish, therefore, to turn my critical attention now to her explanation of the meaning of that standard.

On Rand's account, reason is a faculty of human beings. It is the faculty that directs the process of making use of concepts to discover reality. The process the faculty of reason directs she calls thinking. She says, "Reason is the faculty that identifies and integrates the material provided by man's senses" (OE, p. 20). On her view, however, reason is a faculty a human being may choose to exercise or not. When a human being fully exercises reason, the mind is focused to a full awareness of reality. If one chooses not to use one's reason fully, then to varying degrees one unfocuses the mind. In discussing the virtue of rationality, Rand goes on to add that reason is one's only source of knowledge, one's only judge of values and one's only guide to action (p. 25). When she says, then, that the ultimate standard of value is man's life *qua man*, she means that the standard is the life of a human being as a rational creature, that is, the life of a human being with mind focused to grasp the facts of reality. On her account this is the same as to say the life of a human being with reason fully employed. Since this is the fully human life according to her, with the life of a creature whose mind is less focused being in some way subhuman, it follows that when she says "man's life *qua* man" she means the life of rationality.

Unfortunately it seems that there is a considerable ambiguity in what we are to understand here as being reason or a rational life. Among other possible interpretations of the concepts of reason and rationality in the philosophical tradition, one can recognize two that may be of some help at this point. Some thinkers have conceived of reason as that faculty of human beings which enables them to grasp the nature of the world around them in a strictly factual or descriptive sense. Thinkers have sometimes applied the term *theoretical reason* to this understanding of reason. The important point about this understanding of reason is that it sees reason as a faculty devoted to building a picture of the way the world *is*. This seems to be the kind of conception of reason Rand endorses when she calls reason a faculty that identifies and integrates the material provided by the senses (OE, p. 20). It is important to note, however, that if one takes this kind of conception of reason literally, then reason sets no goals and, in fact, can motivate no actions. Reason is, as it were, an information machine on this kind of conception.

On the other hand, reason and rationality are in some philosophies treated in a way much more nearly related to the goals or ends that human beings may pursue in life. Rather than being understood as merely an information gathering machine, reason may be understood in Hume's phrase as the *slave of the passions*. That is to say, reason may be seen as a faculty that enables one to calculate the most effective means to attain ends taken as given. This is obviously a conception of reason very close to that of the pure information gathering machine, although in this case the gathering of the information is seen as guided by changing ends rather than simply as proceeding along a path set for the faculty involved to gather as much information and understanding as possible. The point to note about both of these conceptions of reason, however, is that the faculty of desire or inclination remains separate from reason on either account. On the second account, which is more concerned with action, ends are taken simply as given. On the first account no mention at that level need be made of how action comes about, since theoretical reason is a faculty for the gathering of knowledge. Rand, however, holds that reason is a guide to conduct and that reason enables one to choose values (OE, p. 25). On the account of reason she has given, however, whether we interpret it in either of the ways I have suggested, reason simply cannot be a guide to conduct in any complete sense. I say "in any complete sense" because reason must be taken to be able to be a judge of ends as well, if it is to be able to guide conduct completely.

To explain my objections here, I wish to distinguish between two conceptions of a guide. Consider that you are in a strange country and you wish to reach a certain city. You might then hire a guide, saying to him, "I wish to reach such and such a city as quickly as possible; please guide me there." On the other hand, if one is in a strange country, knows very little about that country, and has no idea where to go, one might hire a guide, saying to him, "Choose those places that you think would be most interesting for a visitor to see and then take me to them." Notice that the first conception of a guide is one in which the end is completely set and the guide merely chooses the path to attain the end. In the second conception the guide is left open to choose the ends to be attained as well as the paths to be taken in attaining those ends.

Now, in any conception of reason that considers reason to be the faculty that identifies and integrates the material provided by man's senses, reason can serve as a guide only in the first and not in the second sense. If reason is to be confined as merely gathering knowledge of what is, it cannot set goals. The setting of goals will have to be done by desire or inclination. To be sure, desire or inclination may be influenced by what reason tells us about the nature of the paths to certain goals or about the goals themselves, but nonetheless the decision to go in one direction rather than another will have ultimately to rest on desire or inclination.

Reason in either of the two senses I outlined earlier could be taken as expressive of Rand's view, when she calls reason a faculty that integrates and identifies the material provided by the senses. But in neither of those cases is reason able to play the part of a guide that sets the goal to be attained. To allow that task to reason stretches reason from being a faculty which gathers information to being a faculty which approves or disapproves. But, of course, to go so far is to lose the advantage of a faculty account and to return only to the notion of reason as like a little man in the head.

Of course, we know that people can calculate ways both to attain ends and to adopt ends. If reason becomes merely another shadowy person in the head who can do all that real people can, then of course it can do both of these things. If, on the other hand, reason is to be a separate faculty, that is, an identifiable aspect of the activities possible to a human being, then reason, if characterized as an information gathering faculty or a faculty that identifies and integrates the material of the senses, cannot be conceived also as a faculty that sets goals.

This brings us back to the point of criticism raised earlier, that Ayn Rand's account allows an insufficient place for the importance of the activities of preferring, desiring, and the like. I repeat, it is true that such things as desiring and preferring may well be informed by the information gathered by reason. Nonetheless reason, as Rand has explained it, cannot provide motivation toward one alternative or another.

The implication of these problems concerning reason is that Rand's account of the standard of the value of man's life, qua rational creature, would provide us, strictly speaking, no actual standard of action at all. For reason must be provided with ends to seek before it can serve as a guide. These ends must come from outside reason itself. Therefore, to set as a standard for action the life of a rational being is to set no determinate standard at all.

I am quite aware that proponents of Rand's argument may

reply that my conception of reason here is too narrow, that it is positivistic or that it has fallen prey to some other awful philosophical disease. The fact is, however, that the account Rand gives of reason in "The Objectivist Ethics" is an account of reason as a faculty that gathers information. If one takes an account of that sort, then the argument I have advanced follows. Of course, one may try to broaden the account of reason; but in my experience I find attempts so to broaden the account turn out to make reason a shadowy entity that can perform all the usual functions of an actual human being and thus is of doubtful explanatory value. The notion of reason as a faculty, as one aspect of what human beings can do, might have some explanatory value; but simply as a shadowy thing or an all-purpose faculty that can do the things that human beings can do, it is, of course, a piece of metaphysical spare baggage.

Finally, I would hasten to point out that I take up the whole question of treating reason as a faculty of human beings only because it is treated that way in Ayn Rand's work. I would prefer to regard reasoning simply as one of the activities of which human beings are capable, not necessarily to be attributed to some particular faculty of human beings. I am quite willing to admit a good deal of ignorance as to why human beings are capable of some of the activities of which they are capable. We do have, however, a fair amount of information about how it is that human beings can do many of the things they can do. In any case, it is clear that one of the things human beings can do is gather information about the way the world is. They can also profitably bring that information to bear upon choice of the ways to seek their ends and upon choice of ends themselves. However, the fact always remains that when all the information has been gathered, a human being must choose the path he or she prefers to take. That ultimate question cannot be answered by reasoning, because it is not a question of obtaining more information. Even if, as never happens, one had all the information available, one would still in the end have to choose where one wants to go.

As a consequence of the difficulties I have outlined, I am satisfied that the Randian argument is not successful in proving either that life is the ultimate standard of value or that man's life qua rational being is the standard of human beings. There are, however, other issues of considerable interest mentioned in "The Objectivist Ethics." In the next section I would like to discuss two of them briefly.

In taking a broad overview of the points I have been arguing, I would suggest that part of the problem in Ayn Rand's argument has been the fact that she has tried to find a way to make one important human motivation the central and overriding motivation of all appropriate conceptions of the human good. Thus, in attempting to make life the standard of value, she has presented a conception of value that is too narrow to present itself as a standard for many persons who do not fall under her strictures of adopting a subhuman attitude of failing to focus their mind fully and clearly. I might perhaps illustrate this point by appeal to one issue in regard to her discussion of the virtues.

In discussing the virtues of rationality, productiveness, and pride, Rand says, "Productive work is the *central* purpose of a rational man's life, the central value that integrates and determines the hierarchy of all his other values" (OE, p. 25). Now, productive work certainly is essential for the survival of any human being. Furthermore, for many human beings productive work may well be the central purpose of life. It is, however, much too narrow to say that productive work is the central purpose of the life of anyone who is rational.

Consider the person who conducts his life in the following manner. From the years twenty to thirty he works very hard. He arranges his life in such a way that work consumes the greater part of his life, but he does this to earn as much profit as possible as quickly as possible. Suppose that by the age of thirty he has amassed a considerable amount of wealth. Suppose that what he does then is invest his wealth well. He buys stock in Taggart Transcontinental or makes large deposits in a bank run by Midas Mulligan. As a result he has sufficient income to live quite comfortably for the rest of his life, and in the beginning of this thirtieth year he makes the central purpose of his life not further productive work, but the elusive quest for par. Suppose he spends most of his time playing golf or practicing golf, attempting to improve his game.

In what respect are we entitled to say that this man is no longer rational; in what respect, in fact, according to the standards one finds in Rand's writings, are we entitled to view him as some kind of parasite? If he has made investments that represent a voluntary, trader relationship for obtaining his income, he is not to be viewed as a parasite on the person who runs a railroad or the person who operates a bank. That person freely chooses to engage in those activities and has freely chosen to accept an investment to promote the activities in which he or she is interested. Thus, there is no reason to call this golfer either irrational or a parasite.

Nonetheless, I see no reason to suppose that productive work is the central purpose of his life. By hypothesis, playing a game is the central purpose of his life. One may well say, "Ah, yes, but for those ten years productive work had to be the central purpose of his life." Not necessarily so! The central purpose of his life may always have been to able to live the life he lives now; but to attain that, he worked very hard for those ten years to amass the required wealth.

It follows from the foregoing example that productive work simply need not be the central purpose in the life of a rational person. The person in the story is perfectly rational. He has taken account of the facts of reality in order to pursue his own ends. It is pointless to say against him that if everyone did that his course would be impossible. Of course, it would be impossible if everyone did it. Doing most things would be impossible if everyone did them. The point is that he has used his reason to calculate that others will act in particular ways and that they are to be trusted to keep their agreements, and he has therefore acted upon these facts of reality. He is neither irrational, immoral, nor a parasite. It seems clear that he is a person for whom Ayn Rand would feel little admiration. He is doubtlessly far removed from Hank Rearden or Dagney Taggart. But surely the difference is a difference in *taste*, a difference in the kind of life and activity Rand admires and desires, as opposed to the kind of life and activity our hypothetical golfer likes and admires. But that difference is one of taste, not one of failure to abide by some objective standard. Thus it illustrates the difficulty into which Rand falls from her desire to provide an objective standard of value.

Surely the question between our golfer and Ayn Rand's conception need not be settled by saying that one is objectively right and the other is objectively wrong or that one is objectively virtuous and the other objectively vicious. Is it not far more reasonable simply to say that different persons may reasonably value differing kinds of activity? The point about our golfer is that he has not behaved in ways that even Rand need proscribe in attaining the ends he seeks. It is needless, then, for her account of values to impose such a narrow set of constraints upon the kind of life that may rationally be chosen. To be sure, writing in the context in which she was writing, the desire to find an objective standard of value is understandable; nonetheless, our leisurely golfer makes clear, I think, the way in which Rand has been led to an overly narrow conception of values.

Finally, I would mention that my claims that Rand is not entirely clear in her use of the expressions *ultimate value* and *end in itself* are further substantiated when one notices what she has to say in "The Objectivist Ethics" about the basic *social* principle of her view. She says her basic social principle is that every living human being is an end in himself, just as life is an end in itself (p. 25). She further explains that this means that human beings are not the means to the ends or welfare of others and that they must therefore live for their own sakes. I must admit that I remain entirely puzzled as to how this use of the concept of an end in itself will help her to justify a political philosophy.

My puzzlement is not abated by reading Ayn Rand's other works, including the essay entitled "Man's Rights."[11] Rand says that each human being is to be regarded as an end in himself, just as life is an end in itself; but I find no interpretation to put on this suggestion to make it plausible. When we are thinking of each person thinking about his own life, there is, of course, a certain plausibility to saying that each of us finds our life an end in itself; although as I have made clear, I am inclined to doubt that this is necessarily a general truth. Nonetheless, I can see no reason why each of us must regard the other as an end in himself or herself. The notion of an end in itself will be of value for political philosophy or as a social principle only if we are given such a reason.

I could understand an argument to the effect that, when each of us takes our own life as our purpose and man's life as the standard, reason shows us that the only way successfully to pursue our own goals is to exercise the kind of restraint in regard to others that we would hope for them to exercise in regard to us. Obviously this thought could be developed in various ways, and it is not important to follow out a particular one for present purposes. As far as I can see, however, the notion of an end in itself is of no particular value in making the kind of argument I envision here. I must say, therefore, that I remain puzzled as to how Rand believes the notion of regarding each person as an end in himself or herself is in some way related to regarding life as an end in itself. This confirms for me that there is a lack of clarity in her understanding of the notions *end in itself* and *ultimate value* that play a mischievous role in her basic argument, as I have already attempted to show.

CONCLUSION

There are many interesting and helpful points in Ayn Rand's philosophical writings that I have not mentioned. I have been guided by a desire to state clearly my reasons for disagreeing with her central argument concerning life and the theory of value. I believe I have shown reason to reject her argument that man's life is the standard of value.

If, however, one respects and admires Ayn Rand's work as I do, one feels a special desire to point out that reasoned criticism is a high compliment to pay to the work of a philosopher. When criticizing the work of most philosophers, such a disclaimer is unnecessary, but Rand has been treated with such prejudice and disrespect by most intellectuals that I feel it is important to make it clear that my disagreement is not of that order. I have been moved and instructed by her fiction and have read her philosophy with profit. Nevertheless, for the reasons I have explained, I believe that the Randian argument is unsound.

NOTES

1. Robert Nozick, "On the Randian Argument," *The Personalist* 52 (Spring 1971): 282–304.

2. Douglas Den Uyl and Douglas Rasmussen, "Nozick on the Randian Argument," ibid., 59 (April 1978): 184–205.

3. In interpreting Rand's argument, I have relied primarily on the essay "The Objectivist Ethics," in Ayn Rand, *The Virtue of Selfishness* (New York: Signet Books, 1964), pp. 13–35. Further references to this work appear with the abbreviation OE and page number within parentheses in the text. When I refer to other works, a citation is provided; otherwise I am relying on this essay and have provided citations only for direct quotations or particularly controversial claims.

4. Den Uyl and Rasmussen, "Nozick on the Randian Argument," p. 190.

5. Ibid.

6. Ayn Rand, *Atlas Shrugged* (New York: Signet Books, 1957), p. 940.

7. Den Uyl and Rasmussen, "Nozick on the Randian Argument," p. 191.

8. Ibid.

9. Ibid., pp. 190–91.

10. I would not be understood to assert that these terms are synonymous. In fact, there are many differences between them in ordinary language. I assert only that they are similar enough that any of them may be chosen to make my point here. Which one prefers will depend on how one treats other philosophical issues that are not being debated here.

11. Ayn Rand, "Man's Rights," in *Capitalism: The Unknown Ideal* (New York: Signet Books, 1967), pp. 320–28.

7
The Fundamental Moral Elements of Rand's Theory of Rights

◉

Eric Mack

My goal in this essay is to describe, distinguish, evaluate and show the relationships among the key elements in Rand's moral theory as that theory moves toward a doctrine of human rights. This is a substantial task—one which fully requires and merits a more lengthy treatment than is possible here. The many interconnections between Rand's claims within moral theory and her claims about human nature and psychology are important, complex, and difficult to untangle. One device for limiting the scope of this essay will be to consider only a few of Rand's essays, most especially "The Objectivist Ethics."[1] Essentially, the elements to be dealt with are: the grounding of moral theory in the demonstration of the goodness of life-sustaining action; the character of the good to be aimed at or attained in moral action; the connections between moral and political individualism, i.e., between Rand's rational egoism and her doctrine of human rights; and the role of Rand's moral psychology within each of these. In presenting Rand's views I will often employ analogies, parallels, philosophical terms, and distinctions that do not themselves appear within Rand's own writings. The hope throughout is to illuminate rather than render more obscure the character of Rand's thought. This essay is divided into three major sections.

The first focuses on Rand's foundation for ethics. The second raises questions about the nature of the ethical standard thus founded. The third traces the transition to a theory of rights.

I

The two most prominent features of Rand's moral view are her defense of rational selfishness and her insistence on the existence of and respect for human rights. Rand contrasts these doctrines with all varieties of self-negating ethics, i.e., with all versions of the view that individuals should sacrifice themselves or should be sacrificed by others to further the interests of some significant other, e.g., God, Society, the Race, the Noble, or the Wretched. Much of her case for rational selfishness and against altruism lies outside the standard bounds of philosophical argument. It consists in contrasting depictions of self-respecting, self-loving, and independent people and self-sacrificing, self-loathing, and dependent people and accounts of the long-run psychological, sociological, and economic accompaniments of rational selfishness versus the long-run accompaniments of self-abnegation. The entire case involves economic theory, historical analysis, and claims about the connections between ideological commitments and moral and psychological traits. None of this vast aspect of Rand's position can be conveyed here. Instead, we must deal solely with certain of Rand's explicit philosophical arguments or argument fragments.

The crux of Rand's central philosophical insight in moral theory is that there is a far more intimate and profound connection between life and the process of valuation, i.e., the process of forming goals, of planning, of choosing strategies, of acting, than other moral philosophers have realized. It is this connection that, according to Rand, allows us to infer the rightness of certain courses of human action from the existence and nature of human life. The explication of such a connection, justifying such an inference from the existence and nature of human life to the rightness of some courses of action (and the wrongness of others), would close the notorious gap between *is* and *ought*, and between the facts of human existence and beliefs about the right and the wrong, the good and the bad. Only if this gap is closed can moral beliefs be seen as having objective status, as resting upon and being defensible in terms of ascertainable facts rather than being merely more or less elaborate statements or expressions of arbitrary feeling. While Rand intends to establish a specific moral system, success in this endeavor would also put to rest the common twentieth-century doctrine that all systems of oughts are ultimately unfounded, that different individuals or different peoples are simply ultimately *committed* to diverse principles or goals, and that no rational appeal to discernible facts can resolve disputes between such ultimate commitments.

In focusing upon an intimate connection between life and valuation, Rand is not merely maintaining that life continues or florishes only if certain goods, plans, or actions are acquired, formed, or performed. It is not merely that certain valuations are, in this way, necessary to life so that *if* life is esteemed then these life-giving and sustaining processes must also be esteemed. Such an argument would not preclude that esteem for life—in particular an individual's esteem for his own life—was itself just an arbitrary emotive commitment or orientation. An argument having the form, if life is good (and life-sustaining actions are right), then so-and-so specific goals are good as conditions of life and such-and-such actions are right as strategies for life, does not meet the skeptical and relativist challenge that no ultimate value (e.g., life) can be rationally grounded upon the facts of human existence.

We must add, however, that Rand herself often slips or seems to slip into this less ambitious form of argument. As we shall note later in this section, she does not seem to distinguish sharply between arguments for the goodness of life and arguments about what follows from the choice or recognition of the goodness of life. Here, as elsewhere, Rand's philosophical ambitions are endangered by the lack of clear self-conscious and self-critical structure in her exposition.

What then is the argument concerning the intimate connection of life and valuation? Let us take as our initial text for understanding this argument the following two passages.

It is only a living organism that faces a constant alternative: the issue of life or death. Life is a process of self-sustaining and self-generated action. If an organism fails in that action, it dies; its chemical elements remain, but its life goes out of existence. It is only the concept of "Life" that makes the concept of "Value" possible. It is only to a living entity that things can be good or evil. [OE, pp. 15–16.]

Metaphysically, *life* is the only phenomenon that is an end in itself; a value gained and kept by a constant process of action. Epistemologically, the concept of "value" is genetically dependent upon and derived from the antecedent concept of "life." To speak of "value" as apart from "life" is worse than a contradiction in terms. "It is only the concept of 'Life' that makes the concept of 'Value' possible." [P. 17.]

To the latter passage Rand adds, "the fact that living entities exist and function necessitates the existence of value and of an ultimate value which for any given living entity is its own life" (p. 17).

Our initial interpretative problem is that the clearest line from these passages is one which seems to express an uninteresting truism. This is the claim that "It is only to a living entity that things can be good or evil," for surely it is obvious that one must be alive for something to affect one for good or for ill. But this truism certainly does not imply that some particular type of effect on living beings is good, while some other type of effect is evil. Similarly, an uninteresting reading is possible with regard to the sentence "To speak of 'value' as apart from 'life' is worse than a contradiction in terms." Here we might see Rand as merely insisting that nothing is of value to nonliving things, that an entity's being alive is a precondition for anything's being good or bad for it. Surely if this is all there is to the link between value and life, Rand has nothing new or important to tell us. But Rand's claims are deeper, more intriguing and fruitful than these truisms.

We should notice that for Rand the *concept* of life makes the *concept* of value possible. That is, her claim is not merely that the life of an entity is a background causal condition for things being of value to that entity. Rather, her claim is that our concept of value itself somehow incorporates or presupposes the concept of life. It is this dependence of the concept of value on the concept of life that Rand emphasizes in the second passage reproduced above and that she has in mind when saying the former concept is "genetically dependent upon and derived from" the latter concept.

What, then, is the nature of this conceptual dependence? According to Rand the existence of values, i.e., of action, of goal-seeking, of planning, of choice, is necessitated by the existence of living entities. By this Rand means not merely that, given the existence of living entities, one then causally gets the existence of valuing in the way that, for example, given the existence of burning candles one then causally gets soot. Here the concept of soot is not shown to be dependent on the concept of burning candles. One can understand what soot is without knowing anything at all about burning candles. Even if burning candles were, in fact, the only occasion for the existence of soot, soot needn't be understood as that which is (uniquely) produced by burning candles.

Rather, Rand is claiming that valuing is the need of living entities to sustain or attain specific states and conditions to remain in existence as living entities. Valuing is not to be understood as something tacked onto life (and capable of being tacked on only to life). It is something that will exist in any type of living thing in virtue of the nature of life—i.e., its precarious and conditional state. We understand valuing—i.e., we form the concept of valuing—neither by looking at this or that particular instance of action, goal-seeking, or planning, nor by noting its material causal antecedents, but by seeing how life, as the conditional *state* that only remains in existence through adjusting and readjusting to a changing environment, calls forth the existence of life as the *process* of action and reaction, goal-setting, and goal-seeking. Life as this state of conditional existence obtains only insofar as "a process of self-sustaining and self-generated action" obtains (OE, p. 15). As Rand puts it, "Life can be kept in existence only by a constant process of self-sustaining action" (p. 16).

Here again we must emphasize that the process is not something that just happens to be associated with the separate phenomenon of life. Rather, by its (conditional) nature, life requires such a process for its continued existence. It is this requirement, this condition of life, that explains the existence of and illuminates the character of the phenomenon of valuing. Valuing, then, has a teleological explanation—an *in-order-that* explanation. Such an in-order-that explanation for valuing can be understood in a number of ways. We can see a certain phenomenon as that which makes possible a certain outcome and that which is not fully understood until it is seen as making that outcome possible. An example would be our seeing hearts as making possible the steady supply of nutrients and oxygen to the cells of certain types of animals and our not fully understanding hearts until we see them as making this outcome possible. We understand what hearts are when we see them in the context of the requirements—the requirements of body cells for nutrients and oxygen—which the existence of hearts satisfies.

Paraphrasing Rand, we could say that the concept of *heart* is genetically dependent upon the concept of *cellular needs*, and it is only the concept of cellular needs that makes the concept of heart (i.e., the correct concept of heart) possible. In this paraphrase we are not claiming that people were *unaware* of hearts prior to an understanding of heart as that which exists in order that cellular needs may be satisfied. People have known of the existence of hearts for a long time. But their conception of hearts was flawed, or at least incomplete, as long as they remained ignorant of that for which hearts exist. The paraphrase asserts, then, that since the adequate concept of heart includes the understanding of heart as a thing that exists to satisfy cellular needs, this concept of heart builds upon and cannot be cut loose from the concept of cellular needs.

We can also understand claims like hearts exist in order that cellular needs may be satisfied in a quasi-evolutionary way. We can imagine the appearance of creatures with some primitive version of cellular needs and the survival of only those among these creatures who also possessed heartlike organs. Then we can imagine our way up an evolutionary spiral to more specialized needs and more elaborate heartlike organs to satisfy those needs. Within such a picture, it is the existence of such cellular needs and the comparative usefulness of heartlike organs for the satisfaction of cellular needs of organisms that explains the current existence of such organs. If it were not for the cellular needs, there would be no comparative advantage for creatures with heartlike organs and, therefore, no explanation for the current existence of hearts. Hearts, then, can be said to exist because of the cellular needs of creatures (typically) possessing hearts.

The parallel to valuing and life should be obvious. The survival prospects of a living but nonvaluing, i.e., nonactive, non–goal-directed, entity are nil. As life appears and develops, so too must valuing—in order that life may continue. Valuing exists because of the needful nature of life. Valuing exists in order that these needs—instances of the general need to perform life-sustaining activities—may be satisfied. Life is what valuing is all about. But just as we may be acquainted with hearts without being aware of the end for which they exist and may, therefore, unknowingly fail to have an adequate concept of hearts, so too we may be acquainted with valuing without being aware of the end for which it exists and unknowingly fail to have an adequate concept of valuing. In fact, according to Rand, this has been the central failure in the history of ethics. This point merits explanation.

One can easily be acquainted with the existence of valuing, with human goal-seeking and choice, without seeing specific acts as instances of a phenomenon that exists in response to and as a reflection of the needful and precarious status of life. But such an acquaintance with valuing would be on a par with the acquaintance with hearts that does not include an understanding of the functional role of hearts. We can imagine intelligent beings from another planet with bodies very different from ours capturing various human beings and engaging in a variety of biological experiments upon them. They spend, let us suppose, quite a bit of time studying the muscular, pulsating organ they find within the chest of each individual. They weigh each specimen. They record the sounds it produces. They measure the volume of liquid it pumps, and they identify its electrical qualities. But they still remain ignorant of what these things called hearts are—as ignorant as we would be if our understanding of hearts was limited to the sort of information so acquired. They remain ignorant until they determine what the function of hearts is, what needs or requirements within the body explain the existence of these organs. For these aliens finally to become aware of these needs and to see these pumping, three-pound, muscular organs as directed toward the satisfaction of these needs is for them finally to form an adequate concept of heart.

By extending this imaginative example a bit further, we can see the *evaluative* relevance of inquiry into the "what for" of hearts and also into the "what for" of valuing. Imagine that, while our aliens are listening to, weighing, and measuring hearts, but before they have reached a functional understanding of hearts, they are also speculating about which of the hearts are good hearts and which are not-so-good hearts. Some take a liking to the hearts that beat with particular regularity and declare these to be the good hearts—perhaps rationalizing their inclination with the theory that the role of the heart is to serve as a type of internal timing device. Others judge those hearts best that beat most often. Still others discover that some hearts make pleasing (to alien eyes) wall hangings and judge these hearts to be the good ones. Of course, none of these alternative systems of judgment coincides with our evaluation of goodness and badness in hearts. For none is based on a relevant understanding of hearts.

Only when the aliens arrive at a correct functional understanding of human hearts can they correctly grade them. Then the grading, the evaluation, is straightforward. A heart is good insofar as it fulfills the function of hearts. That is, hearts are good hearts insofar as they satisfy the need that explains the existence of hearts, insofar as they satisfy the requirements in the light of which we first understand what hearts are. Once the function of a type of thing—in this case hearts—is known, objective evaluations of things of that type are possible. For a thing of a specific kind is a good thing of that kind if it (or its activity or employment) fulfills the function of things of that kind.

Two points can be made here before returning to the case of life and valuation. The first point is that we now have a more specific reading of Rand's notion of one concept being "genetically dependent" upon another and of the latter concept making the former concept possible. We have seen that in some cases an adequate concept of some kind of thing is formed only when these things are understood in terms of the fulfillment of certain needs. The concept of that type of thing is therefore dependent upon and only possible because of the concept of that needful condition. The dependent concept will involve a functional understanding of that type of thing, since it ties the things understood to certain needs or requirements that explain the existence of such things. The second point is that the notion of function seems to be the natural bridge between *is* and *ought*. That things of a given kind have a particular function, that there is some need to which we must refer to explain the existence of things of this kind, is a factual matter. Whether things of a given kind have a particular function is a matter of how the world *is*. Yet if things of a given kind do have a particular function, then those things can be evaluated. We can judge whether this or that thing is as things of its kind *ought* to be. The notion of function, of the "what for" of things, brings together our understanding of what things are and what they should be.

Let us now return to the case of life and value. Here Rand's claim can be expressed as: the conditional status of life—the need of living things to operate within their environments, to react, to reject, to transform material, and so on, if they are to remain living things—is what explains valuing. If it were not for this needful character of life itself, the whole phenomenon of valuation would never have appeared. And, because valuation reflects the precarious nature of life, it is not to be understood as merely something that happens to appear in living things. Rather, valuation is to be seen as existing because of this need.[2]

Since the function of a type of thing is the satisfaction of the need that explains it, the function of valuation is the satisfaction of the life needs of the valuing organism. We have, then, a standard for evaluating goal-directed activity. When that activity actually satisfies the life needs of the valuing organism, it is good. As valuation it is fulfilling its function. When such activity does not satisfy the life needs of the valuing organism—especially when it hinders such satisfaction—the activity is malfunctioning. It is not fulfilling its function, and it is to be graded as bad goal-directed activity.

Our evaluation of goal-directed activities is not read off from some set of commandments written across the heavens. Rather, it is simply a matter of our seeing valuation as a reflection of and response to the fundamental challenge that is posed for any living entity in virtue of its being a living being. This is the doctrine we may read into Rand's cryptic remark, "The fact that a living entity *is*, determines what it *ought* to do. So much for the issue of the relation between '*is*' and '*ought*'" (OE, p. 17).

In one respect, the analogy between hearts and human goal-directed activity may be misleading. Hearts characteristically fulfill their function. They have no choice in the matter. Hearts do, unfortunately, malfunction—but not through intellectual or moral error on their part. The same is true, according to Rand, of goal-directed activity by organisms below the human level. Such activity automatically tends toward the preservation of the acting organism (pp. 18–19), although the mechanism of such activity can, of course, miscarry. Thus, if in attempting to understand valuation, ethical theorists had focused upon goal-directed activity below the human level, they would have more readily concluded that the function of goal-directed activity was the satisfaction of the life needs of the acting organism. And, therefore, they would have tended to conclude that within any organism the satisfaction of its life needs is the criterion for evaluating its actions.

But in the context of human activity, an additional complication appears. Human action, according to Rand, is not programmed. We survive and prosper by choosing the best alternatives among the many avenues for action available to us. It is this freedom of choice in the case of human action that, according to Rand, makes the evaluation of these actions moral evaluation. But this freedom of choice carries with it the possibility of choosing activities that are less than optimally life satisfying. This is especially true because of the great number and variety of cues that confront us—the sensorial pain or pleasure of an act, its many emotionally felt qualities, our anticipation of its consequences, its felt conformity with past or possible future actions, and so on. Indeed, since we may guide our choices in particular situations by general rules or strategies about how to choose and since these rules or strategies may themselves not be optimally life satisfying, we may end up systematically acting in ways that frustrate life needs. Such actions may, at the same time, be thought of as enlightened and right. So, in the case of human goal-directed activity, we should not expect to arrive at a correct identification of its function simply by observing what characteristically results from human action.

Neither should we focus on existing opinion about what constitutes right action. In very traditional philosophical language, the point is that, because human beings have freedom of choice, the natural end of man's activity (that which fulfills its function) may be neither the characteristic nor the characteristically endorsed end of human action. This is not paradoxical. There is nothing inconceivable about such divergence between a natural (i.e., function-satisfying) end and a characteristic result. If most physicians were concentration-camp personnel, the characteristic result of medical practice would diverge from the end in which its function is fulfilled. If physicians come into existence in ignorance of the function of medical activity, such a divergence is all the more likely.

So, because of freedom of choice, fallibility, and the complexity of choice situations, human beings are in much the same position with regard to understanding the phenomenon of their goal-directed activity as those imaginary aliens are with regard to their understanding of human hearts. In each case the parties are faced with a confusing riches of facts and patterns. What are we to make of these things called hearts? What are we to make of these episodes called goal-directed activities? We have seen that, upon taking a fancy to this or that aspect of hearts, our aliens might formulate all sorts of views about which hearts are good and which are not so good. The sort of surface inspection and disorganized collection of data that results from not wondering why such things exist does not yield an adequate conception of hearts or an adequate standard for evaluating them.

Rand claims that, in a parallel fashion, ethical theorists have taken the existence of valuation for granted. This is why they have not penetrated the vast and diverse medley of qualities and consequences of human valuation. And this is why they have offered us as standards for evaluating human activity only expressions of their own special fondnesses for this or that aspect of human action. Thus Rand says, "Most philosophers took the existence of ethics for granted as the given, as a historical fact,

and were not concerned with discovering its metaphysical cause
or objective validation" (OE, p. 14). Instead, we must ask the
more fundamental questions, What are *values*? and Why does
man need them? (P. 15.) Rand's particular answer, we have
seen, is that valuation exists in order that the life needs of the
valuing organism may be satisfied and that the standard for
judging any particular goal-directed action is its contribution to
the life of the acting entity. "An organisms's life is its *standard
of value*: that which furthers its life is the *good*, that which
threatens it is the *evil*" (p. 17). Thus, Rand reaches the conclusion "that *concern with his own interests* is the essence of a
moral existence, and that *man must be the beneficiary of his
own moral actions*."[3] The second section of this essay will examine, in some respects, what the content of these interests is.

This completes the exposition of Rand's account of the link
between life and valuation and the manner in which this link
provides a basic standard for evaluating action (and results of
action).[4] It remains for us to take note of those passages in
which Rand appears to retreat to the less bold contention that
if each person's life is the fundamental value for that person,
then each person's life-fostering acts can be evaluated as right
and each person's life-hindering acts can be evaluated as evil.
Within this philosophically more modest approach, the only
justifiable evaluations would be instrumental, e.g., this action is
right because it tends toward an end assumed to be good. There
would be no attempt to justify ultimate values. As was indicated
at the beginning of this section, to adopt this approach is to
start from assumed oughts and to give up the attempt to bridge
the is-ought gap. How much of this can we find within Rand?

When Rand asks rhetorically whether ethics is an objective
necessity, "Is ethics a subjective luxury—or an objective necessity?" (OE, p. 14) and "Why does man need a code of value?"
(p. 13), it seems as though she is arguing that not any code of
behavior will sustain "man's existence," that only specific forms
and combinations of actions will in fact sustain man, and that
these forms and combinations are objectively necessary *for that
end*. Hence, objectivity resides in the identification of satisfactory means—not in the choice of ultimate goals.

The natural form of any answer to these questions would be: Because only specific forms or patterns of behavior will get men to state *x*. And the form of such an answer suggests that the value of state *x* (e.g., being alive) is assumed and not proven. That Rand poses her most fundamental question in this way suggests that she herself sees the value of life as an unproven assumption or axiom. Yet this interpretation clashes with her insistence on the *absurdity* of speaking of value as apart from life, i.e., the absurdity of ascribing value to life's alternative, death. Furthermore, if Rand takes herself as merely assuming (postulating) the value of life, it is hard to see how she could expect her position to have any philosophical force against any party who denied this assumption.

But is there any way by which we can account for the air of assumption that Rand's question creates without reading Rand as merely presupposing here the value of life? Perhaps. There is an alternative reading of Rand that ascribes some presupposition to her—but not the presupposition that life is valuable. On this reading, the presumption of the rhetorical question "*Why* does man need a code of values?" is that there is a genuine and valid need for some code of values, i.e., that there is *some* worthwhile end for the attainment of which guided action is necessary. Given this presumption, the rest of the argument follows quickly. If man's worthwhile goal were death, then no code of values would be needed, for inaction or mere random activity would be causally sufficient for death. Hence, death cannot be man's worthwhile goal. But there are only two fundamental alternatives, viz, death and life (OE, p. 15). So it must be life that is the goal worth being guided to.

There is one other, final place in which Rand seems to slip into an ethics that only judges actions against an *assumed* ultimate value. This is in her essay "Causality versus Duty." There she writes:

Life or death is man's only fundamental alternative. To live is his basic act of choice. If he chooses to live, a rational ethics will tell him what principles of action are required to implement his choice. If he does not choose to live, nature will take its course.

Reality confronts man with a great many "musts," but all of them are conditional; the formula of realistic necessity is: "you must if —"

and the "if" stands for man's choice: "— if you want to achieve a certain goal." You must eat, if you want to survive. You must work, if you want to eat.[5]

One cannot deny that the natural reading of these passages is that the choice of life itself is not dictated by "a rational ethics." That Rand here slips into this less ambitious moral theory cannot be plausibly denied. There is, however, a special explanation why, within the essay "Causality versus Duty," Rand should stray from her primary position. In this essay Rand is attacking Kant and the notion that actions should be done simply for the sake of duty. The most obviously contrasting view is that *actions* can only be justified in terms of their effectiveness in realizing desired goals. On this contrasting conception, all justification *for action* is hypothetical. That is, an action is justified if and only if it yields some valued result.[6] However, in pressing her case against Kant and in insisting that all rational action employs causal knowledge, Rand slips into the view that all rationality in human practice resides in actions' being effective in bringing about their intended results—that no practical rationality resides in the choice of goals. That is, she slips into the view that *all justification* (not just for actions) is hypothetical. And to say this is to say there is no justified ultimate value.

Clearly Rand need not have adopted this latter view. This view, of course, conflicts fundamentally with her main line of argument in "The Objectivist Ethics," where she claims: "Without an ultimate goal or end, there can be no lesser goals or means: a series of means going off into an infinite progression toward a nonexistent end is a metaphysical and epistemological impossibility. It is only an ultimate goal, an *end in itself*, that makes the existence of values possible (OE, p. 17). Clearly Rand means that only a *rational, justifiable*, ultimate goal makes the existence of rational values possible.

II

The combination of the stark contrast between life and death as alternative ultimate values leads to the question What is this life which, according to Rand, each is supposed to hold as the ultimate measure of his actions? Answering this question will be a complex matter, for we must consider not only what Rand says, but also why she says it. Furthermore, we must point out where her arguments go wrong and how they might be put right. Let us start by noting the context within which Rand seeks to answer questions about the ultimate measure of a person's actions.

There is a strong suggestion in the language of many of the passages in "The Objectivist Ethics" that the ultimate value for each living being is that being's survival, its remaining alive. This is implied by the sustained contrast between life (being alive) and death. And the use that Rand's argument makes of vegetative and animal life suggests that there is a common denominator among live entities, viz, being alive, which is the standard for evaluating entities' activity.[7]

But Rand certainly wants to deflect this suggestion. She claims instead to favor "man's survival qua man." This means survival with certain character traits—especially rationality, productivity, and self-esteem. It is significant that the problem Rand notices in the contention that survival as such is the ultimate value is *not* that this contention commends survival no matter how painful and miserable. For Rand the crucial task is to build rationality and productivity into the good of human survival.

Rand does not see a comparable need to show pleasure and happiness to be constitutive of a person's ultimate good. While she does hold that happiness is connected with the value of life, her characteristic claim is that it is the "result, reward, and concomitant" of "the activity of pursuing rational goals," i.e., of "the activity of maintaining one's life" (OE, p. 29). And while Rand does say that happiness is "one's highest purpose" (ibid.),[8] nowhere in the several paragraphs devoted to explaining the meaning of the standard *"man's life"* is happiness mentioned (pp. 23–24). Rand, in fact, has a special reason for not wanting to include a person's pleasure and happiness as part of his ultimate good. Roughly and for now, she thinks that to claim this would be to claim that people should be motivated by the desire for pleasure and happiness and that this commends a fruitless hedonism.

Given this context, I can briefly preview my claims within this section. Rand's arguments that are intended to show rationality and productivity to be constitutive of what is ultimately valuable to humans are unconvincing. Rand should have argued for pleasure and happiness as partial constituents of the human good. She was right to want to avoid hedonism but wrong in thinking that accepting pleasure and happiness as ultimate goods portends the type of hedonism she fears. And she should have made out the value of character traits, such as productivity, as a function of the life *and happiness* they yield.

We begin, then, with Rand's struggle with "survival qua man." Central to Rand's understanding of the human condition is her claim that, for human beings, conceptual awareness is the fundamental means of survival. "He cannot achieve his survival by arbitrary means nor by random motions nor by blind urges nor by chance nor by whim. . . . For men, the basic means of survival is *reason*. Man cannot survive, as animals do, by the guidance of mere percepts" (OE, pp. 21, 22). Rand continues:

Since reason is man's basic means of survival, that which is proper to the life of a rational being is the good; that which negates, opposes or destroys it is the evil. Since everything man needs has to be discovered by his own mind and produced by his own efforts, the two essentials of the method of survival proper to a rational being are: thinking and productive work. [P. 23.]

So, for Rand, two of the fundamental virtues are rationality and productiveness. The third fundamental virtue is pride, which consists essentially in esteem for one's life as a rational and productive existence.

But what is the status of these virtues within the Randian system? More specifically, are these forms of behavior valued instrumentally *as likely means* for perpetuating life or are they valued *in themselves* as constitutive of the ultimate value of life? On the first interpretation, the ultimate value for any person is taken to be his biological survival. No character trait, such as rationality or productivity, is a part of that biological survival. So if such traits are endorsed, this endorsement must be on the basis of their being likely means for securing biological survival. If on occasion the prospects for biological survival would be enhanced by abandoning reason and productivity, then on those occasions these traits should be abandoned. On the second interpretation, the life that is of ultimate value includes rationality and productivity as part of its nature. On this view, one should not abandon rationality and productiveness even on those (unlikely) occasions when such an abandonment would enhance the prospects for biological survival.

One unhappy fact about Rand's exposition is that it runs together these two very different positions. On the one hand, Rand is drawn to the hard-nosed criterion of survival—a conception of the "what for" of valuation that seems dictated by the shared life-orientation of goal-directed activity among all living things. On the other hand, Rand rejects mere brutish, "subhuman," survival as the sole ultimate value. We have here something quite parallel to the problem of the ethical hedonist who, having declared that pleasure and pleasure alone is the good, feels uneasy about judging all else by its tendency to maximize the amount of some homogenous stuff called pleasure. So the hedonist begins to talk about "higher," "refined," and "lower," "swinish" pleasure and about how less of the higher pleasure should be preferred to more of the lower. For her part, Rand talks about subhuman survival versus man's survival qua man.

But neither the strategy of the hedonist nor the parallel strategy of Rand is felicitous. If there really are different types of pleasure, the basis for one's ultimate preference for one type over another cannot be in terms of pleasure. There is need to appeal to a principle—refinement is better than swinishness—which is quite independent of the endorsement of pleasure.

Similarly, if there really are different types of survival, the basis for one's preference for one type over another cannot be in terms of survival. If there is human survival and subhuman survival, one's preference for the former must be in terms of the greater value of humanness over subhumanness. There is need to appeal to a principle—humanness is better than subhumanness—which is quite independent of the endorsement of survival. This need is merely obscured by Rand's insistence that human survival is better than subhuman survival, because it is the higher or better sort of survival.

The ambiguous character of Rand's position can be illustrated from the remarks that follow the passage previously quoted, which links survival, rationality, and productiveness. When considering the prospects of those with "unfocused minds" whose survival activity is at best like that of "trained animals," Rand says that the "survival of such mental parasites depends upon blind chance" and that these "are the men who march into the abyss" (OE, p. 23). And when considering unproductive "looters," she says that they "may achieve their goals for the range of a moment, at the price of destruction: the destruction of their victims and their own" (p. 24). Later in the "The Objectivist Ethics" Rand writes that "man is free to attempt to survive by any random means, as a parasite, a moocher or a looter, but not free to succeed at it beyond the range of the moment" (pp. 28– 29). In these passages, Rand certainly appears to be tracing the disvalue of irrationality and nonproductiveness to their negative effect upon survival pure and simple. Such traits are condemned because they endanger the life of the agent.

Of course, the problem with this line of reasoning is the uncertain character of its empirical premises. Do mere imitators who act like "trained animals" tend to live less long than rational innovators? Do criminals and dictators (cf. p. 24) of all sorts tend to live less long than noncriminals and nondictators? Bertrand Russell has been a problem for disciples of Rand just because they did not want to say that he or his actions were predominantly good (for in Rand's eyes he espoused immoral philosophical and political doctrines), yet he lived for a very long time. So seriously is the criterion of longevity taken that some Randian disciples have felt that in order to criticize the socioeconomic order of contemporary Sweden they had to brand as a lie the claim that on the average Swedes stay alive a long time. Rand herself is clearly uncomfortable with this longevity criterion. Often the condemnation of ways of acting that Rand's words convey are clearly intended to be independent of the likely lifespan effect of those ways of acting. For instance, there is the constant refrain in Rand's writings that certain ways of existing are animalistic, brutish, and parasitic. Consider the following passage:

If some men attempt to survive by means of brute force or fraud, by looting, robbing, cheating or enslaving the men who produce, it remains true that their survival is made possible only by their victims, only by the men who choose to think and to produce the goods which they, the looters, are seizing. Such looters are parasites capable of survival, who exist by destroying those who *are* capable, those who are pursuing a course of action proper to man. [P. 23.]

In reality Rand does *not* claim here that the looters will not survive. For, while she does say that they are not capable of surviving, clearly the force of this is that the looter's mode of life-sustaining activity is dependent upon the nonparasitic activities of others. Speaking of their incapacity is only a way of condemning them for surviving in ways that do not involve "action proper to man." Saying that someone is "incapable of survival" simply functions for Rand as the ultimate insult. But is this a justified insult? Is survival *as a rational and productive being* established as the appropriate standard for evaluating human action? If a beaver should manage to adapt so as to be able to survive without building dams, would we judge its actions to be contrary to its life because they don't foster life as a dam-building being? Given that rationality and productiveness are the characteristic survival traits for human beings, if survival is the goal, then each person should *as a matter of general strategy* foster rationality and productiveness in himself. But this in no way excludes the value of animalistic and parasitic courses of action when they are demanded by the longevity criterion.

At this point we should take note of one other way of construing Rand's argument. This turns on her continual use of the generic term *man*. This man is not the collection of individuals who make up mankind. Still less is it this or that particular individual. It is hard to say just who or what this *man* represents. It seems to be something like *man in general* or even *man-ness* or, even more speculatively and peculiarly for Rand the individualist, the collective human species. Consider, for instance, statements like "everything man needs has to be discovered by his own mind and produced by his own effort" (p. 23). This is just obviously false if meant as a generalization about all individual human persons. And it is very likely false if meant as a statement about this or that particular individual. In fact, the most natural reading of this passage is the collective species reading. Any needs discovered in man (the species) can only be satisfied by the thought and work that occurs in man (the species).

However, we can give a less metaphysically collectivist reading to this passage and all those others that speak of man's needs,
man's survival, man's virtues, and so on. This interpretation
also helps to understand why Rand thinks that showing a particular mode of survival (e.g., looting) as parasitic upon another
(e.g., production) is a decisive argument against that parasitic
mode. By focusing on man in general when considering the apt-
ness of some mode of behavior for survival, Rand in effect is
asking whether the *general* practice of this mode of behavior
would be beneficial to the members of a community of such
practitioners. Thus, if a mode of behavior, when generally
adopted, endangers the life of individuals in the group adopting
that behavior, that mode of behavior is deemed bad by the standard of human survival. If some mode of behavior works for
some individuals only if other individuals *shun* that way of acting, e.g., if, like predation, it is parasitic upon nonpredatory
production, then its general adoption would not enhance survival prospects. Hence, it is judged to be bad in any individual
who practices it.

Ironically, in this argument Rand implicitly adopts the Kantian stand that for an action to be morally right it must be of a
sort in which any rational being can engage. A given individual
is not to wonder whether *his* predation might be advantageous
because, in fact, others are engaged in nonpredatory production. We can imagine Rand claiming that such an individual's
predation could not be truly advantageous because it would not
foster his survival qua man. But such a claim presupposes an independent means of specifying the meaning of *survival qua man*.

The tendency to lose sight of the individual and *his* concrete
choice situation is, we shall see, a recurring one in Rand's
thought. But this is not to say that Rand loses all sight of the
distinction between general principle and its application to specific individuals. In fact, she writes: " 'That which is required for
the survival of man *qua* man' is an abstract principle that applies to every individual man. The task of applying this principle to a concrete, specific purpose—the purpose of living a life
proper to a rational being—belongs to every individual man,
and the life he has to live is his own" (p. 25). But notice that the
individual's "concrete, specific purpose" is simply to apply a

general principle to his own case. In the name of survival qua man, all the guiding content is built into the general principle. His purpose is not to act so as to maximize his lifespan or to do what accords with his desires or nature. It is simply to live "a life proper to a rational being." His "task" is to exemplify in his own life this universal model. The *has to live* in "the life he has to live is his own" has a double reading. On the possessive reading, each *possesses* a life, his own, to live. On the more instructive and startling imperative reading, in possessing a life, each *must* live it according to the general standard of survival qua man. Each person, it seems, is to view his life as an occasion for the abstract man being made concrete.[9]

Aside from noticing the weaknesses and ambiguities in these arguments, it is crucial to recall that Rand's aim throughout is to attach rationality and productivity to survival to complete the concept of what has ultimate value for any human being. There is no attempt to establish the ultimate value of (sensorial) pleasure or (emotional) satisfaction. But I want to maintain that Rand's argument would be better if she had set out to show that, not merely being alive, but also attaining pleasure and happiness is constitutive of a person's ultimate good. Here we may hint at how such an argument might go. Subsequently we shall see why Rand mistakenly did not want an argument to this effect and how such an argument might foster the introduction of rationality and productivity at a different, later, place in the doctrine's development.

The argument for pleasure and satisfaction being constitutive of the ultimate good of beings capable of these experiences turns on the structure of the concept of *benefit*. Consider the difference between an entity that is vegetatively alive and an entity that experiences pleasure and pain. The appearance of the latter type of entity can be understood as an alternative evolutionary strategy for the survival of living entities. When such alternative strategies are viable, it is because the capacity for pleasure and pain introduces benefits and costs not previously present and these benefits and costs influence the behavior of the entities subject to them.

Similarly, the appearance of an entity capable of experiencing satisfaction (in the completion of projects) and dissatisfaction (in their noncompletion) can be understood as a further alternative evolutionary strategy. Here new benefits and costs are introduced that further influence the behavior of the entities subject to them. But to say that the pleasure and/or the satisfaction work by being new benefits and that the pain and/or dissatisfaction work by being new costs is to go beyond the claim that the pleasure and/or the satisfaction are *signs* of life-preserving activity and that the pain and/or dissatisfaction are *signs* of life-hindering activity. It is to accept that the pleasure and/or satisfaction is a part of the good of the entity and that the pain and/or dissatisfaction is constitutive of disvalue for that entity.

The reasoning for these last claims is simple. To a being for whom being alive is the *only* value, neither pleasure nor satisfaction would be a benefit, and neither pain nor dissatisfaction would be a cost. Hence, for such a being, the appearance of the capacities for such experience would not represent an alternative evolutionary strategy. But since the appearance of these capacities does represent an alternative evolutionary strategy, pleasure and/or satisfaction must be of value and pain and/or dissatisfaction must be of disvalue to the entities capable of experiencing them. Here is at least a Randian-style argument for pleasure and satisfaction being part of each human's ultimate good.

In the light of this argument, we turn to those features of Rand's views that make her reluctant to consider pleasure and satisfaction to be part of a man's ultimate good. This investigation will allow us to do two things. First and obviously, it will explain this reluctance. But second and more interesting, it will show us how Rand might have gone about, yet nevertheless blocked herself from going about, successfully bringing traits like productivity into her ethical scheme. Our topic here is Rand's views about the relation of reason and emotion. In particular, our concern will be with emotion as the wellspring of action—emotion as desire, interest, fascination, and obsession. I will contend that Rand's appropriate rejection of certain roles for feeling combines with a fear of emotions to yield a disastrous view about the ultimate sources of human actions.

There are at least three possible roles for feelings that Rand opposes. First of all, she opposes subjectivism and emotivism within moral theory. That is, she rejects the view that our most fundamental moral principles must be nothing but statements or effusions of our feelings. She rejects all versions of the view that "ethics is outside the power of reason, that no rational ethics can ever be defined, and that in the field of ethics—in the choice of his values, of his actions, of his pursuits, of his life's goals—man must be guided by something other than reason" (OE, p. 15).

Second, emotions are, in general, rejected as cognitive tools, as guides to truth. Neither one's feeling that so-and-so is true nor one's wanting it to be true is evidence of its truth. And, more specifically, Rand rejects the identification of what is actually in one's self-interest with what one actually desires. Desires may be irrational. Their existence or their satisfaction may be contrary to the real interests of the desirer. "[M]an's self-interest cannot be determined by blind desires or random whims." [10] For "Desires (or feelings or emotions or wishes or whims) are not tools of cognition; they are not a valid standard of value nor a valid criterion of man's interests. The mere fact that a man desires something does not constitute a proof that the object of his desire is good, nor that its achievement is actually to his interest." [11]

Third, Rand denies the viability of ethical theories that make such desired psychological states as pleasure or happiness the controlling goal. As we have already seen, happiness is conceived simply as the by-product of actions that are directed according to the standard, "man's life." Thus we are told that "Happiness is possible only to a rational man, the man who desires nothing but rational goals, seeks nothing but rational values and finds his joy in nothing but rational action" (OE, p. 29). [12]

A standard and decisive philosophical criticism of hedonism is that if one had only a desire for happiness as a source of one's actions, one would achieve little happiness. Since happiness is the product of valued actions and achievements, before the actions or achievements can be valued for the happiness they bring, they must be valued on some independent basis. Only under such circumstances will they bring happiness. I may say that I want to eat roast duck so I will be happy and that here, therefore, is a case in which my desire for happiness is my guiding motive. But unless I independently want (the taste of) duck, eating it will not make me happy and will not be anticipated as making me happy. A desire for happiness will only be satisfied insofar as I have all sorts of other, independent, desires, interests and concerns. If a person were to be stripped of all desires except for the desire for happiness, the paths by which he had gained happiness would lose their interest and their happiness-generating power. He would be left stranded with one, now futile, desire.

Insofar as Rand points to the fact that happiness is a by-product of independently valued action and that, therefore, such a desire cannot itself constitute an adequate guide for action, she joins in this standard criticism of hedonism. But her argument differs from the standard one in a number of important respects. Consider, for example, her claim that "To take 'whatever makes one happy' as a guide to action means: to be guided by nothing but one's emotional whims" (OE, p. 29). This is not just a rejection of guidance by the desire *for happiness*. It is a more general attack on the employment of desires, e.g., my desire for (the taste of) duck, as guiding motives for action. We are told that guidance by emotional whims can at most produce an "alleged happiness" that is really only "a moment's *relief* from [a] chronic state of terror" (OE, p. 28). While the problem with hedonism proper was that the desire for happiness by itself provides too little motivation, the problem with the *whatever makes you happy* theory, according to Rand, is that it sanctions too broad and too indiscriminate motivation.

In attacking guidance by emotional whims, Rand is not intending to deny that people's actions should be ordered and directed by felt desires and interests. She objects, it seems, not to the element of personal desire[13] but, rather, to the unexamined character of some motivating desires. She wants people to act only on rational desires. The problem, however, lies in her conception of rational desire.

Rand's general view about emotions is that they are the products of judgments either implicit or explicit. They are the felt automatic reflections of our evaluations. And, with the sole exception of our wired-in valuing of sensorial pleasure and disvaluing of sensorial pain, all evaluations involve judgment. As

Rand puts it, "Emotions are the automatic results of man's value judgments" (OE, p. 27). Some emotions flow from relatively passive judgments—the judgments we form in unthinking conformity with others' judgments or in accord with paths of least resistance formed by previous judgments and feelings. Such emotions are deemed irrational in two senses: (1) they flow from nonrational judgment, and (2) they are unlikely to generate action that is in the objective interest of the agent. And, of course, emotions that flow from flawed explicit judgments are considered irrational in virtue of their source and irrational with respect to their probable effect on the agent's well-being.

Since Rand holds that emotions are dependent phenomena, she concludes that emotionally we are born tabula rasa.

Man is born with an emotional mechanism, just as he is born with a cognitive mechanism; but, at birth, *both* are "tabula rasa." It is man's cognitive faculty, his mind, that determines the *content* of both. Man's emotional mechanism is like an electronic computer, which his mind has to program—the programming consists of the values his mind chooses. [P. 28.]

Thus Rand arrives at what I call the promulgation view of (proper) desires, viz, that "all of one's convictions, *values, goals, desires*, and actions must be *based on, derived from, chosen* and validated by a process of thought" (p. 26, emphasis added). This view should be contrasted with a validation view of rational desires. On the validation view, one is not directly concerned with the source of a desire but, rather, with the effects for one's life and well-being of affirming, fostering, and acting upon that desire. While tracing the source of some desire might help one judge the effects of acting on it, one would not, as on the promulgation view, refuse validity to a desire simply because it was not *based on* and *derived from* a rational judgment.

Rand is led to insist upon a source in rational judgment just because she thinks the only alternative source for a desire, interest, or disposition is in irrational judgment. But this is a false dichotomy. Many of a person's desires, interests, and dispositions (the emotions that are the well-springs of actions) do not flow from—they are certainly not *derived from*—antecedent judgments. There are, of course, complicated background stories that can be told about all of my desires, interests, and dispositions. But at some point in each of these stories we must make reference to natural (i.e., nonpromulgated) desires, interests, capacities, and propensities that I have in common with all or most other people or that distinguish my personality and hopes from those of others.

Since it is not true that all my desires and interests are derived from antecedent judgments, it is not true that to clear them of the charge of irrationality they must be traced to rational judgments. It seems enough that the possession of and guidance by these desires and interests are advantageous to me, i.e., they serve my life and happiness. Alterations in my desires and interests that on net bring greater safety, riches, or more articulate harmonious experience to my life are to be sought. Passions that are self-destructive or that conflict with the satisfaction of more central goals are to be examined, modified, and, if necessary, overcome. But all this requires only a determination to validate one's desires and not the radically more stringent determination to promulgate them. Such a validation approach seems enough to guard oneself against emotional "unknowable demons" (p. 29). Neither does such an approach make desire "the ethical standard . . . regardless of its nature or cause." Nor could it be fairly said that in its adoption, "the gratification of any and all desires is taken as an ethical goal" (p. 30).

It is false, then, that all my desires and interests have their source in judgments and that they will, therefore, be in some sense irrational if they are not derived from rational judgment. But may not Rand still be right in insisting that we should only act on the subset of desires that do have their source in rational judgment? The answer is no, for such a stricture would rule out the great bulk of human desires. Reason itself has at most a very limited capacity to call forth desire ex nihilo—far too limited a capacity to call forth the forceful and rich fabric of desires and interests that, according to Rand herself, motivates the actions of a rational person.

Some philosophers have even maintained that the dictates of reason as such can have no effect on the passions. On this view, a rational judgment that x is good or right will not as such ever constitute or generate any motive for getting or doing x. On such a view of the relationship of reason and desire there can be no rational desires in Rand's sense. But this is not the view I am maintaining against Rand. For it seems that sometimes we do desire *x*, because we judge *x* right or good (and not merely as a means to something already desired). In such cases desire does seem to be based upon, derived from, (purportedly) rational judgment. For example, my judgment that a particular political crusade is right may itself generate a desire for or interest in joining that crusade.[14]

Nevertheless, the judgment that survival (or survival plus happiness or survival plus happiness and the effective means for these ends) is good is not in itself enough to call forth the *level* of motivating desire for survival (and so forth) that Rand would consider appropriate. Moreover, such a general judgment and its cognate desire (whatever the desire's strength) will not generate the concrete fabric of specific goals and hopes that makes up the motivational structure of any well-motivated individual. No such general judgments and cognate desires will confer on an individual the particular concerns with which he must be blessed to have what Rand would consider a productively purposeful life. Rather, such life-ordering interests appear in us as expressions of our individual natures and personalities. And our choice is whether to embrace and foster such direction-giving interests or to modify or overcome them. To deny validity to any such interest because it does not derive from a judgment or desire affirming survival would be to deny the interests and concerns through which accomplishment and satisfaction can be found. Rand's fictional heroes do not deny validity to such interests. They wisely do not attempt to deduce their specific values and desires from some general rule about living "a life proper to a rational being."

Rand's doctrine that the "emotional mechanism is like an electronic computer, which [the] mind has to program" (OE, p. 29), in effect denies that there is anything essential to a person or his nature beyond the fact (common to all others) that he is living and in possession of a programming mind. Since almost every ethical theory, including Rand's, can be seen as advocating the fulfillment of human nature, it is not surprising that Rand's substantial denial of human nature is accompanied by an in-

ability to find justification for her own specific contentful pre-
scriptions to individuals.

All that Rand need do to break out of this bind is reject the
tabula rasa view of human desires and interests and abandon
the promulgation view of proper human motives. Although the
ultimate value for each person is his life and (we have argued)
happiness, this does not mean that only the desire for life and
happiness can be a proper motive. Instead, any desire, interest,
or obsession—whether promulgated by reason or not—will be
a proper motive if fostering and acting upon it furthers the life
and happiness of the agent. The lesson to be learned from the
critique of hedonism is that the establishment of happiness as of
ultimate value need not—indeed, cannot—establish the *desire
for happiness* as the central, validated, desire. If happiness is established as partially constitutive of human good, then independently esteemed desires and interests must be allowed as proper,
if that human good is to be attained. Being alive, of course, remains partially constitutive of human good, and staying alive is
a necessary condition for any subsequent pleasure and happiness. So, clearly, the survival effects of fostering or pursuing an
interest must be given great weight in anyone's rational validation of that interest. The interest may be judged unworthy of
directing action because such action would conflict either with
other satisfactions or with the agent's very survival.

Given the validation view of proper interests, to establish the
value of rationality and productivity Rand must show that persons can foster rationality and productivity in themselves and
that doing so is itself rational in terms of a person's ultimate
good. Do we have natural (i.e., nonpromulgated) interests in
being rational and productive, and is the fostering of these interests both a source of satisfaction and an enhancement of
one's survival prospects? These are difficult, substantially empirical questions, and answers to them cannot be defended here.

But, clearly, Rand the novelist would want to answer them in
the affirmative; and such answers are plausible when we recall
that rationality is simply the way of interacting with the world
that renders it intelligible and predictable and that gives us confidence in our beliefs, inquiries, and plans. Productivity is simply the way of interacting with the world that places us in active

and creative control of our environment and makes us reliable patrons of our own lives and values. If Rand the novelist is in this respect right about human nature,[15] rationality and productivity can be welcomed into her ethical scheme—as traits to be valued for the life and happiness they bring. Similarly, the more specific concerns and fascinations that help define our individual personalities and aspirations also enter her scheme—as proper motives for those whose fostering of these concerns and fascinations will bring life and happiness. Rand can and should hold that, not some tabula rasa "emotional mechanism," but rather these common and uncommon desires determine (at least in part) the content of an individual's proper motivation.

III

To this point we have been entirely concerned with one of the two distinctive features of Rand's moral view: her defense of rational selfishness. We can now finally turn to the other distinctive feature: her advocacy of human rights. Rand sees her claims about rights as flowing very directly from her claims about the good for each person being survival qua man. In this section I will be concerned with Rand's underlying arguments for rights and with the views about the nature of rights associated with these arguments. I will not be concerned with the specific list of rights that Rand recognizes or with her numerous sound criticisms of "the process of inflation . . . [in] . . . the realm of rights."[16] In general I shall contend that Rand's arguments about rights are not nearly as good as her conclusions or as good as her arguments could have been. More specifically, I claim that her arguments show a failure to understand well the character of rights; that the problems within her arguments are obscured by a continual appeal to the generic *man*; that alternative and more fitting arguments for rights are available to Rand; and that these arguments are more easily advanced if the promulgation doctrine discussed in the last section of this essay is rejected.

Rand proposes to move from certain conclusions about what actions are right for people to certain conclusions about what rights people have. To understand the task involved we must, therefore, take note of the differences between claiming that an action is morally right and claiming that the agent has a right to perform it. The simple and hardly contentious first point is that a person can have a right to do something it is not right for him to do. Having a right to do x involves its being wrong for others to interfere forcibly with one's doing x. And it is more than possible that it will be wrong for others to interfere forcibly against one's doing x even if one's doing x is, in various ways, immoral. For instance, it may be wrong for me to cut off my finger, refuse to befriend someone because of his race, or write essays making fun of someone's religion. But, wrong or not, these are all things I have a right to do. Whatever immorality is involved in any of these acts, it is not of the sort that justifies their forcible suppression. To defend a person's right to do x, one does not have to defend the rightness of his doing x. A theory of rights that had the implication that individuals only have rights to do right actions would be, for this very reason, highly unsatisfactory.

The more complicated point about right actions and rights is that to establish that a person is right to do x is neither to establish that he has a right to do x nor to establish that others have a right that he do x. (A further argument might establish one or another of these claims.) The whole ethical theory that includes the claim that this party is right to do x may yet have no place at all for the idea of rights. For having a right includes having a moral claim *against other people* that they act or not act in certain ways. For example, my right to chop off my finger includes a moral claim against others that they not forcibly prevent me from doing so. Yet an ethical theory might consist entirely of indications to individuals of what actions are right for each of them given what is of ultimate value for each of them. That is, the theory would say: Jones, it's right for you to do this; Smith, it's right for you to do that; and so on, and never thereby include moral claims by one party *against* another party. Indeed, this looks like the Randian position as it has been considered so far. Jones is told that it is right for him to foster his life; Smith is told that it is right for him to foster his life; and so on. Nowhere do we have claims by one party against another to the latter's action or inaction.

Another way of making this point about the possibility of

rightness without rights is to note that rights involve correlative obligations. If Jones has a right against (with respect to) Smith, then Smith has some obligation toward Jones—albeit, perhaps, only a negative obligation not to kill, assault, or cheat Jones. Yet when we affirm that Jones is right in fostering his life, that Smith is right in fostering his life, and so on, we seem to be making no assertion at all about obligations *among* these parties.

Where, then, do rights (and their correlative obligations) come from according to Rand? Unhappily, in Rand's pivotal essay "Man's Rights," she places most of the burden on a passage reproduced from her novel *Atlas Shrugged*. This passage seems oblivious to the distinctions we have just been recalling. Rand argues: "*Rights* are conditions of existence required by man's nature for his proper survival. If a man is to live on earth, it is *right* for him to use his mind, it is *right* to act on his own free judgment, it is *right* to work for his values and to keep the product of his work. If life on earth is his purpose, he has a *right* to live as a rational being: nature forbids him the irrational." [17] Here Rand is saying that various types of unimpeded action and acquisition are right for individuals as conditions of their respective proper survival and that, therefore, each individual has a right to engage in these unimpeded actions and acquisitions.

But how is the conclusion supposed to follow from the premise? If using his own mind is a condition of Jones's "proper survival" then it would be irrational of Jones not to (try to) use his own mind. But how does this imply that it would be irrational or otherwise unjustified for Smith to impede Jones's use of his own mind? How does the rightness *for Jones* of his using his own mind support the claim that it would be wrong *for Smith* to impede Jones's use of his own mind? It is far from obvious that if it would be right for Jones to do *x*, it would be wrong for Smith to prevent Jones's doing *x*. After all, the good that renders action *x* right for Jones is Jones's good (his proper survival) and seemingly it is not in terms of this good, but rather in terms of Smith's good, that Smith is to rationally evaluate his possible actions. Besides, we may wonder, how does the rightness for Jones of his using his own mind create or underlie a moral claim *against* Smith, a moral claim on Smith's action or inaction?

Furthermore, if we have read this passage from *Atlas Shrugged* correctly, Rand's argument for rights has the consequence that persons only have the right to do what is right. If it is the rightness of an activity that confers upon an agent the right to perform that activity, then the agent never will have a right to do anything improper. That Rand is very much in danger of embracing this conclusion can be seen by her characterization of the fundamental right to life as "the freedom to take all the actions required by the nature of a rational being for the support, the furtherance, the fulfillment and the enjoyment of his own life."[18] For it seems that only proper uses of one's life will count as being protected by one's right to life. A person's right to life would not include, e.g., a right to squander life recklessly.[19]

The same theoretically bothersome consequence threatens whenever Rand speaks of rights as "[t]he social recognition of man's rational nature—of the connection between his survival and his use of reason."[20] Rand might reply that since man's survival is most enhanced by self-determined actions, man's right to perform "actions required by the nature of a rational being" must encompass a right to act however he chooses (consistent with others' rights). But can Rand maintain this position in real, concrete cases? For instance, consider the case of Jones freely deciding to amuse himself by playing a solitary game of Russian roulette. Although this action is self-determined, surely Rand would deny that it is among those actions "required by the nature of a rational being for the support, the furtherance, the fulfillment and the enjoyment of his own life."[21] It follows from this that the freedom to perform this action is not included within Jones's rights.

These sorts of questions about Rand's stand on the relationship between actions' being right and persons' having rights arise when we focus, as we did above, on the moral relationships between particular individuals, e.g., when we ask how its being right for Jones to do *x* is related to Smith's having an obligation not to prevent Jones from doing *x*. Rand avoids such questions by speaking more abstractly about what is right for *man* and about *man's* rights. She would, without doubt, claim that this represents the proper, metaphysical approach in contrast to the improper, concrete-bound, and corruptly nominalistic approach that is adopted above. However, it is hard to see Rand's approach as not at least verging on the reification of the species man (or the universal *man-ness*) as a living, acting, thinking being.

In "What Is Capitalism?"[22] Rand argues, for instance: "In order to sustain its life, every living species has to follow a certain course of action required by its nature. The action required to sustain human life is primarily intellectual: everything man needs has to be discovered by his mind and produced by his effort." Rand then claims that freedom is generically valuable because of its connection with productive work: "Since men are neither omniscient nor infallible, they must be free to agree or disagree, to cooperate or to pursue their own independent course, each according to his own rational judgment. Freedom is the fundamental requirement of man's mind."

So, the argument goes, the rightness of man's survival implies the rightness of the generic conditions for man's survival. Each person subject to the standard of man's life must recognize and respect the conditions of man's survival. Freedom is such a condition because man (the species, the generic man, the nonaccidental man?) cannot survive without it. Hence, each person subject to the standard of man's life must recognize and respect man's freedom. Freedom in general makes a claim upon us as a fundamental condition of man's proper end. This seems to be what Rand has in mind when she declares, in "The Nature of Government," that "To recognize individual rights means to recognize and respect the conditions required by man's nature for his proper survival."[23] Thus, Jones's claim against Smith to be free of interference from Smith does not flow from the propriety of Jones's actual current action. It flows, instead—to use Randian language—from the metaphysical importance of freedom for man's survival.[24]

It is difficult to evaluate this argument with confidence because it is difficult to know just what the argument is. Three brief comments that *may* be relevant must suffice. First, even if the survival of human life as a whole or the survival of characteristic human lives requires that *some* human beings enjoy freedom, it does not follow that *all* persons should possess freedom. Second, it does not follow that some or all persons have a *right* to freedom. If "man's life" or people's lives generally require that (some or all) individuals be free, then in the name of man's life or people's lives generally we may value freedom for those individuals. But this hardly shows that respect for this freedom is *owed* to these individuals. It hardly shows that persons have *obligations* to them to respect their freedom in the sense that is involved in their having a *right* to be free. Third, if the argument just sketched is Rand's, it still foreshadows the conclusion that persons only have the right to do what they should, for each is merely to have the freedom to act "according to his own *rational* judgment" (emphasis added). This is the freedom that is valuable for man's life and seemingly the only freedom individuals have a right to—if they have rights at all.

One of the problems with the Randian arguments about rights is that Rand seems to tie an individual's rights to do some action to the *usefulness* of his being in some condition or his doing some action for man's life. But emphasis on such a tie between usefulness and rights represents a misunderstanding of rights. If Jones has a right relative to Smith to do *x*, it needn't be that Jones's doing *x* is useful to Jones, to Smith, to man's life, or to society at large. Indeed, if Jones could only defend his freedom to do *x* by pointing to its usefulness to some party or cause, he would not have a *right* to do *x*. Take the simple case of Jones's having a right to shave off his beard, Smith and all others having a correlative obligation not to (forcibly) prevent Jones from doing so. Clearly Jones can have this right even though his exercise of the right is not useful to Jones, Smith, man's life, or any other favored cause. It is his beard to do with as he chooses, free of others' forcible interference.

If Jones has a right to shave off his beard, then there is something in the very character of Smith's forcible intervention (and not merely in its results) that renders the interference unjustified. Some quality of the intervention taints it morally, so that the intervention can be condemned independently of knowing its results. To ascribe rights to any person, e.g., to Jones, is to insist that there are ways in which he may not be treated, even if treating him in such ways was to promote the good. Rights and their correlative obligations involve deontological claims, i.e., moral claims about how persons must (or must not) be treated that are not determined by the consequences of persons being so treated. Although Smith's respect for Jones's rights may be useful (have good consequences) for Jones, Jones's rights do not *consist in* such usefulness. This ends-do-not-justify-all-means feature of rights is the underlying reason why people's rights cannot directly be read off from some truth about their proper ends.

Although Rand never explicitly acknowledges it,[25] it is clear that Rand steadily employs this notion of rights and that she has a basis for this employment in her doctrine of rational selfishness. Thus, in "What Is Capitalism?"[26] Rand asserts that each man is a "sovereign individual who owns his person" and that no man is a "natural resource" at the (rightful) disposal of others. These distinctions, in turn, reflect the fact that "every man is an end in himself" and that individuals are not to be seen "as members of a pack, each regarding the others as the means to *his* end and to the ends of 'the pack as a whole.'" Similarly, in "Man's Rights"[27] Rand contrasts the conception of man as "an end in himself" with the conception of man as "a sacrificial means to the ends of others." And for Rand it is the treatment of a person as a "sacrificial animal" that constitutes denying him his rights (OE, p. 32).

So the connection between Rand's rational egoism and her belief in rights is this: rational egoism tells us that each person's life (and well-being) is the ultimate value for that person, that there is no higher value (e.g., someone else's life and well-being or society's well-being) to which he should subsume his life. Each person is, in this sense, a moral end in himself. He is not to sacrifice his life and well-being for others. His moral purpose is his own life and happiness. But certain ways of dealing with a person involve treating him, not as an end in himself, but as a means to some end other than his own life and happiness. Such treatment occurs when (by force or trickery) we override a person's own purposes and employ him for our own purposes. Such actions would be justified only if this victim was a sacrificial animal, i.e., a being whose moral purpose was to be of service to us. But, according to Rand's rational egoism, no person is such a sacrificial being. Hence, actions of the type described, in which a person's life, faculties, or activities are disposed of by others, are unjustified. They are unjustified by their very character and not merely because they (typically) fail to advance the interests of the agent, man's life, or the subject of the disposal.

On this interpretation of Rand, the principle that for each person his life and happiness is his highest purpose functions in two distinct ways.[28] When a person evaluates his actions, plans, and choices in terms of an outcome, he should do so on the basis of how well they serve his life and well-being. But a person must also evaluate his activity with regard to the treatment of other people that it involves. If a person's action violates another's control of his own person and life, then the action is unjustified. All parties, in virtue of being ends in themselves, have moral claims against being subject to such treatment. And each person has a correlative obligation toward all others not to engage in such treatment. All persons remain morally at liberty to do anything that does not violate rights; and all others, of course, have obligations to respect such liberties. This is why, and the sense in which, individuals have rights to do many things (e.g., cutting off their own fingers) that it is not right for them to do.

Explicit recognition of the dual role for the principle that each person is an end in himself highlights the *possibility* that self-interested and rights-respecting courses of action might diverge. Perhaps, for some person, the truly self-interested course would involve violating someone's rights. If such a case arose, one would have to choose between sacrificing one's own interests and violating another's rights. Such a possibility represents a problem for the Randian view, with its distinctive emphasis on advocating rational selfishness *and* human rights. Whether such cases truly arise and, if so, how they should be handled is an immensely complicated topic that cannot be done justice here. It is *not* enough to claim, as Rand does, that "human good does not require sacrifices and cannot be achieved by the sacrifice of anyone to anyone" (OE, p. 31). This is either a highly dubious assertion—false at least for some lifeboat cases—or it is rendered trivially true by defining *human* good as good that does not depend upon others' being sacrificed. Rand's task is too difficult to be handled so facilely. Neither does it help for

Rand to put forward, as she does in "The 'Conflicts' of Men's Interests,"[29] the much more bold claim that persons' rational interests never clash. For surely the interests of highly competent competitors for the same highly specialized and attractive position *do* conflict. One can acknowledge this while still denying that it would be in the interest of either of these competitors to violate the rights of the other—by, e.g., eliminating a rival through murder.

What Rand has to show is that, at least outside of special emergency situations that should not in any case be the testing ground for an ethical theory, the best life course for a person is congruent with his respect for others' rights. Of course, whether such a congruence exists is a complex and substantially empirical question similar to and connected with the question of whether rationality and productivity are necessary for the good of happiness. Certainly a start is made by emphasizing the value to individuals of character traits such as rationality and productivity, and integrity, honesty, and independence (OE, pp. 25–26) and by molding these traits into an ambitious and attractive ideal of human life; for such a life is not a predatory and rights-violating one. To these considerations in favor of congruence can be added the simple danger of suffering retaliation for one's rights violations (or the dangers of living in a society in which such retaliation is not likely).

But beyond these factors is the interesting possibility that each person's most satisfactory life course includes the internalization of the principle that each person is an end in himself—an internalization that adds psychological costs to his violating rights, so that such violations are sure to be contrary to his (thus modified) interests. Is such an internalization part of each person's most satisfactory life course? Its costs in terms of actions thereby foregone are not great. For, even prior to such an internalization, it would be (at most) very rare for a rights-violating action to be genuinely crucial to an agent's interest. Internalization would, at most, block only such rare opportunities for the agent to advance his (unmodified) interests.

Are there sufficiently compensating benefits from internalization? For one thing, any person who psychologically commits himself in this way benefits from others' being (additionally) assured of his future rights-respecting course. But, furthermore, Rand might have argued that the internalization of this principle fosters and reaffirms a person's sense of his own worth and the worth of his fellow beings, that it is a precondition of his experiencing his own moral importance (as a being among beings having this moral importance). She might have argued that such an internalization gives play to a natural (nonpromulgated) desire for a sense of moral order among persons and that it gives shape to a natural sentiment for fair dealing and mutual respect. In short, Rand might have argued that a commitment to respect for rights is a necessary correlate to the development of parts of our nature and that, for this reason, a person's fulfillment and his regard for others' rights converge. Rand could and, perhaps, would have argued along these lines—if she had freed herself from the survival conception of ultimate value and the promulgation conception of rational interests.

NOTES

1. Ayn Rand, "The Objectivist Ethics," in *The Virtue of Selfishness* (New York: New American Library, 1964), pp. 13–35. Hereafter references to "The Objectivist Ethics" appear with the title abbreviated OE and the page number within the text. Hereafter *The Virtue of Selfishness* will be cited as VOS.

2. We should note that while Rand proposes a teleological understanding of the phenomenon of valuing that parallels a teleological understanding of, e.g., hearts, we are not to think of either valuing or hearts as having been *designed* for the ends they serve. We are not to think they were created by some Being with the intention that these ends be served.

3. Rand, *VOS*, p. ix.

4. The argument that has been ascribed to Rand here is a recasting of the argument developed in Eric Mack, "How to Derive Ethical Egoism," *The Personalist* (Autumn 1971).

5. Ayn Rand, "Causality versus Duty," *The Objectivist* 9 (July 1970): 4. Note the suggestion in the first paragraph that one need not worry about philosophically refuting the party who does not choose to live, for "nature will take its course."

6. In the third section of this essay I shall maintain that Rand herself should not hold to a simple version of this claim.

7. As Mary Sirridge has pointed out to me, real and fictional people who, e.g., struggled through the Russian civil war and struggled to escape the Soviet Union of the 1920s, at the time of their struggles or even lastingly, may natu-

rally experience and characterize all their thought, planning, and action as fundamentally moves within a battle for survival.

8. Though elsewhere she says "the ethical purpose of each individual . . . is . . . his own life" (OE, p. 25).

9. For a more generous reading of Rand on survival qua man, see Douglas Den Uyl and Douglas Rasmussen, "Nozick on the Randian Argument," *The Personalist*, April 1978, especially pp. 192–94. This essay thoroughly rebuts Robert Nozick's critique of purportedly Randian arguments.

10. Rand, VOS, p. x.

11. Ayn Rand, "The Conflicts of Men's Interests," in VOS, p. 50.

12. There are places in which Rand seems to tie life and happiness more tightly together. For instance, she says, "To hold one's life as one's ultimate value, and one's happiness as one's highest purpose are two aspects of the same achievement" (OE, p. 29); and "It is by experiencing happiness that one lives one's life" (ibid.). Perhaps part of the idea here is that the desire for happiness is the emotional form taken by an esteem for one's life. Still, the first of these sentences *distinguishes* between one's ultimate value and one's happiness. And the second can be read as expressing the "reward and concomitant" view of happiness. In connection with the second sentence, see the argument presented below for the ultimate value of happiness.

13. Cf. Rand's defense of personal desire in this sense against Kantian duty in "Causality versus Duty."

14. We may leave aside the question of whether we should postulate that underlying such cases there is a more basic desire for or interest in the right and the good.

15. For a philosophical defense of similar claims, see the discussion of the Aristotelian principle in John Rawls, *A Theory of Justice* (Cambridge, Mass.: Harvard University Press, 1971), pp. 424–33.

16. Ayn Rand, "Man's Rights," in VOS, p. 95.

17. Ibid., pp. 94–95.

18. Ibid., pp. 93–94.

19. Similarly, in the introduction to VOS (p. x), Rand jumps from saying "man must [i.e., should] act for his own rational self-interest" to asserting "his right to do so." Here, again, it would follow that a person only has the right to do what he should do.

20. Ayn Rand, "What Is Capitalism?" *Objectivist Newsletter* (November-December 1965): 52. Reprinted in Ayn Rand, *Capitalism: The Unknown Ideal* (New York: Signet Books, 1967).

21. Rand, "Man's Rights," pp. 93–94.

22. Rand, "What Is Capitalism?" p. 52. The following two quotations are taken from this essay.

23. Ayn Rand, "The Nature of Government," in VOS, p. 108.

24. For a similar but more sympathetic reading of Rand on these points, see Den Uyl and Rasmussen, "Nozick on the Randian Argument," p. 199.

25. For Rand, to acknowledge any deontological element would be to acknowledge a kinship with her favorite archvillain, Kant. On this, see her essay

"Causality versus Duty" (n. 5 above). As we shall see, some of Rand's worries about the deontic are well-founded—especially the worry about whether deontic constraints will sometimes require a person to compromise his own well-being.

26. Rand, "What Is Capitalism?" p. 54.

27. Rand, "Man's Rights," p. 93.

28. For the development of the idea of a dual employment of the principle that each is an end-in-himself, see Eric Mack, "Egoism and Rights," *The Personalist* (Winter 1973); and id., "Egoism and Rights Revisited," ibid., July 1977.

29. Ayn Rand, "The Conflicts of Men's Interests," in *VOS*, pp. 50–56.

III

Politics

8
Capitalism

◉

Douglas J. Den Uyl
and
Douglas B. Rasmussen

With the possible exception of her ethical views, Ayn Rand's political philosophy is the most notorious feature of her philosophic system. Her unabashed defense of laissez-faire capitalism coupled with a firm denunciation of all forms of collectivism has made her political positions the object of widespread critical attack. Nevertheless, most of the criticisms leveled at Rand's political theories lack an appreciation of the philosophic foundations that support the theory. Whether Rand is wrong or right in her conclusions, any objective reader of her political writings must admit: (1) that her political views flow from a comprehensive philosophy of man and nature, and (2) that her defense of capitalism is insightful and original. The latter point should become evident as we outline Rand's political theory below. A brief discussion of the first point is the natural place to begin that outline.

Rand's political theory centers around her doctrine of human rights. Yet human rights must themselves be understood in light of a prior moral theory. Consider the following passage from Rand.

"Rights" are a moral concept—the concept that provides a logical transition from the principles guiding an individual's actions to the principles guiding his relationship with others—the concept that preserves and protects individual morality in a social context—the link between the moral code of a man and the legal code of a society, between ethics and politics. *Individual rights are a means of subordinating society to moral law.*[1]

Notice that to understand Rand's theory of rights one must first grasp her ethical doctrine and that to grasp her ethical theory one must appreciate her philosophy of man.

In the preceding introductory essays, Rand's theory of human nature was discussed in some detail. In those sections we learned that the mode of activity appropriate to and necessary for human existence is the use of our rational (i.e., conceptual) capacity. This capacity was seen as the foundation for all *human* acts and institutions. Rand's essentially Aristotelian conception of man is modified by her heavy emphasis on the *creative* power of the human mind. Since human beings are not omniscient or infallible, their success in life depends upon their ability to increase their knowledge. The degree to which one's knowledge increases is a function of one's ability to effectively solve the problems confronted. There is no static set of rules that, if followed, will lead automatically to new insights into a given problem. To be sure, there are epistemological constraints, but the creative mind is one that looks beyond the common understanding. Men of genius in both the sciences and the arts are those who do not allow themselves to be held down by received wisdom. In both Rand's fictional and nonfictional writings the creative mind is presented as the motive force of all human progress.[2] Stagnation is synonymous with death, and thus human creativity and innovation must be protected at all cost.

One may justifiably conclude that Rand's doctrine of rights is designed to secure those conditions necessary for the operation of the most significant asset of human nature—the mind. There is ample evidence that Rand links her theory of rights with her conception of human nature. In an article entitled "Man's Rights," for example, she says that "the source of rights is man's nature" and that "rights are a necessary condition of his [man's] particular mode of survival."[3] Elsewhere Rand argues that "it is the basic, metaphysical fact of man's nature—the connection between his survival and his use of reason—that capitalism recognizes and protects."[4] Capitalism is itself "a social system based on the recognition of individual rights."[5]

Reason for Rand is the ability to conceptualize the material provided by the senses.[6] Our survival as human beings depends upon our ability to conceptually attend to the world, to properly interpret and judge the data we confront at each waking moment. The fundamental choice human beings make is whether to direct our full attention to the situations we experience.[7]

If we now add together the foregoing remarks about the choice to think and the creative element of thought necessary for progress, we shall gain a clearer understanding of Rand's doctrine of rights. When Rand claims that rights specify norms necessary for man's survival qua man, she does not mean that any violation of rights results in instant death. Rather, she means that the principle implied by a rights violation is contrary to the principles required for human life. Since men are (and must be) creatures that act and think in terms of principles,[8] a doctrine of rights is meant to insure that the choice to live by those principles required for human life is not impeded by other human beings. Both the choice to think and the creative element of thought are characterized by a process that is volitional and judgmental. What must, therefore, be insured by a system of rights is that those actions not be permitted which limit or destroy the free operation of choice and judgment in action; for any other principle of action would necessarily imply that something besides choice and judgment be the fundamental norm for human action. All this is to say that the moral propriety of attending to the world through the use of our conceptual faculty requires the freedom to act on our judgment. The right of free choice means the right to act on our choices.

Rand argues, as we have seen, that the fundamental alternative facing living things is existence or nonexistence. In the case of human beings, those courses of action necessary for the furtherance of our existence are not automatically determined. Because we are given no automatic means for the furtherance of our lives, we are bound[9] to make choices about which course of action to take. Ethics may give us certain objective standards for the guidance of those choices, but ethics cannot directly dictate how to apply those standards in particular concrete cases. Ethical rules do not tell us *when* we are in a situation that calls for one or another of the rules.[10] We must, therefore, use our judgment in those particular cases and choose accordingly.[11] It is appropriate to conclude, then, that the volitional nature of man's consciousness implies a principle of freedom. To act as if there is some substitute for this volitional feature of human nature is to ignore a fundamental metaphysical fact about our nature.

Now there are numerous ways in which an individual can act that imply principles contrary to the volitional principle just discussed. One such way is to act on the basis of faith.[12] But in the interpersonal realm it is coercion that represents the most significant violation of the volitional principle. Coercion is the attempt to substitute force for judgment and choice—"force and mind are opposites; morality ends where a gun begins."[13] Coercion implies that an independent assessment of the facts is unnecessary and that we can accomplish the business of living a human life by circumventing the necessity of judgment and choice. Since coercive acts violate the volitional principle, rights are meant to be those principles that protect freedom of judgment. Rand puts it this way:

Thus for every individual, a right is the moral sanction of a *positive*— of his freedom to act on his own judgment, for his own goals, by his own *voluntary*, uncoerced choice. As to his neighbors, his rights impose no obligations on them except of a *negative* kind: to abstain from violating his rights.[14]

In essence then, the indispensability of judgment and choice for human existence is given its social expression in Rand's doctrine of individual rights.

It should also be noted at this stage of our discussion that one implication of Rand's view of choice is that choice becomes the foundation for virtue in society. In order to attribute moral worth to an individual's actions it is necessary that the individual be a moral agent, i.e., that his actions be chosen. Liberty is inherently connected with the process of moral perfection. Tibor Machan has made this point in the following way:

The choice to learn, to judge, to evaluate, to appraise, to decide what he ought to do in order to live his life must be each person's own, otherwise he simply has no opportunity to excel or fail at the task. His moral aspirations cannot be fulfilled (or left unfulfilled) if he is not the source of his own actions, if they are imposed or forced upon him by others.[15]

The implication of the preceding remarks for social theory is that even though freedom permits evil actions as well as good ones, the *only* way a society can properly be seen as moral is if its members *choose* the good.[16]

Life, by its very nature, is not guaranteed. In recognition of this metaphysical fact, Rand holds that rights are freedoms of action and not guarantees of anything. Even property rights are not conceived by her to be rights to things, but only the freedom to pursue courses of action with respect to material goods.[17] A system or theory of rights that gives the pretense of guaranteeing certain goods is neither a consistent practice nor a coherent theory. If certain goods are to be guaranteed to individuals—as modern "welfare" rights would have it—some people must be coerced to provide for others. Apart from the fact that what is guaranteed is conditional upon the productivity of some (and hence no guarantee at all), there is in principle no limit to what one could claim must be guaranteed. If the Democratic Party Platform of 1960 can demand that everyone have a right to a "decent home,"[18] then there is virtually nothing human beings desire that cannot also be "guaranteed." But this view of rights makes a mockery of the notion of a guarantee; for if there is no object to which one may not claim a right, then we could conceivably ask the state to guarantee all things equally to everyone.[19]

Even if we were to ignore the foregoing remarks, there are further problems with a welfare conception of rights. In the first place, few arguments are ever advanced for why the coercive apparatus of the state should be the vehicle for guaranteeing certain goods to individuals. It is not enough to assume that the state should provide the goods demanded. One must *show* why initiatory acts of force by the state are not subject to the same moral condemnation we apply to individuals who take such actions. Furthermore, it is imperative to recognize that the welfare conception of rights is inherently discriminatory. That conception of rights demands that the state treat some individuals differently from others, depending on their particular status in society at a particular time (e.g., whether they are rich or poor). Since one's status in society may change over time, the only guarantee we have is that we cannot expect consistent treatment in the course of our lifetime. Robert Nozick makes this very point in *Anarchy, State, and Utopia*.[20] Finally, despite any rhetoric to the contrary, welfare rights do not suppose that people possess rights, but rather that rights are gifts of the state. And like all gifts, the one who has the power to make the gift also has the power to take it away.

Rand's theory of rights avoids the preceding theoretical problems, since all individuals possess the same right to freely pursue their own goals—though there is no guarantee that they will be successful in that pursuit. Since no guarantees are given in nature that men will lead successful lives, it is a kind of metaphysical fraud to act as if this fact were not true in social life. The best we can do is try to establish those *conditions* that will allow for the pursuit of a proper human life, if people so choose to seek that end.[21] Establishing these conditions can be done without reference to anyone's particular circumstances—that is, equally.

It may appear as though Rand is just asking the state to guarantee a different set of goods from those demanded by welfare-rights advocates. One must keep in mind, however, that there is an important difference between a reactive course of action and an assertive one. In Rand's scheme, the state reacts to rights violations—it does not assert itself in the creation of rights. It might be said that the state protects those rights we possess by nature, rather than acting as the instrument of their creation. In other words, the state acts on the recognition of a moral truth, rather than merely stipulating a mode of behavior. Herein lies one reason for considering Rand a natural-rights theorist.

Although we have sketched the basic elements of Rand's theory of rights, we have yet to speak of the importance she attaches to property rights. It has already been noted that her conception of property rights means the right to certain courses of action rather than to particular things. In this sense property rights reduce to the right to life—that is, the right of an individual to pursue courses of action he deems best, provided he does not coercively interact with others. Yet the special importance Rand accords to property rights is expressed in the following passage:

The right to life is the source of all rights—and the right to property is their only implementation. Without property rights, no other rights are possible. Since man has to sustain his life by his own effort, the man who has no right to the product of his effort has no means to sustain his life. The man who produces while others dispose of his product is a slave.[22]

Since human beings are material entities that require material goods to sustain their existence, the use, creation, and disposal of material things must be permitted. Moreover, Rand holds that only individuals act; collectivities are in no sense individuals and cannot act as such. Collectivities, therefore, possess no rights.[23] Since rights specify freedom of action and collectivities do not act, property rights are rights possessed by individuals. Individuals can, of course, form groups and consent to be treated *as if* they were one individual (e.g., a corporation), but this does not detract from the essential truth that rights belong to individual human beings.

But what does it mean to say that an individual has a right to property? In the first place, it means that the individual must not be kept from seeking material goods. Second and more important, the individual must be free to utilize those goods he has noncoercively acquired as he sees fit; for otherwise we have violated the already established principle that it is impermissible to restrict another's freedom of action by the initiation of force. Thus, when Rand says that "without property rights, no other rights are possible," she means simply that freedom of action with respect to material goods is the only way to make manifest the basic right to life. To coercively restrict someone's freedom of action is to say, in effect, that one is free to judge but not to act on one's judgment. This is to advance the principle that there is no necessary connection for human existence between judgments about a course of action and the overt actions implied by those judgments. It would be wrong to suppose that one's judgment about a course of action will necessarily be life-enhancing when the action is performed. What is implied by Rand's comment is that, in principle, the life-enhancing implications of a judgment can never be known unless the judgment is made manifest in overt action. In sum, freedom of choice or judgment implies the freedom to act on one's judgment, and such actions will occur in the material world. All of the foregoing is itself justified in terms of what is necessary for the achievement of a good human life.

Needless to say, freedom of action does not mean the freedom to plunge a knife into someone's stomach, for that would be a violation of the basic right to life. In this connection, Rand holds that a violation of one's property rights is an expression of force against the individual himself.[24] In a very real sense, to steal, to defraud, or to expropriate another's property is to initiate an act of violence against that person. It only follows that if our lives find their expression in the realm of objects—whether those objects be scholarly books or business enterprises—the nonconsensual use of that property constitutes a direct attack on the person himself. Unfortunately, we often tend to see a person's life as extending only to that person's outer epidermic layer. When a new law is passed that forcibly extracts a portion of one's income, we speak of that event as a tax on one's property and not on one's life or personhood. Indeed, we even tend to think of criminal actions, such as theft, as deplorable only because they violate a social rule and not because they represent an assault on someone's life. Rand's argument is that one cannot divorce what one has produced from one's personhood without thereby destroying the proper picture of human existence.[25]

The foregoing argument can be expressed by saying that human beings are ends in themselves and not means to the ends of others.[26] Since life is an end in itself and since life does not exist in the abstract but only in individuals, each individual's life is an end in itself. Rand's doctrine of individual rights is merely the *social* expression of the previous point. In a social context, we show our respect for the concept of each person's being an end in himself by not demanding that he deal with us on any terms but consent.[27] Voluntary agreement is the operative principle of Rand's theory of rights. She calls it the "principle of trade"— exchanging value for value.[28] Granted, there are many complications in determining when one has initiated force, rightfully owns a piece of property, has violated or not lived up to an agreement, and so forth. Rand, however, is more concerned with providing an overall view of the proper social order than with working out its details. The principle of trade and the theory of rights behind that principle constitute the basic structure of that vision. While some may hold that merely arguing for basic principles is not enough to test a doctrine's validity, we believe that the kind of challenge Rand poses for conventional thinking on these issues demands that the overall outline be established before the details can be worked on. Any other procedure would have lost sight of the end to be achieved.

Rand's theory of rights is what informs her defense of capitalism. She defines *capitalism* as follows: "capitalism is a social system based on the recognition of individual rights, including property rights, in which all property is privately owned."[29] Notice that the foundation of Rand's definition is in terms of individual rights and not in terms of the class in control of the means of production or the degree to which government interferes with business enterprise. Capitalism is not simply an economic system. Indeed, for Rand, the essence of capitalism is represented by a moral rather than an economic doctrine. If individual rights are respected in a society, then that society is capitalistic. Rand's conception of capitalism is, in principle, a novel one; for it allows for a society that values primarily art and literature to be just as capitalistic as one that values automobiles and boats—so long as both respect individual rights.[30]

One of the unique features of Rand's defense of capitalism is that she neither considers capitalism a necessary evil (as do many conservatives) nor tries to defend it simply in terms of the benefits it produces (as do many economists). It is not that we must put up with the system to reap its benefits, as we put up with manure to grow a flower garden. Rather, Rand defends the thesis that the very mode of human interaction called for by capitalism is the only morally justifiable way for people to socialize. Consider this passage:

The *moral* justification of capitalism does not lie in the altruist claim that it represents the best way to achieve "the common good".... The moral justification of capitalism lies in the fact that it is the only system consonant with man's rational nature, that it protects man's survival *qua* man, and that its ruling principle is: *justice*.[31]

This is not Adam Smith, F. A. Hayek, or Milton Friedman's defense of capitalism, for these thinkers defend capitalism in terms of its overall social product. Rand, on the other hand, goes to the heart of the issue, because only she has been willing to say that capitalism is an inherently moral social structure.

To make her case for capitalism more plausible, however,

Rand does have to overcome some rather widely held misconceptions about the social effects of capitalism. For example, in one chapter of *Capitalism: The Unknown Ideal*[32] the issues of monopoly, depression, labor unions, public education, inherited wealth, and the practicability of a laissez-faire system are discussed. We cannot undertake an examination of these issues here, and we refer the reader to the aforementioned chapter and the bibliography at the end of that volume.[33] Nevertheless, we can at least indicate Rand's attitude on a few general and more philosophic matters.

It has often been asserted that capitalism is a system that extols the pursuit of self-interest. This statement is usually meant to be a strike against capitalism; but for Rand it is not only descriptively accurate but morally acceptable as well. Some of the issues surrounding the role of self-interest in society have already been discussed in this volume and are further detailed in the following essay by Antony Flew. One does not, however, capture Rand's full view if one's analysis merely shows that capitalism is a social system based on principles that accord with rational self-interest. Rand also seems to hold that capitalism is a system which provides incentives for *advancing* one's self-interest. In the first place, capitalism promotes one of Rand's cardinal virtues—productivity. Whatever one's line of work, a competitive and free market tends to push one toward the achievement of the best one is able to produce within a given context.[34] Because there are no guarantees that past achievements will not be bettered, there are strong incentives to continue to produce at the maximum level. Moreover, those who are innovative and hard-working are not held to the level of the mediocre and the slothful, since there is the full expectation of reaping the rewards of one's efforts. In short, capitalism is a system directed toward achievement.

The push for achievement is given its motive force by the competitive nature of a capitalistic economy. Rand argues that competition is neither the law of the jungle nor a "dog-eat-dog" mode of existence. As Rand put it, "The motto 'dog eat dog' . . . is *not* applicable to capitalism nor to dogs."[35] Competition is not a zero-sum game where someone wins and another loses, such that there is no overall gain between parties. Competition is rather a method of coordinating activities in which those who are most efficient at utilizing a given resource are in a position to do so. A kind of human ecological balance is promoted by the market. An economy of resources develops with the result that the appropriate quantity of goods of optimal quality are directed into those areas where they are most needed or desired. The arguments on the efficiency of the market are not new with Rand, but the emphasis she places upon the market's beneficial effects on one's own sense of worth or efficacy is a novel perspective.

In any case, since the market tends to put resources into the hands of those most adept at using them, all stand to benefit—even those who may have been overcome by a more efficient competitor. As the economists tell us, the benefit of an efficient allocation of resources—through competitive markets—is a higher standard of living for all.[36] Another's success in the market is not achieved at the expense of someone else; for if that were the case, there would be no advance in the standard of living—everyone would simply be changing positions. If we see competition as a directive device,[37] however, we realize that the success of some and the failure of others is a signal about where resources ought to be directed. And since the market order allows the mobility to follow those signals quickly and fully, the efficiency thereby obtained permits sufficient surplus to raise everyone's standard of living.

In this connection it is important to realize that profits (contrary to popular belief) are also not achieved at someone else's expense. In opposition to the Marxist contention that progress in a capitalist order is the result of exploiting the surplus labor of the workers, Rand argues that capitalism is the only system that entirely removes sacrifice from human interaction.[38] Collectivism, in whatever variety, is a system wherein some are sacrificed for the sake of others. The sacrificial character of collectivist social systems stems from their willingness to consider the "needs of society" as overriding the individual's own interests. Rand dramatically states the issue in the following passage:

The social theory of ethics substitutes "society" for God—and though it claims that its chief concern is life on earth, it is *not* the life of man, not the life of an individual, but the life of a disembodied entity, *the collective*. . . . As far as the individual is concerned, *his* ethical duty is to be the selfless, voiceless, rightless slave of any need, claim or demand asserted by others.[39]

The Marxists are, indeed, correct to speak of surplus (i.e., profit) as the motive force for progress in a capitalist society; but that surplus is an individual phenomenon and *not* a class phenomenon. In a capitalist society, production is a process of individual efforts coordinated by a network of contractual agreements. No one is forced to associate with those one finds detrimental to one's interests.[40] This is not to say that capitalism is a fantasy land where one never confronts difficult choices or finds oneself in disagreeable situations. Capitalism, however, does hold out the promise that the products of one's efforts will not be expropriated without one's consent and that one will not have to exert oneself for the sake of an end one has not chosen. It is true that what one has to offer others may not be wanted by them, but the freedom to refuse a product is just the flip side of the freedom to offer it. Thus human relationships are nonsacrificial in the sense that they are consummated only when all parties agree to a specific course of action.

If voluntary interaction among men is morally superior to coerced interaction, then there are no grounds for the forcible rectification of the results of voluntary interaction. Individuals who engage in just exchanges—that is, who voluntarily contract for mutually agreed upon purposes—cannot then be forced to engage in involuntary exchange. Nozick has termed the theory of justice that looks only to past actions to see if current holdings were voluntarily gained an historical entitlement theory.[41] The entitlement theory is opposed to a theory that relies on "end-state" principles—that is, principles which demand that society conform to some specific pattern. The upshot of Nozick's argument is that if past actions were voluntarily undertaken by all parties concerned, there are no grounds for a later attempt to rectify the results of those interactions.

The fundamental place accorded to freedom of choice by both Rand and Nozick would imply that choices to engage in trade detrimental to one's objective interest (e.g., the choice to consume cigarettes) is morally superior to coercive attempts to prohibit the detrimental behavior. Thus, all forced redistributive schemes and all attempts to keep people from harming themselves are inherently pernicious. A society that mixes free and coerced exchanges is one which has chosen to mix two incompatible theories of the appropriate form of human interaction. And just as mixed economies are inherently unstable because the pockets of free trade tend to upset the plans imposed by the state,[42] so also does the mixture of voluntary and coerced exchanges tend to unsettle a society's moral values.

Today we find mass confusion about what are appropriate and inappropriate ways for human beings to interact. The result must be either further restriction on liberty or further removal of already existing restrictions. That is the choice we face. And even though we seem to be choosing the former course, the very fact that we do have a choice means we are not doomed to that alternative.

In all of Rand's discussions of the virtues of capitalism one must remember that no system of laissez-faire capitalism has ever existed.[43] Many of the alleged abuses of capitalism—such as depression, poverty, and war—cannot be attributed to capitalism itself, but to the actions of the state.[44] Thus many of the examples used against capitalism are simply beside the point. To justify this last claim is beyond the scope of this essay. We mention it only to alert the reader to the fact that one must distinguish the results that can be directly attributable to the market from those attributable to the state (or a mixture of state and market). Rand holds that when one has carefully examined the evidence, one will find that governmental action is usually responsible for the abuses normally attributed to the market order.

To claim that the state is often guilty of promoting problems that would have been otherwise nonexistent or less severe in a market order requires at least a general outline of Rand's view of the role and nature of the state.[45] We must know, in other words, what Rand takes to be the permissible limits of state power before we can determine whether a given state has gone beyond those limits. Rand restricts the state's function to the retaliatory use of physical force.[46] The basic principle behind the permissibility of the retaliatory use of physical force is the right of self-defense.[47] Individuals have the right of self-defense, because without that right their other rights could not be protected. The state acts in behalf of this right of self-defense, and the reason the state does so rather than individuals themselves seems to be because of the potential for excessive responses to minor rights violations. Moreover, without a set of rules for evidence and for punishment, there would be no way to adjudicate claims concerning rights violations. And without some method of adjudication, people would be able to deal with one another in *whatever* way their desires happened to push them. Under such a system no rights would be protected at all. Rand does not, however, seem to have either an explicit theory of punishment or a detailed theory about the structure of proper rules of evidence.[48]

The essential role of government is to protect people's rights, not only by preventing physical violence, but also by the enforcement of contractual agreements. Rand considers a breach of contract (together with fraud and extortion) to be an indirect initiation of force. In such cases, values are obtained without consent and then, by mere possession, are retained by force and not by right. Yet it is not only because rights must be protected that governments are justified. A further justification for government lies in the fact that without such protection civilization would be impossible, and civilization is necessary for people to achieve their proper end as human beings. This defense of the existence of government follows, given the fact that rights themselves are seen in terms of what is necessary for a proper human life.

Rand adopts the essentially Weberian view that governments possess a monopoly on the legal use of physical force. The monopoly status of government means that the government possesses great potential to violate rights.[49] The strictures on governmental action are, therefore, the same as the strictures placed upon individuals—actions that initiate force must not be taken. Moreover, since the government possesses a monopoly on the legal use of force, the potential consequences of its violation of rights is more serious than the criminal's violation of rights (even if we collectively aggregate the potential consequences of all criminals at any given time). These potential consequences of governmental abuse require that specific limitations be placed upon government. The regimes of Stalin, Hitler, and Mao are constant reminders that the violation of rights is more often and to a greater degree perpetrated by governments than by criminals.

Now that we have sketched the basic areas of Rand's political theory, we face the question of just where Rand's contribution in this area lies. Apart from the many interesting specifics one might mention, perhaps the most general statement of her contribution is the following. Rand attempts to combine an essentially classical or premodern view of man with a modern political doctrine; that is to say, an Aristotelian view of man's nature is integrated with a liberal political doctrine. The argument, as we have seen, is that freedom of action in society is a function of what is proper to living a good human life—indeed, what is necessary for the fulfillment of our human potential. There have been other intellectuals who have held a basically classical view of man and who were also political liberals. But no one else has shown the connection between those two outlooks as explicitly and successfully as Ayn Rand. Many details still need to be given thought, and there are certainly controversies that must be settled. Nevertheless, Rand offers us the outline of a theory that can motivate much scholarly research and debate. The present volume is the first step in that effort to discuss the merits of the Randian teaching.

Like the ancients, Rand has always strongly adhered to the view that ideas not only have consequences, but also have an important impact on culture. Moreover, Rand never wavers from the belief in the primacy of philosophy. Her emphasis on the role of the intellect culminates in the importance she attaches to the most intellectual of all subject matters—philosophy. Her advice to philosophers, and to other intellectuals as well, is summed up in the following passage:

The best among the present intellectuals should consider the tremendous power which they are holding, but have never fully exercised or understood. If any man among them feels that he is the helpless, ineffectual stepson of a "materialistic" culture that grants him neither wealth nor recognition. . . . let him realize that ideas are not an escape from reality, not a hobby for "disinterested" neurotics in ivory towers, but the most crucial and productive power in human existence.[50]

NOTES

1. Ayn Rand, "Man's Rights," in *Capitalism: The Unknown Ideal* (New York: New American Library, 1967), p. 320. Hereafter *Capitalism: The Unknown Ideal* will be cited as *CUI*. (The essay "Man's Rights" also appeared in Ayn Rand, *The Virtue of Selfishness* [New York: New American Library, 1964].)

2. Cf. Ayn Rand, *Atlas Shrugged* (New York: Random House, 1957).

3. Rand, "Man's Rights," p. 322.

4. Ayn Rand, "What Is Capitalism," in CUI, p. 19. (This essay also appeared in the *Objective Newsletter*, November-December 1965.)

5. Ibid.

6. Ayn Rand, "The Objectivist Ethics," in *The Virtue of Selfishness* (New York: New American Library, 1964), p. 20.

7. Ibid., p. 21: "Psychologically, the choice 'to think or not' is the choice 'to focus or not.' Existentially, the choice 'to focus or not' is the choice 'to be conscious or not.' Metaphysically, the choice 'to be conscious or not' is the choice of life or death."

8. Cf. the discussion of this in chapter 4 of this volume.

9. Henry Veatch, *Rational Man* (Bloomington: Indiana University Press, 1966), p. 46.

10. Aristotle *Nicomachean Ethics* 1.3.1094b12−14.

11. Rand, "Objectivist Ethics," pp. 20−21.

12. This is, by the way, the reason for Rand's rejection of religion.

13. Ayn Rand, "This Is John Galt Speaking," in *For the New Intellectual* (New York: New American Library, 1961), p. 134.

14. Rand, "Man's Rights," p. 322. On the next page Rand also says, "To violate man's rights means to compel him to act against his own judgment, or to expropriate his value."

15. Tibor Machan, *Human Rights and Human Liberties* (Chicago: Nelson Hall, 1975), p. 119.

16. Douglas Den Uyl, "Freedom and Virtue," *Reason Papers* 5 (Winter 1979).

17. Rand, "Man's Rights," p. 322.

18. Quoted ibid., p. 324.

19. Frederic Bastiat, "Stupid Greed and False Philanthropy," in *The Law and Clichés of Socialism*, trans. Dean Russell (Whittier, Calif.: Constructive Action, 1964), p. 14.

20. Robert Nozick, "How Liberty Upsets Patterns," in *Anarchy, State, and Utopia* (New York: Basic Books, 1974), pp. 160−64.

21. In this respect it should be emphasized that Rand's political philosophy

is thoroughly nonutopian. It is a political theory that considers man as he is now, not as something he is supposed to evolve into come the millennia.

22. Rand, "Man's Rights," p. 322.

23. Ayn Rand, "Collectivized Rights," in VOS., pp. 101–6.

24. Rand, "What Is Capitalism," p. 19.

25. In some respects our foregoing account of an individual's relationship to his property is much like Hegel's view (cf. G. W. Hegel, *The Philosophy of Right* (Oxford: Clarendon Press, 1953), p. 40. Given this connection to Hegel, we are led to speculate that Rand, like Marx, would develop a theory of alienation. Alienation for Rand would have to be something like the coercive separation of one from one's property by the state (e.g., by taxation)!

26. Rand, "What Is Capitalism," p. 19.

27. Rand, "Man's Rights," pp. 321–23.

28. Rand, "What Is Capitalism," p. 19.

29. Ibid.

30. Of course, the likelihood of the former society being achieved is another question.

31. Rand, "What Is Capitalism," p. 20.

32. Rand, *CUI*, ch. 5, pp. 72–95. Cf. also ch. 4 on antitrust.

33. Cf. Ludwig von Mises, *Human Action* (Chicago: Henry Regnery Co., 1949); not mentioned in Rand's bibliography but nevertheless very important is Murray Rothbard, *Man, Economy, and State* (Los Angeles: Nash Publishing, 1970).

34. Rand, "What Is Capitalism," pp. 25–28.

35. Rand, "Objectivist Ethics," p. 34.

36. Rothbard, *Man, Economy, and State*, pp. 879–81.

37. The work on competition as a coordination process was begun by F. A. Hayek. Cf. his *Individualism and the Economic Order* (Chicago: Henry Regnery Co., 1972), pp. 77–91; see also Gerald P. O'Driscoll, Jr., *Economics as a Coordination Problem* (Kansas City, Mo.: Sheed, Andrews & McMeel, 1977).

38. Rand, "What Is Capitalism," p. 28.

39. Rand, "Objectivist Ethics," p. 34.

40. Rand would argue that to say nature "forces" a person to work in order to eat is to misapply the concept. It confuses human action taken to alter nature with the conditions given by nature. As Murray Rothbard has stated (*Man, Economy, and State*, p. 581): "The false confusion of freedom with abundance rests on a failure to distinguish between the conditions given by nature and man-made actions to transform nature. . . . Man's condition on earth is that he must work with the given natural conditions and improve them by human action. It is a reflection on nature, not the free market, that everyone is 'free to starve.'"

41. Nozick, *Anarchy, State, and Utopia*, p. 150.

42. Cf. Ludwig von Mises, *Planning for Freedom* (South Holland, Ill.: Libertarian Press, 1962).

43. Cf. Ayn Rand, "America's Persecuted Minority: Big Business," in *CUI*, p. 48.

44. Cf. Murray Rothbard, "The Economics of Violent Intervention in the Market," in *Man, Economy, and State*, p. 765–890.

45. We shall ignore the question of anarcho-capitalism here. This is to say, we shall ignore the possibility of whether a system of competing protection agencies is possible. For Rand's view on this issue, see Ayn Rand, "The Nature of Government," in *CUI*, pp. 334–35. (This essay also appeared in *VOS*.)

46. The following remarks on Rand's view of government are based primarily on her essay "The Nature of Government," ibid., pp. 329–37.

47. Cf. Rand, "Objectivist Ethics," p. 33.

48. It seems likely to us that Rand would not argue that the law could be deduced a priori from the natural right to liberty or could arise from the market mechanism alone. Rules of evidence, standards for judgmental processes in the determination of guilt or innocence, and the mode of retaliatory force would all require experts and the instrumentality for their functioning (the state). Cf. Rand, "The Nature of Government," p. 334.

49. Despite the dismal history of the state, it should be noted that Rand does not consider the nature of government as requiring coercion. Cf. Ayn Rand, "Government Financing in a Free Society," in *VOS*, pp. 116–20. A lottery is suggested by Rand as one of the ways government might be financed; yet this suggestion is rebutted by Robert Nozick (*Anarchy, State, and Utopia*, p. 25).

50. Ayn Rand, "For the New Intellectual," in *For the New Intellectual*, p. 52.

9

Selfishness and the Unintended Consequences of Intended Action

෧

Antony Flew

I

Titles such as *The Crime of Punishment*[1] and *The Virtue of Selfishness*[2] are coined precisely to arrest attention, and they do. For surely both phrases are almost, if not perhaps quite, self-contradictory. Is it possible for punishment, the logico-legal correlate and consequence of crime, to be itself a crime, presumably itself demanding punishment? Also, if and insofar as it is common practice to distinguish among actions the illicit as the selfish, how can selfishness be itself a virtue?

Suppose we open the first of the aforementioned books. Inside we find Dr. Karl Menninger, the longtime high priest of U.S. orthopsychiatry arguing with great force and confidence for what he sees as the progressive, scientifically oriented, forward-looking way of dealing with actually or potentially antisocial elements. Menninger expresses the preference that offenders upon conviction, rather than being imprisoned or otherwise traditionally punished, should, as cross-grained and misshapen social material, be handed over to his professional colleagues for "straightening."[3] All such substandard persons are to be detained, as one might say, at the psychiatrist's pleasure. He thus dismisses the deplorably old-fashioned concept of justice—and with it, of course, the supposedly exploded superstition of choice—in a few chillingly impatient sentences:

The very word "justice" irritates scientists. No surgeon expects to be asked whether an operation for cancer is just or not. No doctor will be reproached on the grounds that the dose of penicillin he has prescribed is less or more than justice would stipulate. Behavioral scientists regard it as absurd to invoke the question of justice in deciding what to do with a woman who cannot resist her propensity to shoplift, or with a man who cannot resist an impulse to assault somebody. This sort of behavior has to be controlled; it has to be discouraged; it has to be stopped. This (to the scientist) is a matter of public safety and amicable coexistence, not of justice.[4]

Even before we open the second book it is possible to cite elevated clerical authority for the point that selfishness is one of the concepts that—as Aristotle remarked[5]—have a negative valuation built into it. In the summer of 1972 the *Times* of London reported that Archbishop Camara of Brazil had asked a meeting of both Houses of the British Parliament, "Why do you not denounce, once and for all, the intrinsic selfishness and heartlessness of capitalism?"[6]

However, although the archbishop certainly has at least common usage on his side in taking it as given that selfishness is essentially deplorable, he is not entitled similarly to assume that, whereas the motives and interests engaged in the working of capitalist systems cannot but be, in this understanding, selfish, this is by no means true of the socialist opposite numbers. No reason whatsoever has been given for believing that Bulgarians or Poles living under socialism are led to perform economic tasks by motives fundamentally different from and higher than those stirring the benighted Belgians or the wretched Portuguese. Yet presumably most of these various desires are interested in the sense that all those who are guided by any of them are—in the immortal words of Damon Runyon—"doing the best they can." But, since this would seem to apply to everyone, there is no ground to be found here for condemning some and not others.[7]

This is awkward for one who, we are told, is "one of the great voices of our time." For no one, surely, is so starry-eyed as to believe that any system of economic organization can dispense with all interested motives. If, therefore, one is upon this basis to be condemned as "intrinsically selfish and heartless," then by the same token all must be. Yet that, of course, is precisely not what is wanted by anyone who, with Camara, denounces capitalism root and branch, and as such, while tolerantly discounting as more or less "serious distortions" whatever faults in the socialist countries they can, however briefly and however reluctantly, screw themselves up to recognize.

II

So what is Ayn Rand about when she so defiantly proclaims the virtue of selfishness? First, she is sometimes tempted into trying to prove far too much. She then suggests, not that unselfishness and self-sacrifice are a thoroughly bad business of which we have had and still are having far too much, but rather that, while still apparently bad things, these are strictly inconceivables. Thus in *For the New Intellectual*, quoting a speech by Howard Roark from *The Fountainhead*, she says: "no man can live for another. He cannot share his spirit just as he cannot share his body. . . . It is impossible in concept."[8]

This will not do at all. In the first place, the conclusion is false: the concepts of unselfish and self-sacrificing action are two that can be, and often are, taught by reference to actual paradigm cases. Such teaching by reference to specimens, that are at the same time models to be imitated is a large part of moral education. In the second place, even if such a conclusion could be proved, the proving of it would deprive Rand of her own chosen enemy.

Rand gets into this mess by confounding what belongs contingently to the individual with what belongs *necessarily*. Thus a few paragraphs earlier she has Roark proclaim:

But the mind is an attribute of the individual. There is no such thing as a collective brain. There is no such thing as a collective thought. . . . The primary act—the process of reason—must be performed by each man alone. We can divide a meal among many men. We cannot digest it in a collective stomach. . . . No man can use his brain to think for another. All the functions of the body and spirit are private. They cannot be shared or transferred.[9]

Yet it is false to say that "No one can use his brain to think for another." All sorts of people are doing it all the time. It is, for instance, a main function of staff officers to relieve the general in command of the impossible burden of working out in detail how the army movements he wants are to be effected. What is true is that when the staff officers tackle this problem, it is necessarily they who are thinking it through.

It would even be false to say that we cannot in principle digest a meal for somebody else. For presumably I can, by employing methods favored by gluttonous banqueters in the period of Roman decadence, make myself vomit up a half-digested meal for penitential consumption by someone else; something of this sort is in fact done by the parents of some other species for their offspring. But what would again be true is that this repellent predigestive performance would necessarily be my performance.

Fortunately Rand recovers herself from this initial lapse, for *The Virtue of Selfishness* includes a little piece, written by Nathaniel Branden but approved by Rand, on the question Isn't everyone selfish? Here Branden takes and makes the point that the popular answer, that everyone always is and must be selfish, depends upon "an extraordinarily crude equivocation." As Branden puts it: "It is a psychological truism—a tautology—that all purposeful behavior is motivated. But to equate '*motivated* behavior' with '*selfish* behavior' is to blank out the distinction between an elementary fact of human psychology and the phenomenon of *ethical* choice."[10]

III

Altruism, therefore, is both a logical and psychological possibility. The fact that every desire is necessarily, if not exactly a desire for pleasure, at least a desire for its own satisfaction[11] does not preclude there being, as there are, desires and actions that are not selfish. It is here, I believe, that Rand begins to set herself apart from the herd, not only and most directly by commending rather than condemning whatever she rates as selfish, but also and more subtly by what she admits or refuses to admit into this class. To cite two dramatic examples—it is, incidentally, a weakness in Rand as a practical moralist that so few of her illustrations are everyday, pedestrian illustrations—to sacrifice your money or even your life for someone you love or for a cause in which you believe is in her cultural circle not self-sacrifice (condemnable) but selfishness (commendable):

Any action that a man undertakes for the benefit of those he loves is not a sacrifice if, in the hierarchy of his values, in the total context of the choices open to him, it achieves that which is of the greatest *personal* (and rational) importance to *him*.[12]

If you wish to save the last of your dignity, do not call the best of your actions a "sacrifice": that term brands you as immoral. . . . If a man dies fighting for his own freedom, it is *not* a sacrifice: he is not willing to live as a slave; but it *is* a sacrifice to be the kind of man who's willing. If a man refuses to sell his convictions, it is not a sacrifice, unless he is the sort of man who has no convictions.[13]

While working on the present essay I read a report of the funeral eulogy for the NBC-TV cameraman who was killed in the minimassacre in Guyana—the murders preceding the mass suicide that took from the Jewish resistance at Masada a long-standing world record. Robert Brown, a colleague said, "died on his feet with his camera rolling because that's the kind of man he was."[14] Both Brown and the zealots of Masada would surely be said by Rand to have displayed "the virtue of selfishness." For Brown refused to let anything obstruct his chosen commitment to being first and always a cameraman, on the spot as it happens; and the zealots, with their eyes wide open, were precisely not willing to live as—in the most literal sense—slaves.

The characteristics that Rand wants to promote as selfish or to diminish as sacrificial are thus by no means exactly the same as those the vulgar depreciate as the one or commend as the other. It is here unfortunate both that Rand's novels are so full of long philosophical speeches and that her contributions to philosophy are so largely a matter of quoting the speeches from her novels. Her moral ideas could have been much better illustrated with the help of detailed accounts of paradigm lives, both good and bad, and developed in contrast or relation with certain classical philosophers.

One obvious contrast of this kind would be with Kant. For it is notorious that Kant held no action, however otherwise admirable, to possess "genuine moral worth" unless it was performed "for the sake of duty alone." [15] The even more obviously classical—indeed, Classical—inspiration is Aristotle. Rand is always eager to speak well of "the Master of those that know." But their relations appear to be those of typical contemporary French intellectuals with Descartes. New intellectuals of that stamp think no elegant essay complete without some dropping of the Cartesian name and perhaps a mention of what—in barbarous miscegenation of French on Latin—they are pleased to label *le cogito*. Yet it is rare for these references to reach the point of actual quotation or to suggest in any other way recent first-hand acquaintance with anything Descartes himself wrote. I will say no more about these relations, or lack of relations, since this volume contains an essay by Jack Wheeler on Rand and Aristotle.

IV

What next demands attention is the perplexing and unbelievable doctrine that there could never be any conflict of interest between true objectivists. This is, to the embarrassment of all concerned, reminiscent of the revelation in the *Communist Manifesto* that, in the upcoming utopia, "the free development of each will be the condition of the free development of all." [16] Rand writes:

The Objectivist ethics holds that *human* good does not require human sacrifices and cannot be achieved by the sacrifice of anyone to anyone. It holds that the *rational* interests of men do not clash—that there is no conflict of interests among men who do not desire the unearned, who do not make sacrifices nor accept them, who deal with one another as *traders*, giving value for value. [17]

In a later chapter Rand acknowledges that "some students of Objectivism find it difficult to grasp the Objectivist principle that 'there are no conflicts of interests among rational men'." [18]

To meet their difficulties—which have certainly been mine—she considers the case of two people competing for one job: "Isn't this a case of a conflict of interests, and isn't the benefit of one man achieved at the price of the sacrifice of the other?"[19]

It is worth saying, by the way, for the instruction of those who, like Archibishop Camara, are inclined to make immediate but invalid inferences from the ordinarily self-interested to the ordinarily selfish, that this case constitutes a perfect counter-example. For the refusal of one to sacrifice one's own interests to those of another would not normally be rated and, consequently, be berated as selfish. Even if we were to allow that the "Boo/Hooray" analysis of moral terms is in substance correct, it would still be wrong to render *selfish* as the equivalent of *self-interested*. Not all self-interest is in that vulgar understanding selfish.

It is also worth saying, this time for the benefit of all those concerned in any discussion of selfishness or unselfishness, that these alternatives, though no doubt mutually exclusive, are not altogether exhaustive. Reusing the example of the previous paragraph, we should have to say that someone who withdrew from competition for some post he himself wanted to leave the field clear for someone else was being in this unselfish. But we have already reminded ourselves that the same person would not ordinarily be condemned as selfish for not thus withdrawing. The situation—Aristotle to note—appears to be that we have words for two opposite extremes, but not for the mean; while that particular mean-in-action could scarcely be rated a positive virtue.

Rand's answer to the question pressed by puzzled students involves collapsing the distinction between rights and interests. This maneuver is facilitated by her insistence that the interests under consideration must be rational—in her own special interpretation of the term *rational*. Notice how that word is inserted and italicized in the statement quoted at the beginning of this section. The collapsing of the distinction between rights and interests is clearest in the concluding paragraphs of the cited chapter:

The mere fact that two men desire the same job does not constitute proof that either of them is entitled to it or deserves it, and that his interests are damaged if he does not obtain it. . . . Whoever gets the job, has earned it (assuming that the employer's choice is rational). This benefit is due to his own merit—not to the "sacrifice" of the other man who never had any vested right to that job. The failure to give to a man what had never belonged to him can hardly be described as "sacrificing his interests." [20]

Notice next that the interests qualified as "rational" are further specified there as both excluding "the unearned" and including only those of "*traders*, giving value for value." Rand is, I suggest, mistaking it that all human relationships are or should be trading transactions. She thus moves invalidly, from a true insight into the essential nature of trade, to the false conclusion that the relationship between two persons could not include that of a flat conflict of interest. The true insight is that trade is not, as is constantly assumed, a zero-sum confrontation. [21] Since trade must be voluntary on both sides, and assuming that both parties are economically rational, then both of them must expect to be—and typically, of course, they actually will be—better off after having made the deal than if no such deal had been made.

"All of the above discussion," Rand insists in a final coda, "applies only to the relationships among rational men and only to a free society." Then she adds, incredibly, that "in a nonfree society, no pursuit of any interests is possible to anyone." [22]

Much more to the present point, the whole discussion applies, if at all, only in a constricted and factitious interpretation of the term *interests*. Nothing has been said to show, what is not true, that there can be in the ordinary acceptation of the terms no conflict of interest among objectivists. To say that the rightly rejected candidate was not entitled to the job and did not deserve it is not the same as saying, and does not imply, that he had no interest in getting it. Very likely he did have such interest. But in that case he and his interest were, in the appointment of the better man, quite properly passed over.

One of the reasons why Rand wants to maintain that among good objectivists there can be no conflict of interest is her overriding concern to deny the legitimacy of any appeal for self-sacrifice. If she once allows that there are genuine conflicts of interest, then perhaps sometimes—though rarely, if ever, in the context of fair competition for scarce employment opportunities—I ought to sacrifice my interest to yours. The same concern leads her to maintain that our only obligations to others are to respect their rights, rights that, as it very reasonably turns out, are all either natural rights to noninterference or artificial rights voluntarily bestowed by us in the course of our contractual activities as "traders, giving value for value."

We can see here a most interesting meeting of extremes. On the one side are the all-providing-from-before-the-erection-till-after-the-Resurrection welfare statists laboring to make out that everything they think it would be good for people to have is owed to them as a right. That this everything should be supplied is, therefore, a matter of (social) justice. On the other side are the objectivists urging that no one ever has any obligation to give anyone anything but noninterference and the fulfillment of any contracts voluntarily effected. Both parties meet in their inclination to make justice the whole of morality. But, whereas one does this by incorporating everything else they can think of into their new ideal of (social) justice, the other achieves a similar result by denying the subsistence of any obligations to others beyond that of yielding what they are entitled to demand of right.

John Rawls provides an excellent example of the former tendency when he offers *A Theory of Justice* as a rival, not particularly and specifically to J. S. Mill's account of justice in the fifth chapter of *Utilitarianism*, but instead generally and comprehensively to classical utilitarianism as a whole.[23] That the latter is authentic Rand comes out well in a speech by Howard Roark: "I came here to say that I do not recognize anyone's right to one minute of my life. Nor to any part of my energy. Nor to any achievement of mine. No matter who makes the claim, how large their number or how great their need. . . . I recognize no obligations toward men except one: to respect their freedom."[24]

V

Another reason why Rand wants to prove that among faithful objectivists there can be no conflict of interest was hinted in the first paragraph of section 4 of this essay. Like Marx, Rand would like to believe, as who would not, that human nature and the human condition are such as to make possible a conflict-free utopia. But nothing we know, either about the universe in general or the evolution of our own species in particular provides the slightest ground for such a hope. That Marx put the fulfillment of a conflict-free utopia forward as not merely possible but inevitable, as the finding of scientific as opposed to utopian socialism, was therefore, remains, and ought to be much more often declared to be grotesque.

Rand can say, by contrast, that the promise of an objectivist morality is far better than a groundless hope. Curiously, when she makes this point it seems always to be made with little if any theoretical backing. Howard Roark says, for instance:

Now observe the results of a society built on the principle of individualism. This, our country, the noblest country in the history of men. The country of greatest achievement, greatest prosperity, greatest freedom. This country was not built on selfless service, sacrifice, renunciation or any precept of altruism. It was based on man's right to the pursuit of happiness. His own happiness. Not anyone else's. A private, personal, selfish motive. Look at the results.[25]

This is no doubt, as far as it goes, all very well. We might even, while moving in this direction, go a bit farther. Recall again the hackneyed yet never too often pondered contrast between the German Federal Republic and Soviet Germany.[26] Throw in then for good measure, pressed down and running over, the almost equally dramatic but much less familiar contrasts between Thailand and Burma, and Taiwan and China.[27] Still, none of this begins to answer the question why an economic system under which all are free to "do the best they can" for themselves should at the same time tend to the enrichment of everyone. It is, indeed, a little extraordinary that Rand, concerned as she is with both defending "the system of natural liberty" and stressing that the consequences of our actions are often other than or even opposite to our intentions, pays no homage to Adam Smith. Let that omission forthwith be repaired. Consider now one of the great passages of *The Wealth of Nations*:

But it is only for the sake of profit that any man employs a capital in the support of industry; and he will always, therefore, endeavor to employ it in the support of that industry of which the produce is likely to be of the greatest value. . . . As every individual, therefore, endeavors as much as he can both to employ his capital . . . and so to direct . . . that its produce may be of the greatest value; every individual necessarily labours to render the annual revenue of the society as great as he can. He generally, indeed, neither intends to promote the public interest, nor knows how much he is promoting it . . . he is in this, as in many other cases, led by an invisible hand to promote an end which was no part of his intention. Nor is it always the worse for society that it was no part of it. By pursuing his own interest he frequently promotes that of the society more effectually than when he really intends to promote it. I have never known much good done by those who affected to trade for the public good.[28]

The nerve of Smith's argument is that investment decisions must tend to be wealth-creating if and insofar as those who make these decisions have a direct and proportionate interest in their being so: if, that is, these crucial decisionmakers know that they are themselves individually going to be richer in proportion to the wealth created by their decisions and, correspondingly, poorer to the extent that these decisions prove to be wasteful. It is an excellent demonstration; although it does not prove, of course, that it is necessary for the decisionmakers either to enjoy individually the whole return on or to suffer individually the whole loss from the capital thus employed. The argument will still go through with the same force wherever and so long as these key decisionmakers have a proportionate and, to them, significant share of the consequent gains or losses.

This apparently weakening qualification carries two strong corollaries, neither of which is sufficiently recognized. The first is that taxes levied at progressive rather than proportionate rates, particularly when extorted from real capital gains, must be a disincentive to wealth creation. The second is that stockholders who hire other people to direct their corporations should in prudence insist that these other people in one way or another acquire, as their own main individual investment, some holding in the corporation they have been hired to direct. It is not necessary that any such holdings be large, either absolutely or relatively to the total assets of the corporation. What matters is that they be large relative to any other investments of the person concerned and that they be held individually rather than collectively. Only thus will those persons acquire individual interests that are significant to them and sufficient to guarantee their commitment. The scope of the principle of prudence just enunciated must also extend to any key employees other than the directors, whose commitment is similarly crucial to the success of the corporation as a wealth-creating enterprise: "A society which wishes for economic growth should nurse the creative talent which its enterprising members possess, and should encourage the development of such talent to its full stature."[29]

It is no doubt impossible even to estimate the amount of economic growth forfeited by those countries that ignore or defy either or both of these corollaries, and such economic detail would in any case be out of place in a book of philosophical essays. But it is in place simply to mention that Britain, with its notoriously abysmal economic performance, has the highest rates of income taxation, from the lowest thresholds, of almost any not yet communist industrial country. It is also especially hard on income from investments, which it singles out for official abuse as "unearned."[30] More peculiarly, the British Treasury, encouraged by the socialist politicians who seem to be always in power, whether in office or in opposition, have a long record of obstructing all schemes to ensure that company directors and other key employees will have substantial individual stakes in the profits and losses of the corporations they are hired to serve.

Returning from corollaries to the main point, we have now to repair Smith's omission of two important further points: (1) that there is no easy or infallible way in which even those with the strongest personal interests in so doing can guarantee to make investment decisions that will turn out to be right; and (2) that "the system of natural liberty" has the enormous merit of providing a feedback mechanism to ensure that those who regularly get them wrong will in the not very long run be replaced by others, whether these be new ventures or established persons with better track records of success. This mechanism consists in the most simple fact that in this system those who make investments which turn out badly lose their own money and, hence, have in the future less to invest, whereas those who back proven winners equally automatically have more.

The force of both Smith's main point and our two addenda will be more fully grasped if we consider for a moment the British socialist alternative. Major investment decisions, our socialists love to say, must be made, not in a rapacious and selfish quest for private profit (Boo!), but through an unselfish determination of the public interest (Hooray!). Genuflections in the direction of their Great Idol, the State, would here be seen as proper.

It is as essential as it is uncommon to demystify such gushes of abstract talk from the indoctrinated devout. We must demand to know precisely who is going to make such vital economic decisions, how, and subject to what incentives or pressures. Once that question is put, its answer in Britain is obvious. If these decisions are not to be made by private owners with a proportionate individual interest in their turning out to be wealth-creating or by the hired agents of such private owners, then they will be made, as to an ever-increasing extent they already are made, by the mandarins of the civil service, by the politicians, and by the creatures of the politicians. Yet such worthies have no ex-officio individual interest in making decisions that are in fact wealth-creating, and they stand to suffer no corresponding domestic loss if, in what is always the rather distant future, their actual decisions turn out to be ruinous. Indeed, Britain is most insistent that her civil servants and her politicians should not have any such private interest in the decisions they make on behalf of the public; and for a long time it has been and still is outstandingly successful in ensuring that in fact they do not.[31]

Thus, to eschew relevant incentives is by itself quite sufficiently imprudent. But that is not the half of it; for civil servants, politicians, and their creatures are humans like the rest of us—no worse, no doubt, but no better either. Therefore, they are all inclined, as the economists put it, to maximize their own utilities. In this they are subject to the various pressures and appropriate incentives of their own several positions. The trouble is that these particular pressures and incentives are not to make decisions that are in fact wealth-creating. Worse still, some of them push or pull in diametrically the opposite direction.[32]

A spelling out of the considerations that have been indicated in the foregoing paragraphs of this section would, I believe, greatly strengthen Rand's arguments against statist monopoly and for competitive capitalism. But usually, if not quite always, Rand appears to be satisfied with appeals to the actual competitive track records of what, following Galileo, we might now call "the two chief systems of the world." Since Rand is an American writing primarily for other Americans, this is perhaps the appropriate emphasis. For although the USA has seen some state ownership and state investment in and into some areas, Americans have had much less direct experience of this form of socialism than those of us who live in less happier lands. American capitalism has, however, recently been crippled, and its once magnificent productivity brought down to an almost British level by the more indirect means of an enormous proliferation of federal and local regulation.

The previous paragraphs of this section have deployed and developed Smith's argument to show that "the system of natural liberty" must tend to generate the most wealth-creating of possible investments. A parallel argument will show that in such a system the consumer must be sovereign and that present consumer decisions, and estimates of future consumer decisions, determine which suppliers will prosper and grow and which will decline or even disappear. There is, I think, notably little emphasis in the Rand corpus upon this side of things. Her works are largely about, and seem in the main to be directed toward an elite of the creative and the actual or potential enterprisers[33] rather than toward the unmemorable mass that may also get rich benefits from the achievements of that elite.

Smith himself does not spell out this parallel argument in another single classic paragraph. But he does have some splendid Randian words on the proper relations between suppliers and consumers:

It is not from the benevolence of the butcher, the brewer, or the baker that we expect our dinner, but from their regard to their own interest. We address ourselves, not to their humanity but their self-love and never talk to them of our own necessities but of their advantages. Nobody but a beggar chooses to depend chiefly upon the benevolence of his fellow-citizens.[34]

Under "the system of natural liberty"—the worse description "capitalism" was unknown to Smith and his contemporaries— it is up to the consumer to decide what to buy, and such purchases are effective votes for the further production of whatever the consumer chooses to buy. The supplier is the servant of the consumer, inasmuch as it is in the interest of the supplier to offer what the consumer wants, better made, more conveniently sold, and cheaper than whatever is offered by the competition. Any supplier who fails to win an adequate vote of purchase from the consuming public will, in the not too long run, be by that very failure driven out of the market. There is, alas, no comparable automatic self-destruct mechanism to guarantee that state organization will disappear as and when it ceases to satisfy the wants of the people outside the organization itself—or that they do not even begin!

Neither is there any guarantee that the directors of a socialist economy will accept and act upon what to Smith appeared a self-evident truth: "Consumption is the sole end and purpose of all production; and the interest of the producer ought to be attended to only so far as it may be necessary for promoting that of the consumer."[35] Thus in the USSR the ruling class devotes a far higher proportion of all investment than in any non-communist industrial country to supplying the armed forces and police. The object is, in fact, not production for use by the Soviet consumer, but production to extend still further the power of the elite. Or, to turn from the menacing to the—to outsiders—ridiculous, consider the large part played in the long-running Concord story by an infatuation with the idea of high technology, unharnessed to and uninhibited by any sordid pressures ultimately to make a profit out of producing and selling something someone would want to buy and use.

It has been a commonplace of socialist propaganda to promise production for use or production to meet human needs as the new, preferred alternative to capitalist production for profit.[36] But, as a moment's thought will show, this is a false antithesis. For no one would stay in business under competitive capitalism making profits unless they were producing what someone else wanted to buy and then, presumably, to use. The true and relevant antithesis is between market and command, between production directed by the choice of consumers and production directed by the command of agents or controllers of the state machine.

A key distinction here is between wants and needs [37]—a distinction clearly related to one Rand develops in the first essay of *Capitalism: The Unknown Ideal.* She there contrasts market value, which is a function of actual wants, with "*philosophically objective* value," which is a matter of what actually is "the best possible to man." Each of us is the prime expert on our own wants, whereas other and superior persons may pretend to prescribe what we most truly need. What people actually want in this less than perfect world may well be deplorable in the eyes of others, and those others not socialist intellectuals only. I myself am not ashamed to regret the kind of music my teenage daughters love, along with most of their contemporaries: music that is either officially disfavored or outright banned in most if not quite all socialist countries. Even more, perhaps, do I dislike the sort of people who produce such music and whom the teenagers, by the free choice of their purchases, vote to enrich. But, of course, freedom comes first; and they, as I, have the right to choose.

Smith—writing before the development of any modern state monopolies of health, education, or welfare services—could go on, in the chapter from which that last quotation came:

Nobody but a beggar chooses to depend on the benevolence of his fellow citizens. Even a beggar does not depend on it entirely. The charity of well-disposed people, indeed, supplies him with the whole fund of his subsistence. But though this principle ultimately provides him with all the necessaries of life which he has occasion for, it neither does nor can provide him with them as he has occasion for them. The greater part of his occasional wants are supplied in the same manner as those of other people, by treaty, by barter and by purchase. [38]

In this respect at any rate, the position of Smith's beggar would seem to have been more free, more influential, and more dignified than that of anyone today dependent on state monopoly provision. For once that beggar had his charity money in his pocket, he could choose between rival suppliers; he could cast his individual purchase vote for this sort and source of supply rather than that; and, as an equal trading with an equal, he could pay cash for what he got. Contrast the situation of the citizen who has no choice, for instance, but to send his children to the neighborhood state school, there to receive whatever education its teachers and the educational bureaucracy see fit to provide.

All would be changed utterly by the introduction of a voucher system such as was suggested by John Stuart Mill, the saint of classical liberalism, which was revived in the '50s and '60s by Milton Friedman and is now advocated in Britain by market-minded radicals associated with the politically neutral Institute for Economic Affairs.[39] In 1978 in California the same idea was strongly plugged by Ed Clark, the gubernatorial candidate of the Libertarian party. The voucher replaces monopoly by a market, and by giving to those who are at present forced to be beggars a kind of money (albeit money to be spent on education only) makes them and not the suppliers sovereign. It is significant that to any suggestion of this kind there are two stock statist responses. The first is that parental choice must introduce or increase that most infamous of all things, inequality; because some parents, especially those of the working-class, are and will remain negligent or indifferent about the education of their children.[40] The second is that, whatever the parents may or may not want, it is the teachers and, of course, the educational administration who alone know and are providing what the children need.

VI

I began in section 1 by seeing *The Virtue of Selfishness* as a paradoxical response to the talk of Archbishop Camara and his like about "the intrinsic selfishness and heartlessness of capitalism." Then, in sections 2 and 3 I came more closely to grips with Rand, who, after the initial lapse of suggesting that unselfish action is inconceivable, took against the Camaras of this world the bold and contrary line that selfishness, albeit selfishness somewhat elusively and idiosyncratically understood, is itself virtuous. In section 4 I unearthed and rejected the unsound foundations of Rand's persistent, false contention that among rational persons ever willing to trade service for service there can be no conflict of interest, taking a little time to indicate an interesting comparison and contrast between the most self-reliant objectivists on the one hand and the most extreme all-providing-from-before-the-erection-till-after-the-Resurrection welfare statists on the other. (Both are inclined to mistake justice for the whole of virtue.)

In section 5 I began to compare Rand's claims about the side effects of objectivist morality with some of Adam Smith's arguments about the unintended social consequences of intended individual actions. The aim throughout was to show how Rand's case for competitive capitalism and against state monopoly may be strengthened by introducing and developing certain of the most characteristic ideas of Smith.

My final suggestion is that we need always to be on guard against any temptation to argue from the motives or intentions of agents to conclusions about the actual consequences of their conduct. Not only is it obvious that all such arguments must be invalid, but also two of the most basic truths of the human condition are (1) that every action has and must have unforeseen and unforeseeable consequences and (2) that the actual outcome of even the best laid plans is often, in whole or in part, contrary to original intentions. Smith's treatment of the capital market, considered in section 5, constitutes a paradigm of social science as the study of the unintended consequences of intended actions.[41] Minimum-wage legislation provides a clear, congenial example of a counterproductive social policy.[42]

For us the immediate, general moral is that, whether or not it is right to go on as Rand does about the virtue of selfishness, we ought to begin by being unmoved by archepiscopal thunderings against "the intrinsic selfishness and heartlessness of capitalism," for the student and critic of social institutions have no business thus to seek windows into men's souls. They should, instead, remember some words of a man whom the archbishop himself must call master, "By their fruits ye shall know them."[43]

NOTES

1. Karl Menninger, *The Crime of Punishment* (New York: Viking, 1968).

2. Ayn Rand, *The Virtue of Selfishness* (New York: New American Library, 1964).

3. This word is borrowed from Samuel Butler's famous fantasy *Erewhon*, of which the second and definitive edition was first published in 1901. In that upside down world—*nowhere* backwards—crime and immorality are dealt with by "a class of men trained in soul-craft, whom they call straighteners, as nearly as I can translate a word, which literally means 'one who bends back the crooked.' These men practise much as medical men in England. . . . They are treated with the same unreserve, and obeyed as readily, as our own doctors." It is a remarkable example of life imitating art that twenty-three years later Menninger and others joined to form the American Orthopsychiatric Association. Their object was to bring together "representatives of the neuropsychiatric or medical view of crime." (It has to be noted that our roots *ortho-* and *psych-* come from Greek words for, respectively, *straight* and *mind* or *soul*.)

4. Menninger, *Crime of Punishment*, p. 17. For discussion of this and several similar manifestos of psychiatric imperialism, see Antony Flew, *Crime or Disease?* (New York: Barnes & Noble, 1973); and, for an outright challenge to the scientific status of such denials of the reality of choice, compare id., *A Rational Animal* (Oxford: Clarendon, 1978).

5. Aristotle *Nicomachean Ethics* 1107a8–13: "But not every action nor every passion admits of a mean; for some have names that already imply badness, e.g., spite, shamelessness, envy, and in the case of actions adultry, theft, murder; for all of these and suchlike things imply by their names that they are themselves bad, and not the excesses or deficiencies of them."

6. "Waiting for a Sign from the Egoists," *London Times*, June 27, 1972. Later in the same week the *Catholic Herald*, June 30, 1972, reported other meetings at which the archbishop—described by Cardinal de Roy, president of the Pontifical Commission for Justice and Peace, as "one of the great voices of our time"—called on British Catholics to fight the forces of capitalist imperialism. It is a pity, yet altogether characteristic, that this "great voice" insisted on thus inserting the word *capitalist* into his denunciation. By so doing he was bound to suggest to any critical listener he might have had that he either actually contrives to believe there is no such thing as a socialist empire or only disapproves of empires when the ruling power has not yet nationalized "all the means of production, distribution, and exchange." If it is the former, he is subject to the commonest and most ruinous of contemporary delusions—willful blindness to the realities of the ever-expanding empire of the Great Russians ruled now by what the Chinese so rightly call "the new czars." If it is the latter, he must be the bearer of a most curiously perverted conscience—nonetheless perverted for being nowadays considered normal in the descriptive sense both at the United Nations and among liberal and progressive establishments elsewhere.

7. For some examination of the economic and moral psychology behind attacks on "The Profit Motive," see Antony Flew, *Ethics* 86 (July 1976): 312–22.

8. Ayn Rand, *For the New Intellectual* (New York: Random House, 1961), p. 80.

9. Ibid., pp. 78–79.

10. Rand, *Virtue of Selfishness*, p. 60.

11. This logical truth is the foundation of the once much bruited doctrine of psychological hedonism: "desiring a thing and finding it pleasant, aversion to it and thinking of it as painful, are phenomena entirely inseparable or, rather, two parts of the same phenomenon: in strictness of language, two different modes of naming the same psychological fact: that to think of an object as desirable (unless for the sake of its consequences) and to think of it as pleasant, are one and the same thing; and that to desire anything, except in proportion as the idea of it is pleasant, is a physical and metaphysical impossibility" (J. S. Mill, *Utilitarianism*, ch. 4).

12. Rand, *Virtue of Selfishness*, p. 49.

13. Rand, *For the New Intellectual*, p. 161.

14. Quoted in *Los Angeles Times*, November 25, 1978.

15. Immanuel Kant, *Groundwork of the Metaphysics of Morals*, trans. H. J. Paton (New York: Harper & Row, 1964), ch. 1. Paton, in "The Analysis of the Argument" prefaced to his translation of *Groundwork* and elsewhere, is right to stress the much less widely recognized point that various Aristotelian elements are, nevertheless, fundamental in Kant's moral philosophy.

16. K. Marx and F. Engels, *The Communist Manifesto*, trans. Samuel Moore (New York: Penguin, 1967), p. 105.

17. Rand, *Virtue of Selfishness*, p. 28.

18. Ibid., p. 57.

19. Ibid.

20. Ibid., pp. 66–67.

21. It is remarkable how often the contrary view is assumed or even asserted, and not only by propagandizing hacks. See again Flew, "The Profit Motive."

22. Rand, *Virtue of Selfishness*, p. 67.

23. John Rawls, *A Theory of Justice* (Cambridge, Mass.: Harvard University Press, 1971), preface and passim.

24. Rand, *For the New Intellectual*, p. 85.

25. Ibid., pp. 83–84.

26. I refuse to soil my pen by using, as opposed to mentioning, the lying official misdescription "German Democratic Republic."

27. Suppose that Vice-Premier Teng, in his peregrinations, really was to learn the lessons that his most flourishing neighbor countries have to teach, and suppose further that he was able to introduce into the mainland the system under which other Han people in Taiwan and in the capitalist city-state of Hong Kong have been and are prospering so ebulliently, then this small planet could scarcely contain the consequent explosion of Chinese economic growth.

28. Adam Smith, *Wealth of Nations*, ch. 4, sec. 2.

29. These otherwise unremarkable words were attributed to Dr. Goh Keng Swee, minister of finance in what perversely describes itself as a socialist government. I copied them in 1969 from a plaque erected in the central marketplace of Singapore.

30. At the time of first writing and before the first budget of Mrs. Thatcher's Conservative administration, the actual top rates—which, it should be emphasized again, start from, by international standards, extraordinarily low thresholds—were 83% for "earned" and 98% for "unearned" income.

31. The suggestion that those who decide to pour tax moneys into state industrial projects, or to print more for this purpose, should be required to back these particular judgments with some of their own private resources has in fact been made by one or two members of Parliament. But, for reasons that sympathetic readers will have no difficulty in conjecturing, it has never been seriously entertained by anyone in or near ministerial office.

32. Once again, this is not the place to go into details. It must suffice to make two points.

(1) Any minister of the Crown is bound to feel pressure from labor unions; and far more so if he is a member of the Labour party, ever aware of the size of their financial contributions to party funds, of their corresponding mass votes at the party conference, and of their consequent decisive influence on his political future. But unions tend to be biggest and strongest in the most overgrown, overmanned, and now declining industries—industries, indeed, that often are in decline in large part because of union-enforced restrictions on productivity. The most effective pressure of these unions will be and has been for throwing good money after bad into such industrial disasters as British Leyland, British Steel, and British Shipbuilding.

(2), Any minister of the Crown is bound to feel pressure from constituents, especially his own, and from those others who likely might shift their political allegiance. Long after it had become obvious to all disinterested and most interested observers that the original investment in the Concord project would never be recovered, that no one would freely buy any token aircraft that might be produced, and that there was in fact no worthwhile technological spin-off, the decision to pour still more money was made, nevertheless—by an above-average, able, and ambitious minister. Could it—I ask aloud—have been coincidence that the main factory concerned was giving highly paid employment to many of his constituents? Or even that we heard no word that he was at the same time throwing down the same bottomless drain any of his own or his wife's substantial inherited wealth? (It was as if, instead of wisely deciding not to subsidize the building of a passenger SST on the sound ground that any commercially promising venture should and would be fully financed by private investors, the U.S. Senate had passed the making of this decision to the, on many counts so admirable and here understandably so eager, Sen. "Scoop" Jackson—"the Senator for Boeing.")

33. This English translation of the usual French import *entrepreneur* is today favored by the dissident reactionaries struggling to reverse Britain's long

downhill drive toward a shabby totalitarianism. Surely there ought to be such a word, native to the language of those forebears who made the first industrial revolution, for the members of the class that led it.

34. Smith, *Wealth of Nations*, ch. 1, sec. 2.

35. *Ibid.*, ch. 4, sec. 8.

36. "One of the familiar phrases of the moment is to say that under capitalism production is carried on for profit, while under socialism it is carried on for use; that socialism is planned production for use. What is meant by this phrase?" John Strachey, *Why You Should Be a Socialist* (London: Gollancz, 1944). This work, first as an enormously wide-selling pamphlet in the thirties and then as a book in the forties was responsible for making generations of socialists, including the generation now holding the highest offices in Britain: "If you seek their—and its—monument, look around you!"

37. See Antony Flew, "Wants or Needs: Choice or Command," in Ross Fitzgerald, ed., *Human Needs in Politics* (Rushcutters' Bay, NSW: Pergamon, 1977), pp. 213–28.

38. Smith, *Wealth of Nations*, ch. 1, sec. 2.

39. See, for instance, Arthur Seldon, *Choice in Welfare*; A. T. Peacock and J. Wiseman, *Education for Democrats*; E. G. West, *Economics, Education, and the Politician*; and A. Maynard, *Experiment with Choice in Education* (London: IEA, 1963, 1968, 1971, and 1975 respectively).

40. Socialist intellectuals are notoriously inclined to despise members of the class favored by their patronage. In fact, though no doubt there are neglectful and indifferent parents to be found in all social groups, when recently the scandal of systematic nonteaching at William Tyndale School erupted onto British television screens, the concerned mothers who came forward to complain that their children "had not been properly learnt to read" by (middle-class) radicals on the staff were themselves conspicuously and incontestably working-class.

41. For a development of this seminal idea and for some assessment of Smith's place in the story of the growth of social science, see F. A. Hayek, *Studies in Philosophy, Politics, and Economics* and *New Studies in Philosophy, Politics, Economics, and the History of Ideas* (London: Routledge & Kegan Paul, 1967 and 1978 respectively).

42. See, for instance, Walter Williams, "Race and Economics," in *Public Interest*, Fall 1978, pp. 147–54; and compare Thomas Sowell, *Race and Economics* (New York: Longman, 1975), passim. Both of these excellent economists, who happen also to be black, show how and why this and other legislation strongly supported by all establishment liberals, has in fact, presumably against their intentions and belief, bit disproportionately hard against certain black groups, particularly the unskilled young. For another example, compare F. G. Pennace, ed., *Verdict on Rent Control* (London: IEA, 1972).

43. Matthew 7:20. Consider as *one* indirect pointer to one of these fruits the following judgment. Joseph Needham, who has for more than three decades played the leading role in a vast investigation of *Science and Civilization in China* (Cambridge: Cambridge University Press, 1954–) offers his sugges-

tion as to why modern science evolved in Western Europe rather than in China, notwithstanding that until sometime in the late 1600s or early 1700s China was technically more advanced. He writes: "The institution of the mandarinate had the effect of creaming off the best brains in the nation for more than 2000 years into the civil service. Merchants . . . were never secure, they were subjected to sumptuary laws, and they could be mulcted of their wealth by inordinate taxation and every other kind of government interference. . . . In other words, not to put too fine a point on the matter, whoever would explain the failure of Chinese society to develop modern science had better begin by explaining the failure . . . to develop mercantile and then industrial capitalism." This tribute is the more impressive coming, as it does, from an unreconstructed member of the Communist party, who was still capable of writing without any sign of shame or embarrassment that in the socialist "Soviet Union . . . the dignity of each man's work is fully recognized, and his participation in the government of the factory and the state is acknowledged." See John Needham, *The Grand Titration* (London: Allen & Unwin, 1969), pp. 39–40, 135.

10
Reason, Individualism, and Capitalism: The Moral Vision of Ayn Rand

◠

Tibor R. Machan

Ayn Rand explains that the world view she sought to express as an aspiring novelist was missing from the contemporary intellectual climate.[1] This required that she turn to philosophy. She realized that only if she first developed a rational philosophy would there exist a foundation and context for her romantic realistic fiction. Such a vision would have to be complex and non-utopian, and inspire men and women to admire and defend the social and political system suitable for its realization, namely, capitalism.

The results of Rand's undertaking are her literary artistry (as playwright and novelist) and objectivism (as philosopher). Together these provide a philosophical foundation for a rational moral and political system and a vision of human life lived in accordance with such a system, superior to all other systems.

Within recent human history the United States has approximated the system of capitalism. The political foundations of capitalism—by no means a mere economic system—were best expressed in the Declaration of Independence:

We hold these truths to be self-evident, that all men are created equal, that they are endowed by their Creator with certain unalienable

Rights, that among these are Life, Liberty and the pursuit of Happiness. That to secure these rights, Governments are instituted among Men, deriving their just powers from the consent of the governed.

Despite the political substance of the Declaration, it is connected to a philosophical point of view and not simply to greedy motives, as alleged by capitalism's critics. Lincoln made this point eloquently in 1859:

All this is not the result of accident. It has a philosophical cause. Without the *Constitution* and the *Union*, we could not have attained the result; but even these are not the primary cause of our great prosperity. There is something back of these, entwining itself more closely about the human heart. That something, is the principle of "Liberty to all"—the principle that clears the *path* to all—gives *hope* to all—and, by consequence, *enterprise*, and *industry* to all.[2]

The priority of commerce or exchange is not implied in the American system, even if we admit that it "clears the path to . . . enterprise, and industry to all." Common sense plainly shows this, even in the face of widespread accusations about the necessary economic motivations of all human action and thought. The principle of liberty to all is not embraced within the American political tradition merely because observance of this principle makes the pursuit of crass hedonistic pleasure possible or because this tradition rests on the view shared by Hobbes and Locke that life is the joyless quest for joy.[3]

But more is required than common sense. Without a firm philosophical base, the free system *is* vulnerable. The critics make the valid point that capitalism has yet to be widely and prominently associated with a comprehensive philosophical ethics, and thus it lacks moral fuel. The problem with western liberal capitalism is that the political liberty it cherishes (at least in the language of its political declarations) has not been adequately justified by the pursuit of human excellence. As Solzhenitsyn has noted: "A society without any objective legal scale is a terrible one indeed. But a society with no other scale but the legal one is not worthy of man either."[4]

The critics are wrong to claim, however, that therefore the system is crass, callous, heartless, nihilistic, purely legalistic, and incapable of inspired support and defense. Capitalism, the social system that has at its political foundation the principles announced in the Declaration of Independence, contains abundant normative elements. Even if understood merely as an economic system, capitalism is quite attentive to values, for it fosters personal responsibility and excludes force from human relationships. It requires the individual's initiative to achieve prosperity, however understood, with the clear implication that others' efforts must be respected. There is ample moral substance in this alone.

The problem has been that, while the political principles of capitalism in the main require every individual to lead the moral life, those political principles are neither sufficient as a moral code nor firmly linked philosophically with such a code. Two approaches to the problem have dominated the work of moral theoreticians—philosophers, theologians, and pedagogues.[5] The first has assumed a need for the religious ethical traditions of earlier times: loyalty and faith in something superior to human life are supposed to sustain a culture. The second has denied that we can identify a moral foundation for any sort of political system; a culture rests only on human drives, vested interests, and economic, psychological, or social instincts.

Looking first at the second alternative, we can see that free society has come to be widely linked with its amoralist tenets. This is due in part to the mistaken association of modern economics with scientific neutrality (especially regarding moral or political values). The point may be stated as follows: modern economics is both scientific and gives support to the free market; introducing moral issues just weakens the scientific integrity of the case for liberty.

Those who have sought religious support for politics have, in turn, been willing to make compromises between liberty and slavery. They have denied Lincoln's premise that "no man is good enough to govern another man, *without that other's consent*"[6] mainly on grounds of faith and tradition. For these individuals (mainly America's conservatives) liberty is a fine and productive thing, but in the end various moral requirements call for its denial as a general principle of human relationships. Those taking this line find the very idea of a rational morality socially destructive, since that would place human beings in a position of self-reliance—reliance upon their own reason.

The welfare-state alternative is but the secular version of the faith that there must be something outside the individual human being and his personal excellence to which each of us owes allegiance. Attempts to ground this supposed allegiance on a sound philosophy have ended in appeals to intuition, utopian visions, and theories of historical progress toward a glorious future all of us are obligated to help usher in. None of these efforts are satisfactory for purposes of grounding a political system, because in none of these is it possible to establish the case for the system objectively so that everyone with normal conceptual and perceptual faculties might arrive at the same conclusions concerning the kind of system best suited for human beings.

Both economic and spiritual welfare statists have rejected any defense of capitalism based on a moral footing. Those who do try to defend capitalism have rejected the possibility of a rational normative approach completely. But, in fact, capitalist society cannot be given sound support unless the rights of *all* individuals can be shown to be founded on a sound, rational, objectively established moral theory which demonstrates that, while altruistic considerations have their place in human relations, they do not play a primary, decisive role or justify depriving others of their liberty.

Adam Smith observed that modern moral philosophy is defective, and the defect to which he pointed suggests that a better philosophical approach to morality would be supportive of the free society:

Ancient moral philosophy proposed to investigate wherein consisted the happiness and perfection of a man, considered not only as an individual, but as the member of a family, of a state, and of the great society of mankind. In that philosophy the duties of human life were treated of as subservient to the happiness and perfection of human life. But when moral, as well as natural philosophy, came to be taught only as subservient to theology, the duties of human life were treated of as chiefly subservient to the happiness of a life to come. In the ancient philosophy the perfection of virtue was represented as necessarily productive to the person who possessed it, of the most perfect happiness in this life. In the modern philosophy it was frequently represented as almost always inconsistent with any degree of happiness in this life, and heaven was to be earned by penance and mortification, not by the liberal, generous, and spirited conduct of a man. By far the most important of all the different branches of philosophy became in this manner by far the most corrupted.[7]

At this juncture the work of Ayn Rand has to be considered, for it is this ancient perspective on the moral life of human beings that she has resurrected—without the flaws contained in its renditions in ancient thought (e.g., its metaphysical idealism and its reification of abstract, collective humanity).

What Rand shows is that man has an objective need for morality, and that the morality appropriate to satisfy this need is one in which "the duties of human life [are] subservient to the happiness and perfection of human life."[8] The ethical theory of rational self-interest, articulated throughout Rand's philosophical works and displayed in her fiction, returns to a view advanced by Aristotle, among others, as to the place and function of morality in human life. But when applied within the sphere of human community life, Rand's ethics of rational self-interest implies a political system of capitalism in its purest form, not the semipaternalistic ideal of Aristotle's polity.

Also, Rand's idea of rational self-interest is entirely different from the Hobbesian and neo-Hobbesian versions of egoism. The reason both Randian ethics and Hobbesian ethics are referred to as egoistic or individualistic is that in each the individual is placed at the pinnacle of the hierarchy of values in human existence, and in neither is any other alternative arrangement seen. But the self for Rand is very different from what it is for Hobbes and his contemporaries, and the principles of morality that flow from these two forms of egoism are very different, which is clearly shown in the preceding chapters on Rand's ethical theory.

The most important criticism of Rand's ethical teaching in our context is hinted at by Michael Novak, who states that to ask humans to seek their own flourishing in life is insufficient inspiration and is, thus, socially and politically self-destructive. To guarantee the self-perpetuation of the social system we need a moral vision. To place the individual at the highest point of our value scale simply is not inspiring enough.[9] It is true that an individualist or egoist cannot construct some kind of collective moral vision. Rand's ethical theory, however, enables each of us to construct our own personal—but always human—ideal; and her philosophical inquiry demonstrates that that is everything there can and should be to a moral vision.

Ultimately, the capacity of a moral theory to provide a bona fide moral vision (as opposed to a fraudulent, utopian vision) confirms the truth of that theory. A valid moral vision is a realizable ideal, not an impossible dream. It will inspire good human beings to defend the conditions that make this ideal possible. But if what Novak and other newfound supporters of capitalism are asking for is a magic formula that can generate an inspired defense of a society without regard to the personal will the individuals of that society do or do not exert, then nothing will satisfy them.

Humans may not always be guided by truth, but when they are guided by falsehood, the likelihood of their becoming frustrated is so great that cynicism will result. What has prevented cynicism wherever corrupt moralities have taken root is an admixture of common sense. Thus, the self-sacrifice that is part of most moralities is tempered with a requirement for honesty and integrity—virtues that promote anything but one's demise. But it is undeniable that cynicism has closed in upon us frequently enough in human history. If it is true today that the West has lost its will, it is true because we lack a sound moral code that nurtures realistic and robust moral visions.

In what sense does Rand's work enable one to create a moral vision? For Rand, as for Aristotle, the question How should a human community be organized? can only be answered after the question How should I, a human being, live my life? has been answered. Rand follows the Greek tradition of regarding politics as a subfield of ethics, although she envisions the actual substance of these two fields in ways that are significantly distinct enough to make it necessary to consider her views on their own. For Rand the right way to live is the ground on which to establish the basic principles governing interpersonal behavior. These principles of community conduct establish the appropriate principles that govern political life.[10]

A moral vision is an image of the state of affairs that arises from living by a particular code of ethics. Virtually any moral point of view offers something akin to a moral vision for those who care to formulate it. Theologically based ethics have been accompanied by an other-worldly vision—a state of ultimate bliss—that would result from leading the moral life on earth. In secular altruistic moralities, images of the (loving) brotherhood of all men (such as that promised in the communist future) are envisioned. The function of such images is to remind one of the concrete implications of subscribing to the life of virtue. In practical terms, the images encourage loyalty to the principles being promoted.

A central feature of the persistent criticism of liberal, democratic capitalism has been that it fails to project an inspiring moral vision. Within the tradition of capitalism, the value of liberty is socially paramount. However, liberty is by definition an absence of coercion, an absence of an evil. Liberty is not the presence of a concrete achievement; although, when possessed of liberty, a free individual can create a concrete good.

So liberalism admittedly lacks a complete moral vision, since it focuses on the political front alone. One of liberalism's greatest virtues, namely its relegation of politics to a discrete realm of human life, is turned against it by a wide variety of collectivist demands. Indeed, it is a contradiction to demand that liberalism offer, in the context of a theory of limited politics, a total moral vision. Yet what liberalism has achieved is to conceive of a political order in conformity with human nature—a system which requires that each individual carry full responsibility for one's own moral achievements and failures. Only where others would obstruct this individual responsibility may the government—the instrument of men's political concerns—make a move, not for any other purpose. Is this liberalism's shortcoming?

Irving Kristol puts it this way: "The enemy of liberal capitalism is not so much socialism as nihilism."[11] If by this Kristol means that liberal capitalism can amount to a sound political system only if its political features alone can avoid nihilism—the abnegation of values—then he accepts the collectivist assumption that it is the function of politics to supply the full substance of morality. This assumption is in direct conflict with the individualist foundations of the capitalist system; and if these ethical foundations are sound, Kristol is simply asking for the impossible.

Another more complex objection to the individualist foundation of capitalism is advanced by Leo Strauss. In his characterization of Locke's view of human nature, Strauss remarks that "Through the shift of emphasis from natural duties or obligations to natural rights, the individual, the ego, had become the center and origin of the moral world, since man—as distinguished from man's end—had become that center or origin." [12] Strauss sees the base of morality in the liberal ethos, not as an ideal to be reached, but as a need to be satisfied. For Strauss, the individual denies the idea of a summum bonum—some highest good toward which to aspire—and "in the absence of a *summum bonum*, man would lack completely a star and compass for his life if there were no *summum malum*" [13]—a worst evil from which to escape (e.g., the death of oneself). However, Rand's view is that man is an end in himself qua man, i.e., that the realization of the rational capacity in one's particular life is a summum bonum. She thereby rejects the possibility of separating human life and human good. [14]

From analyses such as Strauss's, many have concluded that liberal capitalism, the free society, cannot be morally justified. If it is true that only by reference to the idea that human beings are driven (by genes, history, evolutionary forces, or instinct) can the free society be defended, the foregoing conclusion follows. But the conclusion is ill-founded: it is possible, clearly, that the type of society defended on neo-Hobbesian grounds can also be defended on the basis of a quite different understanding of human existence. It may be true that if the Hobbesian viewpoint is correct, then capitalism suits us well. But it is false that if the Hobbesian view is wrong, then capitalism does not suit us well.

Ayn Rand enables us to construct for ourselves a moral vision that is not so deceptively simple as the theocratic and collectivist alternatives. The payoff is that each individual can achieve a credible, realizable moral vision that incorporates private and public (i.e., distinctively political) components. Such a vision is not simple, because it takes into account the individuality of everyone, as well as everyone's essential humanity. Since individuality thus conceived does not occupy some inferior metaphysical and moral position—as with Plato and Marx—it has to be regarded seriously. However, individualism does not boil down to mere quantitative significance, as it does within a nominalist/atomist framework. The idea of the individual as it emerged from the atomistic tradition could not withstand attacks such as Marx's against liberalism, since, as the latter observed, "the freedom in question is that of a man treated as an isolated monad and withdrawn into himself." [15]

In Rand's metaphysics the particular and universal are inseparable. Accordingly, her principles of moral conduct support a moral vision of both aspects of each individual's life—humanity and individuality—equally and inseparably. Each person's excellence involves the process of achieving and sustaining the human life that is one's own, requiring that there be upheld both a unity of person and a distinctiveness, even separateness, of each person from the other.

From an individualist perspective, basic virtues would still guide the life of a good person. But the results of the implementation of these virtues cannot be assimilated into a uniformly applicable concrete picture. Each person can have a moral vision, but there can be no collective moral vision. In lieu of a collectivist vision, Rand establishes a vision of the moral life as it applies to basic human relationships in a political context:

I am neither foe nor friend to my brothers, but such as each of them shall deserve of me. And to earn my love, my brothers must do more than to have been born. I do not grant my love without reason, nor to any chance passerby who may wish to claim it. I honor men with my love. But honor is a thing to be earned.

I shall choose friends among men, but neither slaves nor masters. And I shall choose only such as please me, and them I shall love and respect, but neither command nor obey. And we shall join our hands when we wish, or walk alone when we so desire. For in the temple of his spirit, each man is alone. Let each man keep his temple untouched and undefiled. Then let him join hands with others if he wishes, but only beyond his holy threshold. [16]

The political vision here suggested makes considerable demands upon us, for it must be filled in by each of us with concrete content. It postulates the individual's aspiration to excellence but precludes any guarantee that this social moral vision will be achieved. To give this personal moral vision of individualism public expression is a difficult artistic task indeed. Certain forms of art serve as the medium for this purpose. The novel, play, ballet, and painting all are media for such expression of more or less widely applicable moral visions that exalt and inspire. Unfortunately, this domain of feeling associated with the arts has been almost the exclusive province of religion. Rand explains:

Religion's monopoly in the field of ethics has made it extremely difficult to communicate the emotional meaning and connotation of a rational view of life. Just as religion has preempted the field of ethics, turning morality against man, so it has usurped the highest moral concepts of our language, placing them outside this earth and beyond man's reach.[17]

Given the long history of religion's dominance in the arts and the only recent tolerance of secular artistic expression, it is to Rand's artistic credit that, despite her unambiguous atheism, some have proclaimed her a profoundly religious writer. The meaning of E. Merrill Root's praise of her, for example, is none other than that she has been able to inspire and produce exaltation with her artistry and that many people have no way of explaining this other than by linking it with something mystical, despite the rational philosophical foundations of all of Ayn Rand's ideas and imagery.

It is imperative that those who are concerned with the spiritual revitalization of the West stress the need for a rational morality and an individualist moral vision. But will these be adequate to counter nihilism? Once again, consider Irving Kristol:

In every society, the overwhelming majority of the people lead lives of considerable frustration, and if society is to endure, it needs to be able to rely on a goodly measure of stoical resignation. In theory, this could be philosophical rather than religious; in fact, philosophical stoicism has always been an aristocratic prerogative; it has never been able to give an acceptable rationale of "one's station and one's duties" to those whose stations are low and whose duties are onerous.[18]

With certain widely, though implicitly, accepted assumptions embedded in these observations, what Kristol is saying seems almost commonplace. Hardly anyone is always satisfied, and we all know of some who are entirely desperate, even in the best of times. Does it follow that, for such people to have hope, something of a fancy story—a Platonic "noble lie"—must sustain them?

Not so, once the assumptions are made explicit. First, Kristol flatly accepts the view that at root, morality consists of duties. So conceived, a morally excellent life comes down to a life dominated by chores. This makes it plausible that, to live a moral life, one would need some inducement or incentive beyond life itself—in Adam Smith's terms, "to be earned only by penance and mortification, by the austerities and abasement of a monk."

Second, in Kristol's detached framework the issue of the truth of religion seems to be set entirely aside. From his God's-eye point of view, religion has, in fact, no basis; yet he, unlike the rest of us, is in possession of the aristocratic prerogative and sees that we need religion. If "in theory" morality could be defended philosophically, then religion is not indispensable unless human beings are somehow naturally divided into those who can live with truth and those who require deception. That Kristol finds this the proper attitude toward his fellow humans is indicative of why he believes that life for most must be accepted stoically.

Despite the evidence that supports some of what Kristol says, we would be fooled by what is blatantly apparent—e.g., via newspapers, television, magazines, and the rhetoric of politics—to think that human life is as dismal as he reports. He fails to mention, for example, the private lives of millions who totally escape public notice, news reporting, and sociological inquiry. I am here focusing mostly on the quality of life linked to a so-called bourgeois society. In contrast, one need but examine reports from totalitarian states and consider the fate of millions who have lived through the epochs of feudalism, caesarism, and the varieties of Asian, Middle-Eastern, and African theocracies and tribal ages. When one also recalls what one these days is prominently said to have a natural right to (as explained, for example, in the United Nations Universal Declaration of Human Rights adopted in December 1948 and held up as a model of the just social system ever since), it is not difficult to see that despite appearances to the contrary, stoicism is not what is required. Granted that the state has rigged circumstances even in America so that the lives of many people are legally stymied (or kept artificially at a point of parasitic prosperity), it is only statistically true that these people lead lives of considerable deprivation and genuine frustration. Yes, although this may be so at some point of some lives in some portions of the country, in the majority of cases there is no reason why this needs to remain so for these persons individually.

There is, then, no reason to accept the pessimism Kristol projects. Neoconservatives like him are correct to be concerned with morality, but they are misled about the nature of morality and what is required to explain it and give it force within our culture. They are thus playing into the hands of Marxists, whom they do not like, by seriously advocating religion as the opiate of the masses.

Throughout history in most countries, religion, with virtually absolute links to the state, has monopolized reflection— theorizing, teaching, and criticizing—about morality. Even in the United States, public education evolved very early, usually as a secular substitute for reliance on religious schooling. In both theocratic and democratic traditions, morality has retained its altruistic emphasis (i.e., as officially taught), in the first instance stressing the primacy of one's duty to God, in the second one's duty to the state or one's fellows. Since the message in both instances bodes ill for all those who are being addressed, it is not surprising that either a heaven or a role in making a future heaven-on-earth has been promised to achieve compliance.

Aside from other problems, the idea that hope lies in the revitalization of a supernaturalist religious moral perspective is a will-o'-the-wisp. All that is left is the secular version, which is why Marxism—the most extreme secular altruistic/collectivist perspective on human life—has fared so well in the absence of alternative normative positions. In the end we need to keep in mind that pessimism about the capacity of a philosophical, secular ethics rests mainly on the prior acceptance of the view that ethics requires self-denial. This realization reaffirms the enormous influence of the modern outlook on ethics referred to by Adam Smith as requiring that "heaven [is] to be earned by penance and mortification, not by the liberal, generous, and spirited conduct of man."

But abandoning the pessimistic stance is justified in the light of Ayn Rand's work, the paramount significance of which is that, from an ethical viewpoint, it makes the rational conceptualization of one's own happiness possible and its depiction in works of art a reality. Rand's ethics isn't the promise of making mankind perfect, but it is the promise of the possibility of self-perfection, of being the best person one can be in the context of one's existence. This requires, however, that humans undertake the supreme moral effort to think conscientiously and to live by the judgment of such conscientious thought—and nothing else.

Among the numerous concerns, genuine or otherwise, that have stood in the way of accepting the possibility of a moral vision of rational egoism—individualism within the moral/political framework of capitalism—a final one demands rebuttal. This is the Marxist and theocratically inspired lament that in social terms the ethics of self-interest means mere "egoistic calculation." The question is Does ethical egoism really resolve personal worth into exchange value? Is commerce satanic?

Rand may on first sight appear to be simply classifiable among those who reduce all human relationships to exchange value. In John Galt's famous speech we are told, for example, that "We, who live by values, not by loot, are traders, both in matter and in spirit. A trader is a man who earns what he gets and does not give or take the unearned."[19]

A close look should make clear that this conception of trade has nothing to do with the *homo economicus* conceptions of human relationships. There is nothing purely materialistic in the trader image of man in Rand's viewpoint. For Rand emphasis is on the *terms* of human relationships, not on their motivation or the alleged economic impetus for all human conduct. A rational egoist is not a utility maximizer, a calculating hedonist, but an individual who acts on principle, by reference to a code of values that is not reducible to, but merely subsumes (within a certain social domain), market values.

Rand anticipates the attempt to dismiss her position by those who would assimilate it within the materialist, reductionist tradition. She distinguishes between the sort of subjective value (or revealed preference) stressed by economists and some other defenders of the free society as the only meaningful value and the value various anticapitalist critics find to be in need of emphasis. Rand notes that "the market value of a product does not reflect its philosophically objective value, but only its socially objective value. . . . [The former is] estimated from the standpoint of the best possible for man, i.e., by the criterion of the most rational mind possessing the greatest knowledge, in a given category, in a given period, and in a defined context." The latter is "the sum of the individual judgments of all the men involved in trade at a given time, the sum of what *they* valued, each in the context of his own life."[20]

So, unlike the economic advocates of the free market, Rand does not equate all types of values—e.g., artistic, economic, moral, and scientific. In the marketplace where people know very little of each other, exchange value may indeed be as close a measure of personal worth (between those involved in trade) as can reasonably be expected of the traders. A good chef will gain esteem as such; a bad taxi driver will fail to do so. It is probable that outside of economic engagements individuals reach levels of nobility or dishonor not evident in the marketplace, yet there is no lament about the indifference shown this in commercial relationships. One does not require the total recognition of one's worth or worthlessness from others one knows but slightly.

The market does not prevent a rational communication of value between those who trade with each other, but it does not fancy itself the court of last resort in these matters, contrary to what collectivists imagine to be required for human self-esteem. As Nathaniel Branden explains:

Under capitalism, men are free to *choose* their "social bonds"—meaning, to choose whom they will associate with. Men are not trapped within the prison of their family, tribe, caste, class, or neighborhood. They choose whom they will value, whom they will befriend, whom they will deal with, what kind of relationships they will enter. This implies and entails man's responsibility to form independent judgments. It implies and entails, also, that a man must earn the social relationships he desires.[21]

Replying to Erich Fromm, one of capitalism's long-time and severest neo-Marxist critics, Branden shows just how misconceived is the view that "the principle underlying capitalist society and the principle of love are incompatible."[22] Fromm, following the early Marx (who followed Ludwig Feuerbach), advocates in effect that the intimacy of love between persons can be grafted onto the human race at large. Capitalism is unacceptable, since it does not adjust itself to this fantasy and instead makes "the fairness ethic . . . the particular ethical contribution of capitalist society."[23]

But Fromm's idea and corresponding program are an illusion and horror chamber, as recent history has shown so vividly. Contrary to what some stubborn apologists for Marx still cling to—namely, the view that the Marxist-inspired (though not *caused*) Soviet Union, Stalinism, gulags, and other totalitarian evils throughout the world are merely perversions of an essentially human philosophy—Marxism, as Leszek Kolakowski has observed, may not have been "predestined to become the ideology of the self-glorifying Russian bureaucracy . . . [but] it contained essential features, as opposed to accidental and secondary ones, that made it adaptable for this purpose."[24] To try and make mankind conform to an ideal suited to how one or two people might, if very good and very lucky, relate to each other in personal intimacy is to bring forth barbarism and inner death.

Subsuming some human relationships within the economic-exchange framework is not only inoffensive but morally commendable, even inspiring. Trading with the grocery clerk or plumber, we can only feign close friendship, unless we come to know each other very well by spending a great deal of time together. Close relations require knowledge and appreciation of a person's history, aspirations, character, dreams, foibles, tastes, and so forth. Unless we come to know a person as an individual, we deal with him more justly by rewarding him for the little he has in fact done for us in engaging in a particular transaction. We each can leave the market and find ourselves being appreciated by others for different reasons, and we always have as a last and maybe best resort our own self-esteem. To fantasize about a closer relationship is to build utopian dreams that are the stuff of fairy tales, not of political philosophy.

What we can and should do is pay persons the respect due them for having done admirable work. Via the money we exchange, provided it represents value (honest earnings, not officially inflated "notes"), both can assume the work was well enough done so others might enter the same transaction. In a free market it is this basic trust we can ask of our relations with one another. We can even begin to become friends. All over the world, every hour of the day, humans befriend each other. But it is false that they are duty-bound to do so and intolerable that they should be forcibly organized accordingly.

One lamented consequence of our market dealings—as of some nonmarket ones—is the possibility of benefiting persons of whom, if one knew them, one would disapprove. One might, indeed, be exchanging value with a serious enemy: a Jew might inadvertently trade with an anti-Semite, neither knowing that the other is an antagonist. Yet, is there really something drastically wrong with this? After all, in a free marketplace boycotts and economic pressures of all types are possible, unlike in socialist and other planned economies. In general, the beneficial consequences of market impartiality—the concrete result of the "fairness ethic"—are considerable. Most of this is evident from common sense and is obscured only when we view the world with ideological blinders.

Those who dream of a society that will guarantee for everyone a collective utopian vision will always find the free society objectionable. Those who discuss the moral foundations of capitalism and its capacity to sustain a moral vision are usually theoreticians who assess the issues with the aid of elaborate theories. Or they are unaware of the theoretical support for laissez-faire capitalism, so they tend to accept the distorted history, handed down under ideological influences, that is hostile to capitalism.

Commerce can appear to be satanic to such individuals, especially if they have accepted impossible ideals by which to evaluate political systems and have not questioned the belief that capitalist society is to be viewed on the model of a boxing ring. In the tradition of Aristotelian[25] (not Hobbesian) ethical theories, personal economic well-being is one aspect of a larger concern for all human life. Thus, capitalist human relations need not be crass.

Ayn Rand's ethical conception of human life, personal and

social, enables one to sustain a moral vision that is both realistic and exalting—capable of inspiring humans to heights never before attempted. To date, however, Ayn Rand has not received her due from the intellectual community as advocate of the philosophical and ethical base of a free society. Although her novels have been bestsellers since their original publication, intellectuals have merely alluded to her ideas in asides. Rand's observation on this topic is instructive: "It is only the American people—not the intellectuals—who have given signs of rebellion against altruism. It is a blind, groping, ideologically helpless rebellion. But it would be a terrible crime of history if that rebellion is allowed to be defeated by silent default."[26]

Unfortunately, such default appears to be in the making today. Those intellectuals who would speak of the need for spiritual fuel must recognize the supreme social importance of liberty; and those who value liberty must value morality, the fuel of the spirit. Matters can change, and to any who would seriously consider a change for the better, Rand's words could be of considerable value: "Now is the time to assert, to proclaim and to uphold the ideas that created America—and thus save this country and, incidentally, to offer guidance to a perishing world. But this cannot be done without rejecting the morality of altruism."[27]

NOTES

1. Ayn Rand, "The Goal of My Writing," *Objectivist Newsletter*, October 1963, pp. 37–42.

2. Quoted in Harry V. Jaffa, *How to Think about the American Revolution* (Durham, N.C.: Carolina Academic Press, 1978), p. 1.

3. That Hobbes and Locke share this view is alleged by Leo Strauss, *Natural Right and History*, 2d ed. (Chicago: University of Chicago Press, 1970), p. 251. I address this issue further in Tibor Machan, "Libertarianism and Conservatives," *Modern Age* 24 (Winter 1980). But see John P. East, "The American Conservative Movement of the 1980s," ibid., for a different view.

4. Alexander Solzhenitsyn, "A World Split Apart," *Imprimis* 7 (1978): 4.

5. There are other approaches to take, but all are so hostile to liberty as not to bear discussion. There are extremes of the left and the right where liberty is not even regarded as a value, so the suggestion of a compromise between liberty and some version of slavery does not arise. Certain theocratic political doctrines on the right and totalitarian views on the left would fit this characterization.

6. Quoted in Jaffa, *American Revolution*, pp. 1–2.

7. Adam Smith, *The Wealth of Nations* (New York: Random House, 1937), p. 726.

8. Ayn Rand, "The Objectivist Ethics," in *The Virtue of Selfishness* (New York: New American Library, 1974), pp. 13–35.

9. Michael Novak, *The American Vision* (Washington, D.C.: American Enterprise Institute, 1978), seems to argue this point with the support of, e.g., Bernard-Henri Levy. More recently George Gilder, in *Wealth and Poverty* (New York: Basic Books, 1980), which is regarded as a brilliant Christian, antirationalist defense of capitalism, stresses the view that only an ethics of altruism can defend the free market, by reference to the notion that as an act of faith each person should seek to create, to engage in entrepreneurship and trade, with the motivation of helping others, not of furthering his own proper ends.

10. Ayn Rand, *For the New Intellectual* (New York: New American Library, 1961), p. 182.

11. Irving Kristol, "Capitalism, Socialism, and Nihilism," *Public Interest* (Spring 1973), p. 8.

12. Strauss, *Natural Right and History*, p. 251.

13. Ibid.

14. Ayn Rand, *For the New Intellectual* and *The Virtue of Selfishness*.

15. Karl Marx, *Selected Writings*, ed. David McLellan (New York: Oxford University Press, 1977), p. 53.

16. Ayn Rand, *Anthem* (New York: Signet Books, 1946), p. 111.

17. Ayn Rand, *The Fountainhead* (New York: New American Library, 1968), p. ix. See, in this connection, E. Merrill Root, "What about Ayn Rand?" *National Review*, January 30, 1960, pp. 76–78.

18. Kristol, "Capitalism, Socialism, and Nihilism," p. 12.

19. Ayn Rand, *Atlas Shrugged* (New York: Random House, 1957), p. 1022.

20. Ayn Rand, "What Is Capitalism?" in *Capitalism: The Unknown Ideal* (New York: New American Library, 1967), pp. 24–25.

21. Nathaniel Branden, "Alienation," *Objectivist Newsletter* 4 (1965): 37.

22. Quoted ibid., p. 36.

23. Quoted ibid.

24. Quoted in Michael Harrington, review of *Main Currents of Marxism*, by Leszek Kolakowski, *New Republic*, February 3, 1979, p. 32.

25. See W. F. Hardie, "The Final Good in Aristotle's *Ethics*," *Philosophy* 40 (1965): 277–95, for a discussion of the egoistic aspects of Aristotle's ethics. But this should not be taken as a claim that Rand's case for egoism is the same as Aristotle's. See Tibor R. Machan, "Recent Work in Ethical Egoism," *American Philosophical Quarterly* 16 (1979): 1–15, for a discussion of various recent versions of egoism, Rand's included.

26. Ayn Rand, *The Moral Factor* (Palo Alto: Palo Alto Book Service, 1976), p. 12.

27. Ibid.

Conclusion

The preceding essays have begun the task of measuring Ayn Rand's worth as a philosopher. Whatever one's evaluation of her theories, it should be clear that Rand attempts to provide a systematic philosophical position. Political theory is dependent upon ethics, and ethics in turn is dependent upon metaphysics and epistemology. Whether or not Rand is successful in linking these three central branches of philosophy together, it is clear that she makes the effort to do so. In this Rand stands outside some of the current trends in contemporary analytic philosophy. But it may also be the case that Rand's approach to philosophy is somewhat ahead of its time. The demise of logical positivism has left at least Anglo-American philosophy without the homogeneous core it once enjoyed in this century. Whether a return to systematic philosophizing is forthcoming is an open question. But even if philosophy simply becomes more pluralistic, Rand's systematic vision and suggestive insights may have a place in future philosophic thinking.

Rand did not believe that the philosophical lines of dependency went in only one direction. One's metaphysical or epistemological views can have effects upon one's ethical and, therefore, one's political thinking. This claim is reiterated again in her posthumously published work, *Philosophy: Who Needs It?* (New York: Bobbs-Merrill, 1982). As in her earlier writings, especially the novel *Atlas Shrugged*, this latest book tries to argue that the adherence to certain philosophical theories has practical consequences. Although her most recent book does not contain the kind of significant philosophizing found in her earlier works, the book does urge us to consider Rand's place within intellectual trends that issue in practical recommendations. However much Rand may have done in the more abstract areas of philosophy, she is still considered by many to be primarily a political thinker. We believe that it is therefore best to conclude with some remarks about Rand and current political ideologies.

And since Rand has often been labeled a conservative, our main emphasis will be on that movement.

Conservatism's reaction to Rand's philosophy reflects a tension within the conservative intellectual movement. As George B. Nash notes in his history, *The Conservative Intellectual Movement* (New York: Basic Books, 1976), there have been two warring factions within American conservatism since 1945. These factions result from two opposed views regarding the purpose of government. The first faction, roughly labeled *traditionalist*, sees government's purpose to be the promotion of virtue. Traditionalists—thinkers who regard Christianity as the moral basis of western civilization—see Rand's advocacy of ethical egoism and laissez-faire capitalism as a continuation on the road to hell, both figuratively and literally, taken by modernity in its rejection of Aquinas's synthesis. Rand's criticism of altruism and praise for capitalism are considered an antireligious message of philosophical materialism.

The second faction, roughly called *libertarian*, takes the purpose of government to be the promotion of liberty. Libertarians—thinkers who deny the legitimacy of ethics or consider its enforcement to be beyond the government's purview—are ambivalent toward Rand's conjunction of ethical egoism and laissez-faire capitalism. Rand's defense of the free market is considered magnificent, but her advocacy of natural rights is regarded as troublesome, for Rand's commitment to the existence of moral truths is thought of as the basis by which governments can limit liberty and thus pave the way to fascism. Consequently neither the traditionalist nor the libertarian offers Rand an ideological home.

Rand departs from some conservatives by advocating an ethical theory based on a naturalistic world view. This separates her from the traditionalist who sees no basis for morality without the supernatural dimension. Rand differs, likewise, from the libertarian who fears that if we know what sin is, government must prevent it. The ultimate effect of Rand's efforts in these areas is her status as persona non grata among conservative intellectuals.

Rand's rejection by the conservative intellectual movement is most ironic given the central difficulty faced by that movement. The question, Whether virtue or liberty? which divides conservatives, is unresolved. The late Frank S. Meyer, a libertarian, has argued that liberty is absolutely indispensable for the pursuit of virtue and that, therefore, government should refrain from attempting to legislate it. L. Brent Bozell, a traditionalist, has replied that virtue—an action that conforms to human nature—need not require liberty as a condition for its performance and, thus, government should legislatively encourage virtue. The questions Why is liberty necessary for virtue? and—if not—What prevents conservatism from endorsing authoritarian and even theocratic policies? echo loudly. Debate over these questions has resulted less in answers than in a "fusionist" consensus among conservative intellectuals—a fusion not of two political theories, but of persons who are tired of feuding and who desire collaboration. This issue of the relation between freedom and virtue has, nevertheless, lately reemerged in a major journal of conservative opinion (*Modern Age*, Winter 1980 and Fall 1981) in a series of articles discussing the purpose of government and "fusionism." It is ironic that Rand has been given scant attention by so many conservative intellectuals, for her ethical/political philosophy seems to directly address the problem of virtue and liberty. Indeed, it just may be that the very "stone which the builders rejected" is the "one to become the head of the corner."

Rand's thought is not without important connections to the liberal political tradition as well. Her argument for natural, human rights is unvarying; and she refuses to countenance the sacrifice of the individual for the common good. Rand uses her natural rights doctrine as the basis for a critique of tradition and the status quo. Indeed, she is not a conservative precisely because there is no blind desire to resurrect the past or maintain tradition for its own sake. She is, moreover, as tenacious as any liberal in her attacks on racism and in her defense of freedom of expression. But because economic liberties are as important for Rand as civil liberties, her political doctrines do not tend toward fascism as do those of contemporary liberals.

It has often been noted that the labels *conservative* and *lib-*

eral, when they are understood in traditional ways, are capturing less and less of the current thinking about politics. Ayn Rand was one of the first to reject both of these labels. Perhaps, then, Rand's basic message is correct after all—namely, that a concerted effort to think fundamentally about basic questions is not only appropriate, but required.

The Contributors

DOUGLAS DEN UYL is assistant professor of philosophy at Bellarmine College in Louisville, Kentucky. He has publications in the areas of the history of philosophy and social and political philosophy. He is also author of *Power, State, and Freedom: An Interpretation of Spinoza's Political Thought.*

ANTONY FLEW was formerly professor of philosophy at the University of Reading. He is currently at York University in Toronto, Canada. He is the author of a wide variety of articles and books, including *The Politics of Procrustes.*

ROBERT HOLLINGER is associate professor of philosophy at Iowa State University in Ames, Iowa. He has published numerous articles on various philosophical topics.

CHARLES KING was formerly professor of philosophy at Pomona College in Claremont, California. He has published widely in the areas of social and political philosophy and is currently executive director of Liberty Fund, Inc.

TIBOR MACHAN teaches philosophy at SUNY, Fredonia, and also in the economics department at University of California at Santa Barbara. He is educational director of the Reason Foundation and is the author of numerous articles and books, including *Human Rights and Human Liberties.*

ERIC MACK is associate professor of philosophy at Tulane University in New Orleans, Louisiana. He has published extensively on ethics, legal, and political philosophy in various scholarly journals and anthologies.

WALLACE I. MATSON is professor of philosophy at the University of California at Berkeley. He is the author of many articles, and his books include *The Existence of God* and *Sentience.*

DOUGLAS B. RASMUSSEN is assistant professor of philosophy at St. John's University in Jamaica, New York. His publications are primarily in the areas of metaphysics and social and political philosophy.

JACK WHEELER received his Ph.D. in philosophy from the University of Southern California. He is a noted world traveler and adventurer and is author of *The Adventurer's Guide.*

Index

Popper, Sir Karl, 22, 40, 41, 45, 56,
57n7
Porphyry, 19n19
pragmatism, 39, 45, 55, 56
pride, virtue of, 72, 74, 91–93,
100n64, 117, 137. *See also*
egoism
productiveness, virtue of, 72–74,
117, 136–43 passim, 149–50,
158, 174
psuche, division of, in Aristotle,
88–90
Putnam, 56

Quine, 46, 47, 54–56, 58n24,
58n25

Rackham, 83, 87
Rand, Ayn: controversy over, xi;
philosophic system, xii; as philosopher, 3; primary metaethical
concept, 84; as natural-rights theorist, 170; as political thinker,
224–25
—, works: *The Fountainhead*, 21,
185–86; *Introduction to Objectivist Epistemology*, 21–36 passim,
43, 58n25; "This Is John Galt
Speaking," 43; "For the New Intellectual" (essay), 43, 48; "The
Objectivist Ethics," 43, 69, 81,
107–20 passim, 124–59 passim;
The Virtue of Selfishness, 76, 186,
199; "Man's Rights," 119, 152,
156; "Causality versus Duty,"
134–35; *Atlas Shrugged*, 152,
153, 224; "The Nature of Government," 154; "What Is Capitalism?" 154, 156; "The 'Conflicts'
of Men's Interests," 158; *Capitalism: The Unknown Ideal*, 174,
198; *For the New Intellectual*,
185–86; the novels, 187–88,
206, 222; *Philosophy: Who
Needs It?* 224. *See also* Roark,
Howard
Randall, 81
rationalism, 42–43, 45, 49; classical, 44–45, 54; and religion, 215;
——/nihilism dichotomy, 47–48
rationality, 45, 47, 50–54 passim,

58n15, 69–75 passim, 89–91
passim, 106–7, 113, 115, 135–
37, 140, 142, 144, 149–50, 158;
Cartesian theory of, 51, 53; ——
principle, 51, 54; virtue of, 70,
72–73, 75, 88, 90, 117, 137–39;
and ethical behavior, 88–92
Rawls, John, 191
realism, 51, 54, 59n26; metaphysical, 4; Rand's view of, 17; moderate, 18; commonsense —— of
Rand, 56
reality, 44, 47–50 passim, 54,
89–90
reason, 40, 44–49 passim, 54,
57n7, 57–58n15, 112–16 passim, 137, 143–50 passim, 153,
166; supremacy of, in Rand, xiii;
concept of, 50–51; "pure," 55;
defined, 106–7
Regis, Edward, Jr., 7, 8
Reid, Thomas, 28
religion, 215; Rand's rejection of,
180n12. *See also* faith; God;
morality
rights, 119–20, 169, 177–78,
189–90; property ——, 169–72,
181n25; natural ——, xii, 225;
Rand's theory of, 98–99n22,
149–59 passim, 166–72 passim.
See also human rights
Roark, Howard, 191–92. *See also*
Rand, works, *The Fountainhead*.
romanticism, 42
Root, E. Merrill, 215
Rorty, 47, 55
Ross, 85, 93
Russell, Bertrand, 27, 36, 52, 91, 139
Ryle, 36

Sartre, 53, 57–58n15
science, 42, 50, 52, 204–5n43; philosophy of, 25–26
Scotus, 19n19
the self, Rand's view of, 77
selfishness, 92–93, 183–205 passim; a virtue, xi, 185; rational,
94–95, 123, 156, 157, 210
self love, Aristotelian, 94–95
skepticism, 10, 23, 45, 48, 50, 53;
Humean, 52; classical, 44, 53

234